By the hard work of others, we are led
to the most beautiful things that have been dragged
out of darkness and into the light.
Everyone is invited to experience the light
of every age and every people.
So, let us walk hand in hand with those from every age.
Let us turn from this brief and transient time
and offer our minds and hearts to the past,
which is long and eternal.

—Seneca, *On the Shortness of Life*

THE CLASSICS CAVE
Sugar Land

THE CLASSICS CAVE

the earliest light for a brighter life

www.theclassicscave.com

ARE YOU looking for the best books ever? Or new ways to read and benefit from them? To practice what you've read? To learn and grow a little? Let the Cave be your guide!

THE CLASSICS CAVE (the Cave) is an educational* organization centered on the classics of Greek and Roman antiquity, with an emphasis on the best of ancient Greek literature.

OUR MISSION is to shine the light of the past into the present for a brighter life today.

OUR GOAL is practice—the application of ancient wisdom and ways to our contemporary lives.

WE publish books, develop and provide online content, organize and do outreach, and produce and distribute a variety of print and other media intended to entertain and educate, inspire, encourage, and cultivate.

VISIT THE CAVE online (www.theclassicscave.com) to support our mission and to access a growing catalog of engaging books and other beneficial content designed for individuals, educators, groups, and all others interested in benefiting from ancient literature.

SUPPORT THE CAVE by telling others about our work and by leaving a positive review online. You may also wish to buy a book or join The BAGL Club or the AAGS (to adopt an ancient Greek). Or sponsor the BAGL. Or partner with us by giving a donation. Thanks!

With GRATITUDE, we thank our readers, members, sponsors, donors, and all participants in Cave content—you who make the work and outreach of the Cave possible. Without you, the Cave would not exist!

*For the Cave, **education** is that happy transition from ignorance to knowledge; from foolishness to wisdom; and from mediocrity or vice to excellence or virtue, culminating in good habits and character.

In Praise of Homer & his Poetry

"I rank Homer among the oldest and wisest of the poets."
— Aeschines *Against Timarchus*

"Homer, as always and everywhere, should be first, like a god."
— Charles-Augustin Sainte-Beuve, *What is a Classic?*

"The verses of Homer have continued twenty-five hundred years, or more, without the loss of a syllable or letter, during which the infinite palaces, temples, castles, cities have been decayed and demolished."
— Francis Bacon, *The Advancement of Learning*

"Like the sun, which furnishes with its light the close courts . . . of London, while himself unseen by their inhabitants, Homer has supplied with the illumination of his ideas millions of minds that were never brought into direct contact with his work, and even millions more, that have hardly been aware of his existence. . . . And this universality is his alone."
— William E. Gladstone, *Studies on Homer and the Homeric Age*

"I also wish to recommend the epic poetry of Homer to you. In your fathers' estimation he was an excellent poet of such worth that [the Athenians] passed a law that every four years at the Panathenaea he alone of all the other poets should have his works recited."
— Lycurgus, *Against Leocrates*

"When young, any composition pleases which unites a little sense, some imagination, and some rhythm, in doses however small. But as we advance in life these things fall off one by one, and I suspect that we are left at last with only Homer and Virgil, and perhaps with Homer alone." — Thomas Jefferson, *Thoughts on English Prosody*

"Homer may seem divinely inspired. . . . He was the very best poet in the serious style, since he alone made his representations not only good but also dramatic." — Aristotle, *Poetics*

"As Achilles is among warriors, so Homer is beyond all comparison among poets. . . . He has given us a model and an inspiration for every branch of eloquence. Most will admit that no one has ever surpassed him in the sublimity with which he endows great themes or the propriety with which he handles the small. He is at once luxuriant and concise, sprightly and serious, remarkable at once for his fulness and his brevity, and supreme not only for poetic but for oratorical power as well." —Quintilian, *Institutes*

"In the age which preceded or introduced the first formations of Human Society . . . we may dimly discern an almost mythical personage, who . . . may be called the first Apostle of Civilization. . . . He was to do such great things, and to live in the mouths of a hundred generations and a thousand tribes. . . . At length an Athenian Prince took upon him the task of gathering together the scattered fragments of a genius which had not aspired to immortality, of reducing them to writing, and of fitting them to be the textbook of ancient education. Henceforth, [Homer] . . . was submitted . . . to a sort of literary canonization, and was invested with the office of forming the young mind of Greece to noble thoughts and bold deeds. To be read in Homer soon became the education of a gentleman."
                              —John Henry Newman, *The Idea of a University*

"When Aristodemus was asked who he admired for wisdom, he told Socrates: 'In epic poetry Homer comes first.'" —Xenophon, *Memorabilia*

"[They say that] Homer has been the educator of Greece, and that for the education and government of humans, we should take him up and learn from him, and that we should build up our entire lives with the assistance of this poet." —Socrates in Plato's *Republic*

"Where did godlike Homer obtain honor and glory if not from useful teaching in tactics, virtues, and the arming of men?"
                              —Aristophanes, *Frogs*

"Hesiod and Homer . . . are the ones who taught the Greeks the descent of the gods, and gave the gods their names, and determined their spheres and functions, and described their outward forms."

—Herodotus, *Histories*

"I have heard a man say who is skillful at closely examining the mind and meaning of a poet, all Homer's poetry is a commendation of virtue. . . . Homer practically shouts it aloud in these passages, saying, 'You must care for virtue, men . . .'"

—Basil the Great, *How to Benefit from Reading Greek Literature*

"In his *Miscellaneous History*, Favorinus says that Anaxagoras was the first to maintain that Homer in his poems treats of virtue and justice."

—Diogenes Laertius, *Lives and Opinions of Eminent Philosophers*

"[Homer] teaches more clearly, and better than Chrysippus and Crantor, what is honorable, what is shameful, what is profitable, and what is not so. . . . Excellent Homer . . . animated the manly mind to martial achievements with [his] verses."

—Horace, *Epistle* and *The Art of Poetry*

"Everything Homer wrote is both beneficial and useful, [so] it would be a vast undertaking to go through everything he has said about virtue and vice. . . . Both [Homer and Socrates] spoke about the same things . . . human virtue and vice, and things done poorly, and things done well, and truth and deceit, and how many have only opinions while the wise have true knowledge. . . . Homer is a marvelous and truly divine herald of virtue."

—Dio Chrysostom, *Discourses*

"The grammarians describe . . . the rules of poetry out of the poems of Homer." —Thomas Hobbes, *Leviathan*

"Homer's book is a delightful treasure. All that he has touched has turned to gold. . . . Everywhere he entertains and never grows tired. A happy warmth animates his speeches. . . . Love his writings with a sincere love." —Nicholas Boileau-Despreaux, *The Art of Poetry*

"To one only . . . has it been given to draw characters, by the strength of his own individual hand, in lines of such force and vigor, that they have become . . . the common inheritance of civilized man. That one is Homer. . . . We may . . . find an admirable school of polity . . . in the writings of Homer. . . . There is an inner Homeric world, . . . a world of religion and ethics, of civil policy, of history and ethnology, of manners and arts."

—William E. Gladstone, *Studies on Homer and the Homeric Age*

"This is the age of Homer, the golden age of poetry. Poetry has now attained its perfection: it has attained the point which it cannot pass."

—Thomas Love Peacock, *The Four Ages of Poetry*

"[May] Homer's works be your study and delight. Read them by day, and meditate [on them] by night."

—Alexander Pope, *An Essay on Criticism*

"Wisdom among the gentiles began with the Muse defined by Homer in a golden passage of the *Odyssey* . . . It is Homer's privilege to be, of all the sublime, that is, the heroic poets, the first in the order of merit as well as in that of age."

—Giambattista Vico, *The New Science*

"Homer surpassed all the poets whom he encountered, each in his own area of expertise." —Philostratus, *On Heroes*

"Homer was the most ancient and greatest of all poets."

—Diodorus Siculus, *Library*

"We're going to translate [for] you part of a Greek novel, . . . the best novel that was ever written, Cyril, The *Odyssey* [of Homer]."

—Julian, in *Julian Home* by Frederic W. Farrar

"Homer himself is eternally interesting. . . . The epic form . . . has attained, in the poems of Homer, an unmatched, an immortal success."

—Matthew Arnold, *On the Modern Element in Literature*

THE BEST OF
HOMER'S *ODYSSEY*

THE BEST OF
HOMER'S ODYSSEY

The Best Parts in Translation
with
a Narrative Summary of the Rest

selected, introduced, and edited by
The Classics Cave

CAVE BEST OF SERIES
the best of the classics for today

THE CLASSICS CAVE
Sugar Land

The Best of Homer's *Odyssey*:
The Best Parts in Translation with a Narrative Summary of the Rest

ISBN 978-1-943915-08-8

Published in the United States by
The Classics Cave
P.O. Box 19038
Sugar Land, TX 77496
contact@theclassicscave.com
www.theclassicscave.com

The Classics Cave (the Cave) is an educational organization centered on the classics of Greek and Roman antiquity, with an emphasis on the best of ancient Greek literature. Our mission is to shine the light of the past into the present for a brighter life today. Our goal is practice—the application of ancient wisdom and ways to our contemporary lives. We publish books, develop and provide online content, organize and do outreach, and produce and distribute a variety of print and other media intended to entertain and educate, inspire, encourage, and cultivate.

   Visit the Cave online (www.theclassicscave.com) to support our mission and to access a growing catalog of engaging books and other beneficial content designed for individuals, educators, groups, and all others interested in benefiting from ancient literature.

For the one entering this great work . . .
Pause for a moment before its door.

Such is the holy gift the Muses give to human beings.
—Hesiod, *Theogony*

CONTENTS

POINTS OF WISDOM & WAYS OF PRACTICE
from Homer

OTHER MATTERS OF INTEREST
Related to Homer's *Odyssey*

Cave Best of Series
Introduction
the best of the classics for today

HAVE YOU EVER considered how many excellent works of ancient Greek and Latin literature there are to read? Think of all the significant works of poetry and prose—of all the epics, tragedies, comedies, histories, philosophies, orations, biographies, and more!

The problem, of course, is in the approach. How should you read them all? It is The Classics Cave's goal to offer a possible solution—and so the Cave Best of Series, which presents the best of an author, title, or group of authors.

Take the author, title, or group you have in hand. Of the available versions of the work, the Cave Best of Series version is unique for a few reasons. One, it is much shorter than most renditions of the work—oftentimes the number of pages totals anywhere from one-third to one-half of other versions.* Consequently, if you are pressed for time or do not know how many hours you would like to invest in reading the work, then the Cave Best of Series version may be for you.

That is not to say you will not get the whole work—the whole story or discourse or whatever the work centers on. Rather, you will get it in two forms—another unique feature of the Cave Best of Series presentation of a work. Whereas most versions offer either the whole or parts of a work (without any significant explanation of what happens in between each part), the Cave Best of Series version gives you the best or most significant parts in translation, along with a narrative summary of the rest that will tell you exactly what is going on in between. This means you will get the full content, feel, and experience of the work without missing out on anything essential.

And that's important. Unlike study guide versions that offer summary outlines alone, you will have extensive passages and narrative summaries of the whole work that will allow you to judge for yourself what is happening, what characters are central, what themes are significant, what the arguments are and whether they succeed or not, and the like—all depending on the work itself.

This is what the Cave Best of Series offers: the whole work in translated and narrative summary form, making for a relatively quick read that will let you come to terms with the work by yourself.

Not only that but there is also an information-packed introduction that is meant to draw the reader into and answer the most significant questions about the author and the work. Why should we care about *this* author and *this* work? What are the essential facts we should know? What are the work's most important ideas and themes? There is always a full exploration of these points that references the work itself as well as any pertinent scholarship.

Toward the end, there is a section presenting a "Plan of Life" (or something similar), "Points of Wisdom," and "Ways of Practice" related to the author. The latter "Ways" consist of workbook or journal-like prompts and exercises intended to motivate the reader to feel, think, and act in beneficial ways according to the author's "Points of Wisdom" (just as ancient readers or auditors would).

Finally, there is a unique section called, "Other Matters of Interest Related to [the Author]." It offers additional information about the author, whether a summary of the work, a cast of characters found therein, maps, a glossary of relevant Greek terms, suggestions for further reading, and so on.

In the end, when you read the work as presented in the Cave Best of Series, you will be entertained, educated, and, we at The Classics Cave hope, motivated to practice—to act in an intentional, specific manner toward a better life. With this in mind, welcome to the . . .

Cave Best of Series
the best of the classics for today

---

* Even so, whole, or mostly whole, works are sometimes included in the Cave Best of Series if the work is particularly short.

INTRODUCTION

[They say that] Homer has been the educator of Greece, and that for the education and government of humans, we should take him up and learn from him, and that we should build up our entire lives with the assistance of this poet. —Socrates, reporting the view of "Homer enthusiasts"

L ET'S FACE IT. Homer has fallen on hard times. Very few read the *Iliad* or the *Odyssey* anymore. When most people hear the name Homer, they think of Homer Simpson—the same yellow cartoon character that invades the screen upon doing a simple image search for "Homer." For the online Urban Dictionary, *this* Homer is synonymous with an "American Bonehead." *D'oh.*

Others may recall the nineteenth century American painter Winslow Homer, who is famous for his landscapes. It's possible diehard baseball fans will mistake the word for a homerun. *There it goes . . . it's flying . . . a homer over the right field fence.* A small number may remember their childhood hometown of Homer, New York, named after the poet. Others may have been to Homer, Alaska, christened for the late nineteenth century gold seeker Homer Pennock. It's now the halibut fishing capital of the world, and, according to the city's website, it is "quickly becoming known as the Eco and Adventure tourism capital of Alaska."

But Homer, the ancient poet of the *Iliad* and the *Odyssey*?

Sure, most have heard of (or even read about) Odysseus' renowned adventures, including the man-eating Cyclops and the stunningly beautiful but deceptive Sirens. Or of Helen's legendary beauty. Or of the Trojan Horse that brought down a whole city. Or of the broader Trojan War—thanks to Brad Pitt in Wolfgang Petersen's epic film *Troy,* or the far more recent Netflix-BBC version, *Troy: Fall of a City.* But fewer and fewer people know the full story of the *Iliad* and the *Odyssey,* let alone anything about Homer.

It is the goal of The Classics Cave's rendition of Homer's *Odyssey* to change that. If only a little. And if only beginning with *you.*

WHY SHOULD WE CARE ABOUT HOMER?

Go back a few thousand years and Homer was the best thing on television, the hottest new album, or the summer blockbuster. The great Cambridge classics scholar Moses Finley once claimed that "if a Greek owned any books—that is, papyrus rolls—he was almost as likely to own the *Iliad* and the *Odyssey* as anything from the rest of Greek literature."[1] Homer was the thing to have, the thing to know about, and the thing to love.

The first reason we should care about Homer, then, is because millions of others deeply cared about him for well over a thousand years.

Everyone who was anyone in ancient Greece name-dropped Homer in their own works. To give a handful, there was the epinician poet Pindar; the earliest historians Herodotus, Thucydides, and Xenophon; the encyclopedic philosopher Aristotle; and the orators Isocrates, Aeschines, and Demosthenes. Plato, perhaps Europe's greatest philosopher of all, dropped his name the most, though, citing Homer over fifty times in his dialogues and letters. Later Greek authors, such as the geographer Strabo, the essayist and biographer Plutarch, and the Stoic philosopher Epictetus, did the same.

Although we don't literally see Homer's name in other Greek literature, we may nevertheless easily spot his spirit and influence. Take the Spartan Tyrtaeus' seventh century BC notions of courage; or Sappho of Mytilene's conception of great poetry early in the next century (she, by the way, positively compared herself to Homer); or Simonides' pessimism regarding the flux of life late in the same century; or the tragic content of Aeschylus, Sophocles, and Euripides during what has been called the Golden Age of Athens in the fifth century BC. A few anonymous authors even wrote humorous Homeric-style epics pitting frogs against mice, or cats against the same mortal enemy. In the latter, a mouse army gathers against a cat after the cat kills their intrepid mouse hero, Trixos. Regretfully, we don't know how the story ends as we only have a few fragmentary passages. Still, it goes to show how much the ancient world appreciated and imitated Homer.

To give a specific example regarding how adored Homer was, there was the philosopher Socrates (fifth century BC), who was, we may confidently assert, addicted to the poet throughout his life thanks to the immense pleasure he felt in hearing or reading Homer's emotionally powerful poems. In Plato's *Republic*, Socrates readily admits that "a certain love and respect for Homer possessed me from the time I was a child to now."[2] Did you hear that? Homer's poetry *owned* Socrates; it had him by the head and heart!

Observing Homer's rather flatline status now, at least the appearance thereof, it is hard to believe that anyone, let alone someone with the creative and revolutionary mind of Socrates, could have been addicted to him. But Socrates wasn't the only one utterly enamored with Homer. No, the poet was incredibly important to everyone in the ancient world. For centuries ancient Greeks read and listened to him, memorized his lines, and used his poetry to make arguments. In short, Homer's *Iliad* and *Odyssey* influenced their feelings, thinking, speech, and behavior, and so the way they navigated and endured life. There was a passage of Homer for everything—healthcare, warfare, politics, business, education, rhetoric, culture, and every other aspect of public and private life.

This is the second reason we should care about Homer. More than anyone else, Homer formed the Greek mind, shaped Greek sensibilities, inspired Greek culture, and encouraged Greek behavior. It was common for ancient Greeks to spend years studying the poet and, therefore, to be profoundly influenced by him. Diogenes Laertius reports that Menedemus, one of Socrates' students, "applied himself to the study of Homer."[3] He wasn't the only one. We know that others memorized large portions of Homer's *Iliad* and *Odyssey* in order to improve themselves. The Athenian Niceratus, the son of Nicias, for example, told Socrates that he was happy that his "father was careful to see me develop into a good man." By good, we should understand noble and brave. Describing how this development came about, he revealed that, "As a means to this end, he had me learn every word of Homer." He did so, apparently, by listening to the recitation of Homer's poems "nearly every day," as Xenophon reports. Yet more. As Socrates explains, Niceratus not only learned the literal words of the poem but their "deeper sense," that is, what they really meant.[4] Similarly, the fifth century BC epinician poet Pindar recommended the memorization of and adherence to Homer's wisdom. "And among the sayings of Homer, treat this one with care and observe it."[5]

Given Greece's leading educators at the time, this appreciation of Homer only makes sense. For the wealthy and those with influence—men like Niceratus' father, Nicias—these teachers were the sophists, a group of educator-philosophers that dominated Greek learning during the fifth century BC. Interestingly, Plato (through Glaucon) labels Homer himself a sophist in the *Republic*.[6]

According to Werner Jaeger, the author of the landmark history of Greek education, *Paideia: The Ideals of Greek Culture*, the "sophists regarded Homer as an encyclopedia of human wisdom . . . a mine of prudential wisdom for the conduct of life."[7] In this way, ancient Greeks looked upon Homer's works as ancient Indians did the similarly encyclopedic *Mahabharata* or ancient Hebrews the Old Testament (the *Tanakh*). Socrates, for example, reports that "some men claim that Homer and the other poets know all human arts and skills—everything having to do with human virtue and vice." He later goes on to say that there are certain "Homer enthusiasts" who "declare that Homer has been the educator of Greece, and that for the education and government of humans, we should take him up and learn from him, and that we should build up our entire lives with the assistance of this poet."[8]

The point is that Homer was Greece's chief educator and coach. The first century AD Stoic philosopher Heraclitus recognized Homer's influence at every time and on every aspect of life: "From the very earliest infancy, young children are nursed in their learning by Homer . . . it may be said that the same limit is set to both Homer and life."[9] The Roman orator and educator Quintilian put it this way: "As Achilles is among warriors, so Homer is beyond all comparison among poets. . . . He has given us a model and an inspiration for every branch of eloquence."[10]

Recent assessments of Homer's influence have reached similar conclusions. In his classic work on Greek religion, Walter Burkert explains that "to be a Greek was to be educated, and the foundation of all education was Homer."[11] In a short book describing his own academic interests and life, the influential Bernard Knox observes that since the Greeks had no authoritative religious text, they would oftentimes appeal to Homer and the other poets "on questions of conduct and belief."[12] In his own work, Cambridge archeologist Anthony Snodgrass concurs, noting that "there was one huge sphere of action where Homer was widely held to be an infallible guide, and that was good conduct. Not only poets, but politicians, teachers, and thinkers were happy to inculcate a code of behavior that was derived from Homer." Again, Snodgrass reveals that "we know of relatively late compilations which actually spelled out in detail how Homer could be used as a guide for every sphere of life."[13]

The last observation leads us to the third reason why we should care about Homer. Imitating the ancients and the many who lived after them in the Medieval (both Latin and Greek-Byzantine), Renaissance, and early modern world, we can learn much from Homer about how to live and flourish today. I heartily agree with the University of Chicago's James Redfield, who admits, "I find much truth in the Homeric way of seeing the world."[14] In my mind, the truth in the Homeric way is the raw material that may be utilized by us to think about and practice the good life. Not only did Homer help ancient men and women live better lives but if we let him, he can show us the way, too.[15] Along with independent scholar and writer Adam Nicholson, we can accept Homer as "the most truly reliable voice I had ever known," and as "a guidebook to life," even as "a kind of scripture"—in short, as "a source of wisdom" (about which Nicholson at one point admits that, after encountering Homer anew in midlife, he "felt like asking, 'Why has no one told me about this before?'").[16]

Some may find this suggestion absurd—that we can learn much from Homer about how to live and flourish today. That's fine. The truth is that not everyone appreciated Homer in the ancient world. This was particularly true for some during the early centuries of the Christian Church. Theophilus, for instance, the second century bishop of Antioch (in present-day Turkey), questioned the point or profit of Homer, who, he claimed, "deceived many."[17] About the same time, Justin Martyr suggested that Homer's "Odysseus made a virtue of vice."[18] And, perhaps most horrible of all for aspiring orators, St. Augustine, the outstanding Christian theologian and bishop of Hippo, judged Homer dull—this despite the fact that Homer was frequently and positively referenced in ancient Greek and Latin textbooks of composition and rhetoric (for instance, in his *Exercises*, Aelius Theon [first century AD] explains that "we praise Homer first because of his ability to attribute the right words to each of the characters he introduces").[19]

But let's not forget that the first Christians were not only following their own theological tradition but also the example of earlier Greek critics. For instance, the sixth century BC poet and philosopher Xenophanes criticized Homer for "attributing to the gods all things that are shameful and a reproach among mankind: theft, adultery, and mutual deception."[20] A bit later the enigmatic philosopher Heraclitus declared that "Homer deserved to be chased out of the assembly and beaten with rods."[21] And recall that Socrates (or Plato through him), though he loved and learned from him, felt he had to give up the pleasure of Homer for something better—that is, philosophy. In fact, in an early instance of European censorship and editing for the political common good, Socrates wanted to cut out parts of Homer or get rid of him all together. No matter how enjoyable he was, Socrates felt this would be better for everyone. Even though he admitted that "Homer was the best of the poets," he concluded that a truly healthy city could not admit him or similar poetry within its walls. "For if the city gives itself over to the sweet and salty Muse in lyric songs or epic poetry," he warned, "then pleasure and pain will rule your city instead of custom and the law and . . . the best possible deliberations."[22] So it was that his was a call for the sober clear-mindedness of water over the intoxicating euphoria of wine—a call for sanity in place of addiction.

Fortunately—as we've already noted—everyone's view was not negative. Some early Christian theologians, for example, used Homer's tales as grist for the mill of delivering moral lessons. Take the significant fourth century bishop of Caesarea, St. Basil the Great, who is counted among the chief teachers for both Roman Catholic and Orthodox Christians. In contrast to Justin Martyr, who saw nothing but vice in Odysseus (the chief hero of Homer's *Odyssey*), Basil approvingly reveals, "I myself have heard a man, who is skillful at closely examining the mind and meaning of a poet, say that all Homer's poetry is a commendation of virtue. And with Homer, everything apart from what is incidental leads to this end." He goes on to explore how Odysseus was, in his interaction with Nausicaa and the Phaeacians, an encouragement toward virtue.[23]

This idea—that "all Homer's poetry is a commendation of virtue"—was nothing new. In his work on Basil, Oxford classics professor N.G. Wilson concludes that, in his claim about Homer and virtue, Basil was likely referencing Horace (first century BC) or Dio Chrysostom (first century AD).[24] We see, for instance, a strong admiration for the moral side of Homer's poems in Horace's second epistle. There he explains to the Roman politician Lollius that he has been going over the "writer of the Trojan War [Homer], who teaches more clearly, and better than [the Stoic] Chrysippus and [the Platonist] Crantor, what is honorable, what is shameful, what is profitable, and what is not so."[25] As for Dio Chrysostom, he asserts in one discourse that "since everything Homer wrote is both beneficial and useful, it would be a vast undertaking to go through everything he has said about virtue and vice." In another discourse comparing Homer and Socrates, Dio explains that "both were devoted to and spoke about the same things . . . human virtue and vice, and things done poorly, and things done well, and truth and deceit, and how the many have only opinions while the wise have true knowledge." Finally, he cites Alexander the Great's view of Homer with approbation, that "Homer is a marvelous and truly divine herald of virtue."[26]

Before moving on, we should briefly note that the "Homer is about virtue" thesis is one that had deep roots. In his third century AD *Lives and Opinions of Eminent Philosophers*, Diogenes Laertius reports that "Favorinus in his *Miscellaneous History* says that Anaxagoras [fifth century BC] was the first to maintain that Homer treats of virtue and justice in his poems."[27] And recall Socrates' report that "some men claim that Homer and the other poets know all human arts and skills—everything having to do with human virtue and vice."

The big question, of course, is this: why did it matter so much to the ancients that Homer was singing or writing about virtue? It did for the same reason that certain literature matters to us today. Considering the many reasons why we read, somewhere toward the top of the list is that we read for know-how and wisdom. Most importantly, we read to know how best to live. It was this "how best to live" that ancient Greeks were interested in. They wanted to have the best, to do the best, and to be the best.

To understand this, we need to take a brief detour into the land of language. The Greek word for "best," *aristos*, is etymologically related to the word for "virtue" or "excellence," *aretē*, which is, in turn, related to *aretaō*, meaning "to thrive, to prosper" and "to flourish." To complete the circle and to answer the question, then, the Greeks devoured Homer to find out how to flourish as human beings, to thrive and prosper. All that to say they wanted to be virtuous or the best, to be outstanding.

But we should understand that the Greek term *aretē* shifted significantly in meaning during the millennium following Homer (roughly from c. 700 BC to 300 AD).[28] During that time, we see *aretē* in non-animate things as well as animals, human beings, and gods. As for humans, it could mean anything from valor, courage, success, and merit, to moral or ethical goodness having to do with the perfection of the soul (such as wisdom, courage, moderation, and justice). So, when we read that "Homer is all about *aretē*," we must keep in mind what the one making the claim would have meant by *aretē*. Regardless, each believed Homer was a profitable guide to virtue, to excellence.

In general, and for one reason or another, Homer was looked on favorably by those in the later ancient world. Among the many Romans who adored Homer, Virgil was perhaps his greatest admirer, writing his own epic poem, the *Aeneid*, in the manner of the poet. Well over a millennium after Homer's poems were first written down, the Neo-Platonic philosopher Proclus (fifth century AD), who wrote a commentary on them, declared that Homer's epic cycle was a "compendium of 'useful literary knowledge.'"[29]

A thousand years later, Homer continued to shape Greek (and Byzantine Roman) thinking and life down to the end of the

Byzantine Empire, when its capital, Constantinople, fell to Ottoman Turk canons in 1453.[30] And even though Homer's pull lessened during the western Middle Ages, the desire and admiration for his poetry strongly returned during the Renaissance and the following centuries. For instance, in his 1605 work *The Advancement of Learning*, the scientist and philosopher Francis Bacon remarks on the staying power of Homer's epics relative to seemingly far more durable human creations: "The verses of Homer have continued twenty-five hundred years, or more, without the loss of a syllable or letter, during which the infinite palaces, temples, castles, cities have been decayed and demolished." In *The Art of Poetry* (1674), Nicholas Boileau-Despreaux declares "Homer's book . . . a delightful treasure," advising his readers to "love his writings with a sincere love." A century and a half later, Thomas Love Peacock judges Homer and his age "the golden age of poetry" in his *The Four Ages of Poetry* (1820). Finally, in his *Thoughts on English Prosody*, Thomas Jefferson similarly recognizes Homer's ongoing power to please:

> When young, any composition pleases which unites a little sense, some imagination, and some rhythm, in doses however small. But as we advance in life these things fall off one by one, and I suspect that we are left at last with only Homer and Virgil, and perhaps with Homer alone.

The title page of George Chapman's 1616 translation of the "whole of Homer" suggests that Homer was the "prince of poets." As prince, he went on to oversee, as it were—through the influence of the Romans—the flourishing of European literature. As a later commentator wrote, without Homer "there would be neither an *Aeneid*, [Dante's] *Divine Comedy*, [Milton's] *Paradise Lost*, nor the comic epics of Ariosto or Pope or Byron."[31] During the last five-hundred years, Homer has universally inspired admiration in Europe.[32]

Homer was important to many until recently when there was a sharp decline in interest some fifty to one hundred years ago. Writing just after World War II, W.H. Auden judged that "the days when classical studies were the core of higher learning have now passed."[33] Homer included. For several reasons, George

Chapman's prince has been buried under a mound of other authors, concerns, approaches, and ways of thinking about life.

But let me say it again: The Classics Cave hopes to change that.

If nothing else, we should care about Homer because his poems are the earliest Greek literature we possess. Consequently, they most clearly reveal the earliest feelings, thoughts, and behavior of this dynamic people that profoundly influenced the Romans, who, in turn, influenced every other European kingdom and nation-state. And whether for good or ill—doubtlessly both, though on balance for good—Europe went on to influence American culture and thus, directly or indirectly, the culture of most peoples.

These early Homeric Greek "first words," and the feelings, thoughts, and actions or behavior they reveal, are somewhat like those we have, however well-formed or not, when we first wake up in the morning—the feelings and thoughts that guide the rest of the day. To leave off with them—to forget them—would be like forgetting why we are doing whatever we are doing *right now* on *this* day. Have you ever had that feeling? Well, the same can happen to all of us, collectively. Why are we here? Why do we feel as we do? Why are we thinking *this* among all possible thoughts? Why are we doing *this*? Behaving *this* way? Reading Homer will help us remember our first feelings and thoughts, and how we first behaved. And perhaps if we carefully look at the beginning, we will feel a bit more comfortable with who we are now, and we'll know how to better trudge forward in the minutes and hours to come in this long human day.[34]

What were we doing? Oh yeah, *that*. So with Homer in hand—Homer the adored, Homer the culture-creator, Homer the life-guide, and Homer manifesting some of our first words, feelings, thoughts, and behavior—let's confidently move ahead, knowing we are engaged with someone whose work truly matters.

BASIC FACTS ABOUT HOMER

Who was Homer? In the ancient world, Homer was the divine "adorner of warrior heroes, the godly Homer."[35] At least that is what one epigram we have claims. Alongside Hesiod, he was "the most inspired of poets."[36] More specifically, for most ancients, Homer was known as the sole creator or *maker* of several long epic poems that brought to life and glorified many heroes among the ancient Greeks.[37]

In more recent times, however, and for good reason, scholars have doubted that one man alone was responsible for these poems. Rather, in one way or another, they have suggested that the epic poems are the evolved result of a long process through time. Consequently, various answers have been given to the *who was Homer* question. Of them, two stand out. What follows simplifies each thesis considerably.

One is that no one man called Homer ever existed. Rather, following the nature of oral poetry—with its basic themes, type scenes, and formulaic phrases combined like Legos or the colorful shapes in that old video game Tetris—, the epic poems were created or composed by countless bards over hundreds of years and just as many performances before live audiences. Some have called this the creation-by-committee approach. Bard A would recite a version of the poem following the usual poetic conventions and restrictions, yet putting it together in his own way to suit the audience listening to him. Bard B would do the same with another crowd, as would bards C, D, and E. When they all got together, as it were, for their annual bard convention in Chios (or when they met over the years and ensuing centuries), they would discuss their performances over cups of wine—what they sang and how they sang it. Their conversation about certain points of difference may have gone something like this: *What terms do you use to describe ships? How do they work—metrically, rhythmically? You regularly call Diomedes that? Is Achilles' anger the major theme for you? Oh, so that's how you describe Hector's death. Are the gods always* makar *(blessed) in your recitation? And what about arming or sacrifice—how do you depict them?* And ultimately—or so goes this view of Homer and Homeric poems in a nutshell, and all-too simplistically—the committee-originated poems were written down by some scribe once the Greeks had access to a suitable alphabet.

The other major view is that the poet who gave final shape to these epic poems *was* Homer himself—or, at least, a bard who came to be called Homer. Cambridge classics scholar G.S. Kirk shares this view when he writes that "Homer was an individual singer who came near the end of a long tradition of heroic poetry; he presumably acquired a repertory of songs from other singers and reproduced them in his own manner."[38] In this manner, this one poet was responsible for the poems in a way that the scribe of the committee-originated poems was not.[39] Though not creating them *ex nihilo*, from nothing, he was nevertheless the creative force behind the poems, a creativity that can be detected throughout.

What are Homer's major works? The sixth century AD Byzantine Hesychius of Miletus tells us that Homer's "undisputed poems are the *Iliad* and the *Odyssey*." Modern scholars all tend to agree. Therefore, we may safely say that Homer's most important works are the *Iliad* and the *Odyssey*. The one narrates a portion of the tenth year of the Trojan War. The other tells of the hero Odysseus and his travels home to Ithaca after the same war.

Were any other poems attributed to Homer? If we were to time travel back a few thousand years and ask the ancient Greeks this question, many would tell us that Homer composed the *Homeric Hymns*, some thirty-plus poems meant to glorify one god or goddess or another—Dionysus, Demeter, Hera, Zeus, Helios the Sun, and Earth, the mother of all, among others. Despite this ancient testimony, however, modern scholars deny Homeric authorship, dating the hymns to the few centuries (seventh century BC and on) after the *Iliad* and the *Odyssey* were written down. Otherwise, one life of Homer tells us that the poet composed a series of "fun poems" for a group of boys he was teaching in Chios: the *Cercopes*, the *Heptapaktike*, the *Epikichlides*, and some truly entertaining ones, the *Battle of Frogs* and the *Battle of Starlings*. The *Margites*, a comic narrative poem, fits in with these fun poems. Still others attribute the whole epic cycle to him, those poems narrating the events surrounding the Trojan War.[40] Today, as we have noted, the *Iliad* and the *Odyssey* alone are ascribed to Homer.

When were Homer's epics written down? Most contemporary scholars argue that, utilizing a modified version of the Phoenician alphabet, Homer or a scribe probably wrote the epics down sometime toward the end of the eighth century BC.[41]

What time does Homer represent? Without entering the academic battlefield that is this question, Homer's epics represent the world and values of not only the end of the eighth century BC, when the poems were written down, but also the three or four (or more) centuries before, including the Greek Dark Age and the earlier late-Mycenaean period. The reason why this is the case mirrors the long evolution of the *Iliad* and the *Odyssey*. When the poems were first recited—possibly as long ago as the very late-Mycenaean Age, let's say—they had certain features and reflected certain cultural elements and artifacts that were carried through time to recitations during the Greek Dark Age (c. 1100-776 BC) and onward into the Archaic period (776-479 BC). The result was that the poems came to represent the time when the scribe or final poet wrote them down, as well as the long centuries before. Consequently, relative to the first feelings, thoughts, words, and behavior mentioned in the previous section, the *Odyssey* represents some of our first words and the like from as far back as three thousand years ago.

THE BIG THEMES AND IDEAS OF THE *ODYSSEY*[42]

The journey (the odyssey). Whether by land or by sea, journeys—or odysseys[43]—were common in Homer's world. Since much of Greece consists of shorelines and islands, many of these expeditions were by ship. As we observe them in the *Odyssey*, there were at least four reasons to launch these voyages. One was to profit by means of trade. Another was to collect wealth by engaging in piracy. Waging war for the sake of sustenance or glory—yet another reason—was related in some ways to piracy. There was also the need to obtain news in other lands, from men who were friends or other men. The news might be specific, as with Telemachus, who wished to learn his father's fate, or general, as was the case with Odysseus, who "wandered much," Homer reports, after the Trojan War, and "visited many cities and knew the mind and thoughts of many men."[44]

As Homer presents it, the initial purpose for Odysseus' journey—*the* archetypal odyssey—was straightforward: he joined the Achaeans, the army of men gathered from many cities and led by

Agamemnon, in order to conquer the Trojans. After this was accomplished, his motivation for travelling was equally straightforward: he wanted to get home.

So it is that we glimpse the whole arc of Odysseus' journey in the *Iliad* and the *Odyssey* together.[45] He leaves home, voyages to Troy, plays a significant role in vanquishing the Trojans, and returns home, learning much and suffering a great deal along the way.

We may well wonder about the significance of the journey. On one level, the point is clear: it is an entertaining, even thrilling, storytelling device, where the hero leaves behind everything of significance to accomplish a challenging task, all the while leaving the one experiencing the story to wonder, *Will he succeed?* And, *Will he ever make it back home?* On another level, though, there is something much deeper going on. This, anyway, is how later Greek philosophers came to understand the *Odyssey*. Before we get to that, however, let's look at getting back home — the corollary of the departure. To do that, we must first grasp the significance of the Homeric home or household.

The Homeric home or household (oikos) and homeland. The first thing to know is that in Homer's world, households were typically multigenerational affairs consisting of and based on the abilities, efforts, and commitments of many household individuals. In the *Odyssey*, for instance, Odysseus' household is made up of Odysseus himself; his wife, Penelope; his father, Laertes; his son, Telemachus; and many serving men and women.

The second point is that the household was essential to one's identify. This is why Homer's Greeks are so eager to present their lineage to others — *who* they are in terms of fathers, grandfathers, gods, and so on. To a large extent, they *are* their household identity. Consequently, the last thing a man or woman wants to be is "unconnected to a household."[46] Odysseus puts it this way: "Nothing is worse for mortals than roaming without a home."[47] But this is precisely his position through much of the poem.

Odysseus often affirms the enormous value of a man's household and homeland. For example, while speaking to Antinous, the king of the Phaeacians, he says, "There is nothing sweeter to a man than his own homeland and his parents. However rich a home he may have in a faraway land, if it is distant from his mother or father, he does not want it."[48]

The sweetness itself had to do with what the homeland and household offered the Homeric hero. In short, it was his defensive and offensive team according to which he either had or did not have what was required to live and be satisfied. As one author notes, it was "the household that procured the basic goods of life that allowed you to flourish in terms of not only mere survival but also enjoyment, wealth, rule, status, and glory. . . . The household got you what you wanted and therefore assured for you some measure of happiness."[49] This was true for everyone attached to the household, whether the head of the household — say, Odysseus — or his wife and children, as well as household guest-friends and servants.

Because of the great value of the household for securing everything desired in life, it was dangerous for a Homeric hero to forget his home — something that occurs quite a few times in the *Odyssey*. It first happens in the land of the Lotus-eaters, when a handful of Odysseus' men eat the lotus, "a food that is like flowers." The problem is that "whatever man ate the sweet fruit of the lotus, he no longer wished to bring back a report to the ship, nor did he wish to return home. No — his only desire was to stay among the Lotus-eating men, feeding on lotus and forgetting his return." Later, the sorceress Circe gives half of Odysseus' men a potion that includes "mournful drugs to make them wholly forget the land of their fathers." Odysseus himself nearly forgets his desire to return home during his year-long stay with Circe. It is his men who have to remind him to go. "My faithful comrades called me out and said to me, 'God-possessed man, it is now time to remember your fatherland." Finally, Athena tells the assembly of gods that the goddess Calypso "detains Odysseus, wretched and weeping, and makes him forget [his home in] Ithaca by means of soft attractions, wheedling flattery, and beguiling enchantments. Regardless, he's tired of life with her and wants to die. He can think of nothing more than how to return [home] — even if only to see the smoke rising up from his own land."[50]

To conclude, then, the home or household was all-important to Homeric Greeks. Though a man journeyed away from home, the outward venture was always to enrich himself—which is to say his household. Accordingly, his focus was always on his home and homeland.

The return home (nostos). Since the Homeric Greek was always thinking about home, how he could profit his household with riches or glory, he was always—on some level—contemplating his return home. As we've noted, anything done, anything suffered while away from home, was valuable or had a deeper significance thanks to his home and thus his return, if he was able to achieve it. In the *Odyssey*, Odysseus and his men are not merely wandering aimlessly; rather, they are attempting to "win . . . their return home." Homer explains that, of the leading Achaeans who fought at Troy, Odysseus alone is "longing to return home," while the other heroes—Nestor and Menelaus, for instance—are already "at home having fled both the dangers of the [Trojan] war and the sea."[51]

The notion of the "return" or "return home" (*nostos*) played a significant role in the wider ancient Greek epic cycle. Therein, *Nostoi* or *Returns Home* relate the homeward journeys of different Greek heroes. The *Odyssey* is Odysseus' *nostos*. Homer lets us know this early on when he reveals that "all the gods" have finally "agreed it was his time to return home to Ithaca."[52]

The deeper significance of the outward and homeward journey.[53] To return to the deeper significance of the journey and the return home mentioned a moment ago, later philosophers such as the Neoplatonist Plotinus (c. 205-270 AD) gave this cycle—the journey out and the return home—spiritual significance. We see this in one of his philosophical treatises, where he urges each one of us on in our own return home:

> "Let us flee then to the beloved homeland." This is unerring counsel. But what is this flight? And how do we flee? It seems to me that Odysseus is a hint or parable for us when he talks about his flight from the sorceress Circe or from Calypso. He is not satisfied to remain even given all the pleasure presented to his eyes and all the sensual beauty he experienced. The "homeland" for us is where we have come from. And there in that place is the father. What, then, is our journey? And what is the nature of

the flight? We should not go by means of our feet . . . or by a horse or by some ship belonging to the sea. We should let go of these and not think of them. Rather, we should close our eyes, exchanging this way of seeing for another, waking up. Everyone possesses this way, but few use it.[54]

The journey or pattern or cycle of going out from the ideal reality of the One, existing in the material, mundane reality of the many, and returning to the ideal reality was later summed up in the Latin phrase *exitus et reditus*, exit and return—or leaving and returning home, we might say. It was a pattern recognized by other Neoplatonists— Porphyry, Iamblichus, and Proclus, to mention a few—and by later philosophers, such as the Medieval Christian theologian St. Thomas Aquinas, who patterned his *Summa Theologica* on the same general idea—that, in some manner, all things come from and return to God.[55]

Of course, life in this—*our*—realm of "the many" involves a great deal of struggle and suffering. We see this clearly with Odysseus and many other Homeric Greeks.

Suffering. The *Odyssey* is full of suffering. We need only think of the anguish of Telemachus and Penelope, who desperately miss Odysseus in so many ways—as father and teacher, husband and defender, to name a few. Then there is the quiet suffering of the swineherd Eumaeus, stolen from home when young and now under the thumb of cruel masters, the suitors, rather than the caring direction of a gentle master, as Odysseus was. We may also mention the suitors themselves, whose very desire for Penelope and power is a form of suffering that leads them to shameful behavior and a bloody death, and results in further misery for their fathers and other relatives, who not only suffer the loss of their sons but ultimately the anger and violent action demanded by revenge, including death—for one, at least. Most of all, though, the poem is about Odysseus' suffering. As Telemachus observes, "Beyond all men did his mother bear [Odysseus] to sorrow."[56] According to Robert Fagles' translation, his name may be given as "Son of pain."

Odysseus' twenty-year-long journey involves much suffering, both physical and emotional. This is true relative to the ten years he spends fighting before the walls of Troy—about which Nestor reports there was so much misery that no "mortal man could possibly describe all the harm we suffered"—and to the ten years he takes returning home. "Come," Odysseus says to the Phaeacians, "I will tell you of my grievous homecoming, full of many troubles that Zeus permitted while I was venturing home from Troy." Homer himself begins the epic by asking the Muse to tell him about the man who, "when he was out to sea . . . suffered much pain in his spirit in the attempt to save his own life and win his comrades their return home." As it happens, Odysseus suffers so much that he more than once contemplates suicide.[57]

The need to endure and the endurance rule. When Odysseus encounters the Phaeacian princess Nausicaa, he beseeches her from afar first by praising her beauty and then by cataloging much of the suffering he has undergone and what he further expects to experience:

> Sorrow that is hard to bear has come upon me. Yesterday, on the twentieth day, I escaped from the wine-faced sea. During all that time, waves and rushing wind carried me away from the island of Ogygia. And now some god has tossed me ashore here so that I may yet surely suffer even more evil. My guess is that the misfortune will not stop yet—not until the gods give me more.

Nausicaa responds with what we might call *the endurance rule*, that one *must* endure whatever suffering one experiences:

> Stranger, since you do not seem to be a base or senseless man, and since Olympian Zeus himself dispenses fortune and happiness to men, to both the good and the bad as he wills, whether he be a brave man or a coward, noble or base—so I believe that surely he has given misfortune to you. Regardless, *you must endure* it either way.[58]

The endurance rule is simple: to continue on, to go where you hope to go, *you must endure.*

We see the observance of the rule in action throughout the *Odyssey*. Odysseus endures many monstrous creatures on the way home, including the Cyclops, the Laestrygonians, and Scylla and

Charybdis. They all attack him and his men, most slaughtering and devouring at least a few of his comrades. When home, he bears the outrageous behavior of the suitors and his disloyal servants before fighting them in a battle he must, yes, endure.

But by what method does Odysseus endure? We see it in action when he chooses to maintain his cover by putting up with "the evil deeds" of his disloyal maidservants. He endures, first, by means of self-talk, by admonishing himself to go on: "Endure, my heart!" Second, he recalls a time in the past he has had to bear up with something horrible. This gives him the strength to undergo what he must now endure. "You once endured an even worse thing than this when the irresistible Cyclops devoured your mighty comrades." Third, he relies on the wisdom he has to leave the terrible situation behind. "But you endured until your cunning wisdom led you out from the cave where you imagined you would die." Finally, he finishes by simply obeying the endurance rule. "In complete obedience [Odysseus'] heart continued to endure even though he himself tossed from side to side."[59]

Of course, Odysseus would not have had to endure the maidservants' wicked conduct and that of their lovers, the suitors, if the latter had behaved nobly and received him as a guest-friend in the house—such as was usually expected.

Hospitality (the guest-host relationship[60]). Fortunately, not all was so horrible in Homer's world. In contrast to the reception of the suitors, men often supported one another in friendship and in the warm reception of hospitality resulting in the guest-host relationship.

Such hospitality and guest-friendship (a man received with hospitality was a guest-friend or *xenos*[61]) was the command of Zeus Xenios—the god of strangers or hospitality, who was concerned with defending the welfare of strangers in a strange land, those without the present security and benefit of a household. Upon Odysseus' sudden and rather shocking arrival at Scheria, the island of the Phaeacians, Nausicaa explains Zeus Xenios' command to her maiden friends, who are cowering in the distance: "This man who has come here is some unhappy wanderer. And now we must take care of him since all strangers and beggars come from Zeus."[62]

In both Homer's *Iliad* and *Odyssey*, the hosting of a *xenos*, whether a stranger or an already established guest-friend, involves formulaic steps both in his reception and his departure. Upon arrival, the host welcomes the *xenos*, offering *xenia*,[63] guest-gifts or gifts of hospitality, including food and wine, and regularly a bath or some other means of refreshment. After the *xenos* is satisfied and comfortable, the host asks questions about his identity, business, and needs. Following these formulaic steps, Telemachus acts as a perfect host when he welcomes Mentes (Athena in disguise). "Rejoice, *xenos*! Here you will be regarded with affection, welcomed as a friend. And then, when you have eaten, you will tell us about what you need." Later, after Mentes has washed up and has satisfied himself with bread, roasted meat, and wine, Telemachus asks the customary questions: "Who are you among men and where do you come from? Tell me about your city and parents." The point is to ascertain his identity in terms of his homeland and household. He finishes by getting to the most important point of all: "Declare to me the truth of this so that I may know it well: is this your first visit to our house, or are you my father's *xenos*?"[64] We see the same steps of reception time and again in Homer's poems: arrival, welcome, refreshment, and questions.[65]

The departure of a *xenos* also follows formulaic steps. First is the recognition, whether spoken or unspoken, of an ongoing duty of friendship and mutual hospitality. Such is implied in the ongoing friendship Mentes claims with Odysseus, and in the way Nestor and Menelaus respond to Telemachus once they realize that he is the son of their friend Odysseus. Such is also behind Odysseus' refusal to fight or engage in strife with his host Laodamas when he is hosted by the Phaeacians.[66] The other step is the exchange of gifts. When Athena-Mentes departs, Telemachus promises to send him away glad in spirit: "I will . . . give you a present so that you may go to your ship rejoicing. I will give you one of great beauty and value—a treasure such as only dear guest-friends give to guest-friends."[67] Likewise, the Phaeacians give guest-gifts to Odysseus upon his departure.

In Homeric Greece, the purpose of such gift giving and gifts was twofold. One, it was a means of exchange among the nobility, who tended to look down on mere trading—a form of exchange, they judged, that was about profit alone instead of friendship. Two, gift giving was a means of achieving glory and honor, in that the friend would report the host's great wealth and generosity upon returning home.

From all these points, we see how important the custom of hospitality was in Homer's world. Thanks to Zeus *Xenios*, the *xenos* could hope for safety and care in a strange land. Moreover, the establishment of the guest-host relationship conferred immediate and ongoing benefits in the form of hospitality and entertainment, an expanded network of friendships and alliances, and an amplified reputation among other men.

Given the significance of this custom and these relationships, we understand why there was such a feeling of revulsion, even horror, among Homer's Greeks and those later Greeks who would have been listening to his poems when the demands of hospitality and guest-friendship were not met or were blatantly rejected. We see this failure or rejection with the Laestrygonians, the sorceress Circe (at first), and the Cyclops Polyphemus. The last reverses the typical formulaic steps by asking questions first, eating his guests, and proposing a terrifying guest-gift in the form of eating Odysseus last.

We also see this with the suitors, who, as though they were sackers, act to take Odysseus' wealth and position rather than fulfilling their obligations as friends—as they and their families had been—to his household.[68] Such a reversal, one expressing a sacker-defender relationship, demanded a response—revenge.

Revenge. When Odysseus first encounters Nausicaa, he wishes her well by blessing her with the most important goods a young Homeric woman could ask for—a husband and a household. In doing so, he highlights the significance of household unity and friendship, on the one hand, and household revenge against enemies, on the other.

May the gods grant you as much as your heart eagerly desires—a man for a husband, and a house. And may a noble unity of mind and feeling accompany these. For nothing is greater and nothing better than when a man and woman dwell in their household with the same thoughts, feelings, and mind—a huge pain to their enemies and joy to their friends.[69]

In the *Odyssey*, revenge is the successful and ongoing defense of oneself and one's household. So it is that Eurycleia rejoices when Odysseus slaughters the suitors, who have behaved as enemies to her master's, and so her own, household. The slaughter of the suitors is the great and necessary act of revenge in the poem. Even so, the slaughter itself demands retaliation since the suitors' fathers and relatives must exact revenge for their deaths. With this, we see that revenge is not a matter of some abstract right or wrong—after all, the suitors were acting contrary to the custom of hospitality, and so they were actually in the wrong. Rather, as said, it is simply the defense of oneself and one's household. Beyond defense, revenge is also the way to avoid shame—which, in itself, is a kind of defense. As Eupeithes, the father of the suitor Antinous, declares: "Let's go or our eyes will forever be downcast in the future. Forever we'll be shamed in future times if we do not take revenge on those who murdered our sons and brothers!"[70]

Loyalty or faithfulness. In the example of the suitors' fathers and of individuals such as Eurycleia, we see how important loyalty was in Homer's world. We have already observed that one friend had an ongoing duty of friendship to another. Within the household, a similar duty existed in terms of loyalty. For the household system to work well, that is, for the survival and prosperity of the household and its members, everyone had to fulfill his or her own role, carrying out his or her own proper function.

Fortunately, Odysseus' household had many faithful members. The swineherd Eumaeus stands as the perfect example of a loyal servant. When Odysseus is away, Eumaeus continues to care for his master's property even though no one directs him in what he should do. Further, when Odysseus, still disguised, returns home, Eumaeus properly welcomes him in a way that is fitting for one who is representing his master. Later, Eumaeus wholeheartedly agrees to fight on behalf of Odysseus when his master reveals himself. Telemachus equally shows himself to be loyal as a devoted son who searches for his father and battles alongside him when he returns. Finally, there is faithful Penelope. When speaking to the dead suitors in Hades, Agamemnon praises her commitment and virtue:

Happy son of Laertes, much-able Odysseus! You acquired for yourself an excellent wife, one of great worth. How good was the heart in blameless Penelope, the daughter of Icarius. How faithful in mind to Odysseus, her wedded husband. The glory of her excellence will never fade, but the immortals will make among men on earth a graceful song for thoughtful Penelope.

By contrast, Agamemnon lambasts his own wife for treachery:

[Penelope] didn't plot evil works like the daughter of Tyndareus [Clytemnestra], who killed her wedded husband. Her song will be hated among men—and harsh will be the judgment that follows womankind, bringing a bad reputation even to those women who are upright.[71]

For those who betray the household, there can be grave consequences. For example, Clytemnestra is butchered by her own son, Orestes, in revenge for her betrayal of his father. We witness this as well when Odysseus ruthlessly hangs all the disloyal serving women soon after he slaughters all their lovers, the suitors.

Seen in the context of Homer's do-or-die world, where survival was no guarantee, such harsh punishments were perhaps necessary, as everyone had to do his or her part so the whole, the household, could survive and thrive. Acting well together meant survival. Acting poorly and against one another meant the opposite.

A similar rule—that consequences follow upon behavior—held for the Homeric world at large.

Human behavior has consequences. Early on in the *Odyssey*, Zeus expresses the general idea or rule that human behavior has consequences—particularly bad behavior. Speaking to the gods in assembly, he declares, "How shameful it is that the mortals even now blame the gods! From us, they say, come all sorts of bad things." Then he gives the general rule: "But it is through their own recklessness that they have sorrows beyond those that are fated."[72]

There are many examples of how this (bad) human-behavior-has-consequences rule works in the *Odyssey*. One example, offered by Zeus himself, is the reported demise of Agamemnon's wife,

Clytemnestra, and her lover, Aegisthus. They had engaged in a love affair, which Zeus through Hermes had advised against. And they had murdered Agamemnon upon his return home. Of Aegisthus, Zeus states, "He did this even though he knew it would mean his own utter destruction!"[73] Another instance is the death that Odysseus' comrades undergo after they eat the cattle of the sun god Helios. As with Aegisthus, they had been warned. Zeus ends up blasting their ship with thunder and lightning, and they all perish. A last example is the death of the suitors that follows upon their outrageous behavior. Here's what Odysseus says to them after he shoots their leader Antinous through the throat:

> You dogs! You thought that I would never come home again from the land of the Trojans, and so you squandered my household goods, and you forced yourself on my servants to sleep with them! And while I was still alive, you unlawfully wooed my wife, having no fear of the gods, who possess the wide sky above, nor do you fear the indignation of men that will come in due time. But now the ropes of destruction have been tied around all of you![74]

After slaughtering the suitors, and as if to justify his own action, Odysseus proclaims to Eurycleia:

> The fate of the gods and their own cruel deeds have conquered these men. They honored no one on earth, whoever came among them, whether a noble or a base man. Therefore, they brought on themselves a shameful death because of their foolish recklessness.[75]

The gods, fate, and human perception of the gods. With Odysseus' last remark, we see that, even though men experience consequences resulting from their own behavior ("their own cruel deeds"), they are nevertheless also fated or directed by the gods. "The fate of the gods and their own cruel deeds have conquered these men."

The role of the gods—led and managed by Zeus—in human life may be witnessed most clearly early on in the *Odyssey* when the gods sit in council discussing various human matters, including the

fate of Aegisthus and what should happen to Odysseus. "Come,"
Zeus prods, "let us all consider his return home, how he will go."
Later, Zeus declares the outcome of their deliberations: "It is [Odys-
seus'] fate to see those who are dear to him, to come to his high-
roofed house in his own fatherland."[76] At the end of the *Odyssey*, it
is also Zeus who, from deep within his mind, subtly directs Athena
to bring Odysseus and his enemies together in peace. In response
to Athena's question regarding what she should do and what will
happen (she asks, "Will you stir them on to destructive war again,
. . . or will you establish them in friendship?"), Zeus replies, "Did
you yourself not propose the plan to have Odysseus come and pun-
ish these men? So do as you wish. Still, I will tell you what is fit-
ting."[77] Athena follows Zeus. As always, it is *his* suggestion, *his*
plan, that directs human fate by means of the other gods—Hermes
and Iris, for example, or Athena.

Regarding human perception of the gods, though not impossi-
ble, it is a challenge for humans to recognize the activity and direc-
tion of the gods. Speaking to Athena, Odysseus declares, "It is
difficult, goddess, for a mortal to know you when he encounters
you face to face."[78] The reason it is difficult is because Athena takes
on so many ordinary disguises, whether man, child, or bird, rather
than making an extraordinary appearance as one might expect, a
divine manifestation in all its glory. In other words, who is to say
the man, child, or bird is not simply *that* rather than a god or god-
dess? The same may be said for the other gods who appear in one
way or another to human beings. So it is that it is difficult to recog-
nize the gods when encountered.

Human intelligence and skill (versus strength alone). Aside from an
occasional conversation with a god or goddess—as when Athena
speaks with and helps Telemachus, or Calypso gives Odysseus the
background story of the gods' response to his comrades' slaughter-
ing and eating of the cattle of Helios, the Sun, or various signs and
omens that are sent by the gods, such as bird omens sent on the
right signifying a positive outcome—Homeric Greeks have to rely
on their own intelligence to navigate life. Survival and happiness
require wits in Homer's world. Frequently, such wit and

intelligence involve wisdom and cunning—clever assessment, shrewd calculation, guile.

Odysseus possesses these forms of intelligence in abundance in both Homer's epics. He is "much-able," an epithet that particularly refers to his intelligence in devising plans that will accomplish the unthinkable.[79] When, for instance, Odysseus appears alive in Hades, Achilles marvels at his ability. "God-born son of Laertes, much-able Odysseus, you never stop! Tell me—what exploit will you plan that is greater than this? How did you dare to come down to Hades?"[80] Otherwise, Odysseus is always ready with a story, a clever response, or a disguise that will help him survive a situation—so much so that Athena is exasperated with him for his ever-readiness after he tells yet another story, doubtlessly in the name of caution for survival. She says:

> There's no getting by you! Whoever wants to outdo you in guile must truly be cunning and full of wiles—even if it is a god facing you! You cruel man of many counsels, you cannot get enough of deception! It appears that even in your own land you cannot stop all the trickery and all the made-up stories that you adore from the bottom of your heart![81]

As for clever responses, we may cite the ingenious name Odysseus offers to the Cyclops Polyphemus when the latter asks him to identify himself. "My name is Nobody," he announces. The name eventually leads the Cyclops to declare, "Out of all his friends, I will eat Nobody last." And when the other Cyclopes come to see what is wrong with Polyphemus, when he is shouting and crying after Odysseus has violently blinded him, he reports, "Friends, Nobody is killing me by guile or by strength!"[82]

So it is that intelligence and skill in the form of wisdom and craft outperform physical strength alone in the *Odyssey*. We see this not only when Odysseus devises his plan to blind Polyphemus to escape his cave ("you endured until your cunning wisdom led you out of the cave"[83]) but also in the story told by the bard Demodocus about Ares' adulterous love affair with Aphrodite, the wife of Hephaestus. The smith god Hephaestus is himself physically disabled.

Relative to the war god Ares, who is strong and quick, Hephaestus is weak and slow (at least in his lower body). Nevertheless, when Hephaestus brilliantly traps Ares and Aphrodite in an adulterous act, Demodocus, in the voice of the gods, makes clear the moral lesson: "Bad deeds do not thrive. The slow overtakes the swift—just as now Hephaestus, slow as he is, has seized Ares, even though he is the swiftest of the gods who hold Olympus. Lame, he has seized him by craft. Ares must pay the fine for adultery."[84]

Truth and falsehood (reality versus appearance). Reality—or truth, what actually is—is not always readily apparent in the *Odyssey*. When gods appear as humans and humans seem divine; when the old turn out to be strong and the young weak; when the best behave in shameful ways and the apparently shameful are actually the best; when all of reality is a shape-shifting thing like the sea god Proteus, who appears as one thing and then another and only reveals himself if one holds on to him long enough;—when the world is such, the question is, How can one *know*? How can one assess the truth when what appears to be may not be after all?

The problem of reality versus appearance is particularly striking in the case of the identity of persons. When one asks another, "Who are you?" it is possible, of course, to offer the truth or to tell a lie. This is why Odysseus is able to pass himself off as someone else so many times throughout the poem. Several times he is a man from Crete. Another, he is from Alybas. Homer expresses the problem this way: "As Odysseus spoke [to Penelope], he made the many falsehoods of his tale [regarding his false identity] seem like the truth"[85]— which is to say Odysseus passed off appearance (what actually is not, what is falsehood) as truth (what actually is, what is reality).

Telemachus recognizes the binary possibility of speaking the truth or telling a lie when he asks for the truth upon the introduction of a visitor (Athena-Mentes). "Tell me this, and recount it accurately. Who are you among men and where do you come from? . . . Declare to me the truth of this so that I may know it well: is this your first visit to our house or are you my father's guest-friend?" These expressions demanding truth—"recount it accurately," "declare to me the truth so that I may know it well"—appear time and again in the *Odyssey*.[86]

Given the possibility of truth or falsehood, people are sometimes skeptical when another introduces himself and offers information. Both Eumaeus and Penelope, for example, remain unconvinced when Odysseus, who claims he is from Crete, testifies that the *real* Odysseus is nearby and near to returning home. Eumaeus declares, "Ah, wretched stranger, you've truly moved my spirit in telling me about how you have suffered and where you have wandered. But in this one thing I suppose you have not spoken appropriately. No, you won't convince me with this story about Odysseus [and his return]."[87]

Sometimes, it is only a physical sign that can demonstrate the truth of a person's information or the identity of an individual. For instance, there is the revelation of a sign that only a few would recognize, as with the olive tree bedframe that Odysseus and Penelope alone know; or there is the detection of a unique physical feature, such as the scar just above Odysseus' knee; or there is the accurate description of an article of clothing, as when Penelope questions the "Cretan" Odysseus:

> Now, stranger, I believe I will question you to see whether, as you say, you truly hosted my husband and his godlike comrades there in your halls. Tell me what sort of clothes he wore upon his body. And describe the kind of man he was, and the comrades who followed him.[88]

In some cases, there is no possible way to identify with certainty the identity of a person. Such is the case with male ancestors, and, more specifically, with Telemachus' own father. Telemachus knows what he's been told, that Odysseus is his father. But how can he really know the truth? When Athena-Mentes asks him, "Are you, so tall as you are, truly the son of Odysseus?" Telemachus skeptically responds, "My mother tells me that I am Odysseus' son. But me—I don't know. For what man has ever known his male ancestors with certainty?"[89]

Spiritual growth (Telemachus and Odysseus). Fortunately, Telemachus' uncertainty morphs into certainty when Odysseus returns. This is not the only change he undergoes. From the beginning of the *Odyssey* to its conclusion, Telemachus experiences significant change or growth—from boyhood to manhood, inexperience to experience, timidity to boldness, helplessness and inhibition to power and authority. Facilitated by the gods, particularly by the strong influence Athena has on him, the shift comes about, as most changes do, thanks to circumstances: his absent father, the presence of the adversarial suitors, his journey to the Peloponnese to learn news of his father's fate, the demand to get revenge and slaughter the suitors, and the final need to defend his family and allies against the suitors' relatives. To some extent, the change is merely the same as or coincidental with "growing up." Whatever we term it, though, it involves a profound transformation on a spiritual or psychological level. If at the beginning Athena descends to Ithaca to "put courage into [Telemachus'] heart,"—which is to say battle might and prowess,—by the end, he has become a man of courage, vying "with [his father] over excellence" in battle.[90]

Along the way, Telemachus himself and other people recognize the alteration. For example, when Athena "instill[s] strength and courage into Telemachus' spirit," he "feels the change and [is] astonished." "Thus emboldened," we are told, Telemachus goes "straight to where the suitors [are] sitting, a godlike man." Moments later, when he orders the suitors to disperse and gather together in the morning, they are "amazed at Telemachus because he spoke boldly."[91] Much later, after he returns home from journeying abroad, "all the people" of the town are equally overcome at his transformation. Homer reports that as he walks through the place of assembly, they stare at him as one who is so full of "wondrous grace."[92] Penelope similarly notices a change in her son. From a boy who earlier complains about a lack of power and control in his own house, Telemachus shifts to the opposite: "No man here will thwart my will," he forcefully declares to his mother, late in the *Odyssey*, "even if I wished to give this bow to the stranger as a gift for him to take away." He turns and orders her to "go to your chamber and busy yourself with your own tasks." In the end, he claims the status of a man for himself and exercises the authority appropriate to this status. "As for the bow, the men will worry about it, but I most of all since I have the authority in the house." His mother is correspondingly impressed—at her son and his alteration. "Seized with amazement," Homer relates, "Penelope went back to her chamber, storing the wise saying of her son in her heart."[93]

As for Odysseus, he also transforms, though his growth is far more subtle, a shift that is, in the end and in its fullness, only hinted at or prophesied (about which, more in a moment under "*Happiness*"). For now, we may note an apparent shift that is hinted at just after the slaughter of the suitors. When the nurse Eurycleia witnesses them sprawled out in bloody destruction in the great hall, she cries out for joy, celebrating her master's mighty deed. Odysseus' response is revealing. He "stopped [Eurycleia] and checked her in her eagerness, speaking to her with winged words, 'Rejoice in your own spirit, old woman, but hold yourself back and do not cry aloud. It is an unholy thing to glory-boast over slain men.'" The command is surprising given the fact that it was the norm in Odysseus' world to glory-boast over the dead—something that repeatedly occurs in the *Iliad*. Moreover, it comes from the man who, at the very beginning of his battle for revenge, prays to Apollo for the "glory-boast," the very thing he now forbids to Eurycleia. But now something has changed—something that leaves us to speculate as we do not have much else to go on aside from the peace and friendship rather than conflict and enmity that eventually come to Odysseus and the suitors' relatives in the final lines of the poem.

Happiness or happy prosperity. That admitted, we know that a profound change is in store for Odysseus, one that will ultimately result in a settled happiness or "happy prosperity" for him and his people.[94] We know this thanks to the prophecy the blind seer Tiresias gives to Odysseus when he visits him in Hades:

> But when you have slaughtered the suiters in your halls, . . . then go abroad, taking a shapely oar with you. Go until you come to men who know nothing of the sea and do not eat food mixed with salt. Indeed, they know nothing of ships with purple cheeks or of shapely oars that serve as wings for ships. And I will give you a sign that will be readily apparent to you, one that will not escape your notice. When you meet up with another traveler, and he says that you have a winnowing-fan on your

shining shoulder, then plant your shapely oar in the earth and make fine offerings to lord Poseidon . . . Then, go home and offer sacred hecatombs to the immortal gods, who possess the wide sky—offer them to each one in due order. And death will come to you away from the sea, a gentle death that will lay you low when you have grown old. And your people will exist in happy prosperity around you.[95]

Most significantly, Odysseus's life, his focus, will shift away from the sea and everything the sea represents—being away from home, instability, suffering—to a prosperous existence among his people in his homeland at home. Interestingly, this shift will occur for Odysseus thanks to, or in some unexpressed connection with, a people who do not even know the sea, so much so that they do not use salt to enhance their food.

How do we know the hero of the *Odyssey* will actually experience this transformation? How do we know he will end happy? The short answer is we don't. But if we take Tiresias at his word, which is a reasonable thing to do given Homer's world, it *will* happen. "With these words," Tiresias declares to Odysseus, "I speak unerring truth to you." With his people, Odysseus will be happy. And rather than a violent death in battle or an agonizing end at sea, he'll experience a gentle passing in his old age.[96]

So it is we understand that the *Odyssey*—and more so the *Iliad* and *Odyssey* together—is about happiness. It is about that shift, that transformation, that leads to a better, more peaceful life.

Perhaps ancient philosophers such as the Neoplatonist Plotinus were right to see in it something deeper than an exciting story with battles, warrior-heroes, and monsters. We'll end, then, with Plotinus:

"Let us flee then to the beloved homeland." This is unerring counsel. But what is this flight? And how do we flee? It seems to me that Odysseus is a hint or parable for us when he talks about his flight. . . . What, then, is our journey? . . . We should not go by means of our feet . . . or by a horse or by some ship belonging to the sea. We should let go of these and not think of them. Rather, we should close our eyes, exchanging this way of seeing for another, waking up. Everyone possesses this way, but few use it.

Of course, what this means for the one who encounters Odysseus and his odyssey, his going out and return home, will depend on the one listening to or reading the poem, and perhaps a good deal of creative imagination.

LET'S GO!

From what we know about ancient sailing and ships—as, for instance, from the late fourteenth century BC wreckage found at Uluburun off the southern coast of Turkey—, Odysseus would have made his voyage from Ithaca to Troy and back, and everywhere in between, in a relatively small ship. When there was wind, the ship would have cut along the surface of the sea with its sails unfurled. When there was not, his men would have propelled the ship forward by means of long oars, with Odysseus, perhaps, perched in the rear steering, the *kubernētēs* or pilot (governor) of the ship.

The Classics Cave invites you to venture along with Odysseus and his men in a dangerous world where survival is anything but certain. Encounter horrific monsters, angry gods, and arrogant men, all hoping to cause you pain, take advantage of you, and murder you. Know what it means to suffer and to endure and, finally, to make it home, to achieve your goal, only to realize that your journey and everything it entails is not yet over—that there's more suffering to come. Even so, you'll come to recognize the good as well, the good of the help of wise gods, of courage and dogged determination, of family, friendship, hospitality, and loyalty, of food and wine, storytelling, music, and sport—and more, much more.

However you come, whether by ancient ship or a comfortable armchair, get ready to learn something about the way ancient Greeks felt, thought, spoke, and behaved thousands of years ago, as well as how we humans still feel, think, speak, and act today. *Let's go!*

Note: As you read along, observe that you will always know where you are in *The Best of Homer's* Odyssey in a few ways. First, the very top of the righthand page will let you know what book you are in, along with the book's title—say, Book 15 • STORIES AND RETURNS. Second, you will notice line numbers for both translated and summarized passages. Translated passages have an overall block number, for example, 158-220 (as appears in Book 1), which signifies lines 158 through 220 (that is, lines of the poem). Translated passages are also numbered every ten lines, indicated by bracketed numbers such as [160]. Narrative summary passages (in *italics*) are likewise assigned a block number, say 96-157 (as appears for the narrative summary passage that comes before the aforementioned passage in Book 1). The only exception to this system of block numbering is beginning passages, which are not numbered. The reason for this is that all beginning passages start with line one. The ending line number may be determined by looking at the first narrative summary passage and subtracting one. For instance, if that number is 96-157, as in the example above, then the translated beginning passage's range would be 1-95.

NOTES

[1] Moses Finley, *The World of Odysseus* (New York: The New York Review of Books), 12. See also Raffaella Cribiore, *Gymnastics of the Mind: Greek Education in Hellenistic and Roman Egypt* (Princeton: Princeton University Press, 2001), 194 ff.

[2] For Socrates' admission and what he has to say about Homer, see Plato, *Republic* 10.595b-c. For Socrates, Homer was "the beginning of the poetic tribe" and "the first teacher and beginner of all these beauties of tragedy." Still, he level-headedly asserts that "we must not honor a man above truth, but, as I say, speak our minds." More recently, but similarly relative to addiction, Adam Nicholson has explained that "Homer-love feels like a disease" (*Why Homer Matters*, 32).

[3] See Diogenes Laertius, *Lives and Opinions of Eminent Philosophers* 2.133.

[4] See Xenophon, *Symposium* 3.5-6. Socrates goes on to explain that Niceratus "overlooked nothing valuable or worthwhile in the poems."

[5] See Pindar, *Pythian* 4.277-278.

[6] See Plato, *Republic* 10.596d. In this case, the label was no compliment. In Plato's *Theaetetus* 152e ff., Socrates calls Homer and his sophist allies the philosophers of flux or becoming. Since Plato preferred being to becoming, this assessment was tantamount to saying that the sophists didn't know what they were talking about.

[7] Werner Jaeger, *Paideia: The Ideals of Greek Culture*, vol. 1, trans. Gilbert Highet (New York: Oxford University Press, 1945), 296.

[8] See Plato, *Republic* 10.598d-e and 606e. In this case, the Greek words for virtue (*aretē*) and vice (*kakia*) may also be given as "excellence" and "mediocrity" or "success" and "failure."

[9] Heraclitus, *Homeric Problems* 1.5-7. Cited in Richard Hunter, "Homer and Greek Literature," in *The Cambridge Companion to Homer* (Cambridge: Cambridge University Press, 2004), 235.

[10] Quintilian, *Institutes* 10.2.

[11] Walter Burkert, *Greek Religion*, trans. John Raffan (Cambridge: Harvard University Press, 1985), 120.

[12] Bernard Knox, *The Oldest Dead White European Males and Other Reflections on the Classics* (New York: W.W. Norton and Company, 1993), 94.

[13] Anthony Snodgrass, *Homer and the Artists: Text and Picture in Early Greek Art.* (Cambridge: Cambridge University Press, 1998), 2, 4, 6.

[14] James M. Redfield, *Nature and Culture in the Iliad: The Tragedy of Hector.* Expanded edition. (Durham: Duke University Press, 1994), xv.

[15] For how this may be the case, see *The Wisdom & Way of Homer: Pocket Edition* and *Homer Workbook & Journal* (Sugar Land: The Classics Cave, 2022).

[16] See Adam Nicholson, *Why Homer Matters* (New York: Picador, 2014), 11, 32. For Nicholson, this "scripture" is "for me, an ancient book, full of urgent imperatives and ancient meanings . . . to be puzzled out" (32). Similar to Nicholson, though in different terms, for William E. Gladstone, the long-time, on-again-off-again nineteenth century prime minister of Great Britain, "Homer was," as Richard Jenkins explains in *The Victorians and Ancient Greece* (1980), "quite literally, a sacred book." This conclusion fit well with the general Victorian view that "Homer had been the Bible of the Greeks." Indeed, Homer (and other Greeks) was a "preparation for the gospel," whose "religion contained memories of God's revelation to primitive man" (202-204).

[17] See Theophilus of Antioch, *To Autolycus* 3.1-2.

[18] See Justin Martyr, *Discourse to the Greeks* 1.

[19] For St. Augustine's response, see Cathy Gere, *The Tomb of Agamemnon: Mycenae and the Search for a Hero* (London: Profile Books, 2007), 5.

[20] Xenophanes, fragment 11, in Kathleen Freeman, *Ancilla to the Pre-Socratic Philosophers: A Complete Translation of the Fragments in Diels* (Cambridge: Harvard University Press, 1948).

[21] Reported by Diogenes Laertius, *Lives* 9.1.

[22] Plato, *Republic* 10.607a.

[23] See Basil the Great (here slightly modified) in the Cave's *The Best of Basil the Great on Reading Literature and Education* (2021), 54. Commenting on the scene when Odysseus, naked, is introduced to the beautiful Phaeacian princess, Nausicaa, Basil observes that "Homer portrays Odysseus as adorned with virtue instead of clothing" (54). Therefore, he concludes, there was no shame in being seen naked. What other moral points or comparisons does Basil find in Homer? Elsewhere, to give a few examples, in his *Letter* 147 to Aburgius, he compares the unsettling plight of the prefect Maximus to Odysseus' own, "who had great wealth, but returned [from the Trojan War and his adventures] stripped of everything." In *Letter* 148 to Trajan, he mentions "the *Iliad* of misfortune in which

Maximus is involved."

[24] *Saint Basil on Literature*, ed. N.G. Wilson (London: Gerald Duckworth & Co., 1975), 52. For the whole of Basil's text, see his short work, *How to Benefit from Reading Greek Literature*, found in the Cave's *The Best of Basil the Great on Reading Literature and Education* (2021).

[25] Horace, *Letter 2*.

[26] Dio Chrysostom, *On Homer* 53.11 (or 36.11); *On Homer and Socrates* 54.9 (or 38.9); *On Kingship* 2.6.

[27] Diogenes Laertius, *Lives* 2.11.

[28] To understand how the Greek understanding of *aretē* shifted during this time, see *Aretē: Excellence or Virtue—What the Ancient Greeks Thought and Said about Aretē* (Sugar Land: The Classics Cave, 2021).

[29] For Proclus, see Caroline Alexander, *The War that Killed Achilles: The True Story of the Iliad* (London: Faber and Faber, 2010), 13.

[30] For the influence, see, for instance, N.G. Wilson, *Scholars of Byzantium* (London: Gerald Duckworth & Co., 1996).

[31] W.H. Auden, ed., *The Portable Greek Reader* (London: Penguin Books, 1977), 10.

[32] This was particularly true during the late nineteenth and early twentieth centuries. See, for instance, "Homer and the Edwardians," in R.M. Ogilvie, *Latin and Greek: A History of the Influence of the Classics on English Life from 1600 to 1918* (London: Routledge & Kegan Paul, 1964).

[33] W.H. Auden, ed., *The Portable Greek Reader*, 3.

[34] It goes without saying that other examples of early world literature are also vitally important to the project of knowing who we are as humans and how we are joined together as a human family. Not only is there the literature of Greece and Rome but there is that hailing from ancient China, India, and the Near East, as well as (though recorded much later) the great variety of Native American and early European literature, Aboriginal storytelling, and the rich narrative tradition originating with the many peoples of Africa.

[35] See *The Contest of Homer and Hesiod* 1, in *Homeric Hymns, Homeric Apocrypha, Lives of Homer*, ed. and trans. Martin L. West (Cambridge: Harvard University Press, 2003), 319.

[36] Ibid., 18, 353.

[37] The English words *poet* and *poem* are derived from the Greek verb *poieō*, "to make." Accordingly, one life of Homer tells us that Homer "made [*poieō*] the *Odyssey* . . . having already made the *Iliad*."

[38] G.S. Kirk, "The Search for the Real Homer," in *Homer*, ed. Ian McAuslan and Peter Walcott (Oxford: Oxford University Press, 1998), 39.

[39] The sixth century AD Byzantine Hesychius of Miletus had this to say about the making and writing down of one of Homer's poems: "He did not write the

Iliad all at once or in sequence, as it has been put together: he wrote each rhapsody and performed it as he went around from town to town to make a living, and left it there, and subsequently the poem was put together by various people, above all by Pisistratus, the Athenian tyrant [sixth century AD]." See "From Hesychius of Miletus: Index of Famous Authors," in *Homeric Hymns, Homeric Apocrypha, Lives of Homer*, ed. and trans. Martin L. West (Cambridge: Harvard University Press, 2003), 429. Hesychius' report reflects the two major positions scholars have historically taken since the late eighteenth century (and the analysis of Friedrich Wolf) regarding the fundamental unity (the Unitarians) or lack of unity (the Analysts) of Homer's poems. The poems were either composed "all at once or in sequence," or they were "put together by various people" over time. The debate shifted emphasis in the early twentieth century with Milman Parry's observations regarding the oral composition of the poems (though similar ideas may be traced back to the nineteenth century).

[40] Poems in the Epic Cycle include, among others, the *Cypria*, the *Aethiopis*, the *Little Iliad*, and the *Nostoi* or *Returns*.

[41] We should nevertheless note that there are some who argue for a later date, suggesting the latter part of the sixth century BC in keeping with the above remark (among other considerations) of Hesychius of Miletus that "the poem was put together by various people, above all by Pisistratus, the Athenian tyrant."

[42] Before launching into the themes and ideas of the *Odyssey*, we may briefly note that, thanks to the profundity of Homer's poem, such an endeavor could be a nearly endless process. Consequently, the themes and ideas covered in this section are the ones the Cave believes are the most significant or interesting. That said, we could have added others or highlighted aspects of certain themes and ideas we have not. Some examples include: the function of "testing" (whether of loyalty or identity); the nature and significance of omens and other signs (such as bird signs, dreams, and even sneezes); geography and the journey (the meaning of the sea, dry land, and human geography, whether "wild" or "civilized"); proper shame and boldness (relative to Telemachus); the device of storytelling and the role of the storyteller (whether that of Homer, various bards, or Odysseus himself); the notion of hiddenness (as we see with Calypso, whose name means "the one who hides" or "concealer," and the various guises we encounter throughout the poem); various "recognitions," particularly when Telemachus and Penelope and others come to know Odysseus' real, as opposed to apparent or claimed, identity; the dangers of falling asleep (for Odysseus) and temptation (for both Odysseus and his men); the importance of family and relatives (whether Agamemnon's, Odysseus', Nestor's, Menelaus', the suitors'); and, finally, a more allegorical reading of the poem, such as was commonly done in the ancient world, particularly among the Neoplatonists (though we include this briefly). On the latter note, see, for instance,

Porphyry, *Porphyry on the Cave of the Nymphs*, trans. by Robert Lamberton (Barrytown: Station Hill Press, 1983). See also Dennis Ronald MacDonald, *Christianizing Homer: The Odyssey, Plato, and The Acts of Andrew* (Oxford: Oxford University Press, 1994). For a nineteenth century allegorical reading, see Thomas Taylor's 1823 essay, "On the Wandering of Ulysses."

[43] The word "odyssey" means "a long, adventurous journey." It is derived from the name of the hero of the poem you have in hand—though you should understand that Odysseus' name does not mean "journey"; rather, it means something like "son of pain."

[44] For evidence illustrating the reasons to journey, see the following:

For "profit by means of trade": When, for instance, Odysseus comes to the land of the Phaeacians, Euryalus, one of his hosts, queries whether he and his men are merchants or traders out for a return. "You look like a man occupied with many-benched ships," he says, "the leader of sailing men, who are traders, ever mindful of your cargo, keeping watch over your freights and grasping for gain" (*Odyssey* 8.161-164). See also 3.72, where Nestor asks Telemachus and Athena (disguised as Mentor) if they are on "some trading voyage." Earlier (1.182-184), Athena gives hint of the nature of such trade when she (disguised as Mentes) reveals, "I have come here with my ship and crew on a voyage over the wine-faced sea to men of a strange tongue. We are bound for Temese with a cargo of iron, and we hope to bring back copper."

For "to collect wealth by engaging in piracy": When Nestor asks Telemachus and Athena (disguised as Mentor) if they are out "on some business" or on "some trading voyage," he adds a seemingly common alternative: "Or," he asks, "do you aimlessly wander, as pirates roam the seas, risking their lives and bringing misfortune to people in another land?" (3.72-74). The Cyclops Polyphemus puts the same questions to Odysseus and his men in 9.252-255. The ancient Greek historian Thucydides confirms the reality and extent of early Greek piracy and raiding in his *History of the Peloponnesian War* 1.2-12.

For "waging war for the sake of sustenance or glory": When Odysseus explains how men generally go about satisfying hunger, which is to say their desire for survival and everything else that contributes to a good life, including glory, he offers what may be considered the *why* or origin of raiding and warfare: "But there is no hiding a hungry belly. It is an accursed, destructive thing, which introduces many evils to all men. It is because of hunger that well-benched ships are made ready to sail the barren sea and carry misery and sorrow to hostile men" (*Odyssey* 17.285-289). In other words, alongside farming and other peaceful means of production, raiding others by sea was a legitimate way to satisfy desire—or hunger. Broadly speaking, this sort of raiding is what was behind the Trojan war, the great event that was waged as much for securing profit and winning glory as it was for retrieving Helen, Menelaus' wife, and getting revenge.

For "the need to obtain news": When Telemachus journeys to Pylos to speak with Nestor and to Sparta to speak with Menelaus, both men friends of his father, Athena (disguised as Mentor) explains that he should not feel any shame in speaking up since he "sailed across the sea for this reason—to discover news about your father" (3.15-16). For general news and Odysseus, see 1.1-3.

[45] It is a journey summarized in the first few lines of the *Odyssey*: "Man—tell me, Muse, of the versatile man of many adventures, who wandered much after he had sacked the holy town of Troy. He visited many cities and knew the mind and thoughts of many men. When he was out to sea, he suffered much pain in his spirit in the attempt to save his own life and win his comrades their return home" (1.1-5).

[46] See Tim J. Young, *A Hero's Wish: What Homer Believed about Happiness and the Good Life* (Sugar Land: EuZōn Media, 2015), 129.

[47] See *Odyssey* 15.343. To the point, in the *Iliad* (9.63), Nestor explains that a man would never wish to be without a family or home. It would be on par, he claims, with having an outlaw status. Much later, when the goatherd Philoetius first encounters the hero, he is right to observe that such a homeless, "much-wandering" man—as Odysseus appears to be—is a miserable man, "plunged . . . into misfortune and wretched pains" (*Odyssey* 20.195).

[48] Ibid., 9.34-36.

[49] Tim J. Young, *A Hero's Wish*, 130.

[50] See *Odyssey* 9.84, 94-97; 10.236; 10.471-472; 1.55-59.

[51] Ibid., 1.11-13.

[52] Ibid., 1.5, 12-13, 17-18.

[53] Admittedly, the "deeper significance of the outward and homeward journey" is not directly a "Big Theme and Idea" of the *Odyssey*. Still, we at the Cave believe it is important to know how others have creatively read the epic poem, and consequently how you—if you wish—can read it with imagination and deeper application.

[54] Plotinus, *Enneads* 1.6.8. The "father" may be understood as the intelligible world—that is, the spiritual world of Forms or Ideas, which is itself an emanation of the One, the Absolute or God.

[55] For the pattern or cycle observed relative to its broader ancient context, see Thomas McEvilley, *The Shape of Ancient Thought: Comparative Studies in Greek and Indian Philosophies* (New York: Allworth Press, 2002).

[56] *Odyssey* 3.95.

[57] For Odysseus' suffering, see ibid., 9.37-38 and 1.4-5. For Nestor's declaration, see 3.113-114. For the contemplation of suicide, see 10.49-52, where the options are to die or endure.

Regarding suffering, part of Odysseus' suffering has to do with human na-
ture—the general nature of human beings. As he describes it: "Of all things
that breathe and move along the earth, there's nothing weaker than a human
being—I tell you, the earth nurtures no frailer thing. For as long as the gods
give him excellence, and as long as his knees stand strong, he thinks he'll never
suffer misfortune in the days to come. But when the blessed gods send him
misery, he must bear it with an enduring spirit even though it is against his
will" (18.130-135).

Otherwise, we see that Odysseus suffers on both the sea and dry land. As the
enchantress Circe puts it, "I know about all the pain and distress you have suf-
fered on the fish-filled sea. I know as well all the damage hostile men have done
to you on dry land" (10.456-459). Part of Odysseus' suffering has to do with the
sea itself, over which he must travel to make it home. The sea is unpredictable,
even as the winds are that a sailor relies on to sail. It is the ever-shifting stage
upon which Poseidon stirs up his dark storms that give rise to towering waves.
The latter sport with the ships of men—ships that mimic the stability of dry land
but only as long as the sea and its god cooperate. Then again, dry land is also
unpredictable and thus a problem (or those things are that happen on dry land).
It is not so much a problem in a natural sense—though Odysseus struggles with
cold and a fear of wild animals when he first lands on Scheria, and some lands
do not provide enough food. Rather, it is a problem in the sense that a traveler
encounters other human beings while ashore. Odysseus expresses the fear this
way: "Ah me! To what land of mortals have I come? Are they violent and inso-
lent men? Are they uncivilized and wild, without justice or the proper ob-
servance of custom? Or are they hospitable men, loving strangers?" (6.119-121).
If a man encounters "uncivilized and wild" creatures such as the Cyclopes, then
he can expect to face danger and possible suffering. If, by contrast, he meets up
with someone such as the princess Nausicaa, as Odysseus does on the Phaeacian
island of Scheria, then he can expect to be treated humanely as a guest-friend.

58 Ibid., 6.187-190. Athena similarly explains that Odysseus must endure the
trouble that he is destined to suffer in his house upon his return: "Nevertheless,
you must endure the trouble and pain—you have no choice. . . . But in silence
suffer all the pain and distress, and patiently bear the violent abuse of men"
(13.307-310). Odysseus himself recognizes the rule in what was already cited
under *suffering*: "But when the blessed gods send him misery, *he must bear it*
with an enduring spirit even though it is against his will."

But are humans strong enough to endure? In Homer's *Iliad*, we learn that
we humans fortunately "come well-equipped to handle suffering," as the "In-
troduction" to the Cave's *The Best of Homer's Iliad* explains. See *Iliad* 24.49,
where the god Apollo reveals that "the Fates put an enduring spirit into men."

[59] To observe Odysseus' method of endurance in action, see *Odyssey* 20.18-21, 23-24. It may also be seen in Odysseus' words to his frightened men found in 12.206-212: "I went through the ship and I encouraged my comrades with soothing words, standing by each man saying, 'Dear friends, up to now we have not been ignorant of suffering and misfortune. Surely this misfortune that is upon us now is no greater than when the Cyclops shut us in his hollow cave by his mighty bodily strength. Yet even then we escaped thanks to my excellence, both my counsel and understanding. I believe someday we will remember these terrors, too.'" We can guess that Odysseus' speech to his men in the cave of Polyphemus included similar encouraging words — words intended to help his men endure, when he "spoke to [his] comrades to give them courage so that under the influence of fear no man would hesitate or draw back" (9.376-377). Finally, we may detect the method of endurance beneath Odysseus' speech to Calypso revealing his readiness to endure (see 5.220-224).

[60] In Homer's dangerous zero-sum world, the guest-host relationship itself is the opposite of what we may call the sacker-defender relationship, a relationship of hostility where one (whether an individual, a household, or a larger alliance) violently attacks another (of the same) for the sake of gain. We see the latter, for instance, when Odysseus and his men attack the Cicones on the way home from Troy (Ilium): "The wind took me from Ilium and carried me to the land of the Cicones, to Ismarus. There I sacked the city, bringing destruction to all the men. As for the women, we seized them and took them from the city along with much property and wealth that we later divided equally so that no man was cheated" (9.39-42). For the terms as well as a discussion of the "sacker-defender relationship" and the "guest-host relationship," see Tim J. Young, *A Hero's Wish*, 209 ff.

[61] Our word "xenophobia," fear (*phobos*) of foreigners (*xenoi*), is based on *xenos*. *Xenos* is a word that ranges in meaning from "foreigner" and "stranger" to "guest" and "friend" — thus, "guest-friend." *Xenos* is also the friend that hosts a guest-friend, that is, the "host."

[62] *Odyssey* 6.206-208. The swineherd Eumaeus later makes the same point to Odysseus, who, at the moment, is disguised as an old, wandering beggar. When Odysseus blesses him for taking him in, Eumaeus declares, "Stranger, it is not right for me to dishonor someone like you — not even if one more unfortunate and of lesser account than you came to my shelter. I say this because all strangers and beggars come from Zeus" (14.56-58).

[63] In the United States, there are at least two towns called *Xenia* — Xenia, Ohio and Xenia, Illinois, both founded in the first half of the nineteenth century. Each presumably wished to be known as welcoming towns, offering "guest-gifts."

[64] Ibid., 1.123-124, 170, 175-176.

[65] For other examples, see Menelaus' reception of Telemachus and Peisistratus (4.22-62); Nausicaa's reception of Odysseus (6.206-216) (though she leaves the questioning to her parents, Alcinous and Arete, who welcome Odysseus in a similar manner [7.146-239]); and even reception among the gods, when Calypso hosts Hermes (5.77-97).

[66] We see this ongoing duty of friendship most clearly, though, in the *Iliad*, when the heroes Diomedes and Glaucus recognize longtime friendship between their households ("then you are an old guest-friend [*xenos*] in my father's house") and so vow abiding friendship ("I must be your dear host [*xenos*] when you are in middle Argos, and you must be mine if I should ever go to Lycia"). The abiding friendship is even more striking when we realize they are actually enemies fighting on opposite sides—that is, before they recognize each other, acknowledge the deeper bonds of friendship, and plant their spears in the ground, agreeing to "avoid each other's spears when men come together." See 6.215, 224-226.

[67] *Odyssey* 1.311-313. The same also happens with Diomedes and Glaucus (mentioned in the previous note). When the two separate, they exchange gifts as is usual upon the departure of a friend. In their case, they exchange armor just as modern athletes sometimes swap jerseys. See *Iliad* 6.234 ff.

[68] The same is true in the *Iliad*, when Paris, even though he had been received as a guest-friend, behaves as an enemy by taking Menelaus' wife, Helen. When Menelaus prays to Zeus for revenge, that Paris might pay the penalty for his wrongdoing, he declares that the god should fulfill his prayer "so that among men to come a man may shrink from doing harm to his host, to the man who shows a guest affection and offers him friendship" (see *Iliad* 3.353-354).

[69] *Odyssey* 6.180-185.

[70] Ibid., 24.432-435. Since glory is the converse of shame in Homer's world, revenge is also a way of getting glory.

[71] Ibid., 24.192-198.

[72] Ibid., 1.32-34. Generally speaking, destruction (*olethros*) or sorrow, pain, distress, or trouble (*algos*) follow upon reckless behavior (*atasthulia*) or insolence, arrogance, or wantonness (*hubris*). Note that Zeus is fully admitting that the gods *do* cause some bad things, "those that are fated." Humans are fated and therefore receive some good things and some bad things (see, for instance, Achilles' explanation in the *Iliad* 24.525 ff.). Yet in a way that is not explained by Homer, but simply presented as fact, humans are able somehow to act *beyond* fate and so experience results—whether success or failure, joy or suffering, pleasure or pain—that are "beyond those that are fated." For a discussion of fate in Homer, see Tim J. Young, *A Hero's Wish*, 155-158. For a general discussion of Fate or *Moira* in the Greek world, see William Chase Greene, *Moira: Fate, Good, & Evil in Greek Thought* (Cambridge: Harvard University Press, 1944).

[73] *Odyssey* 1.37. For the whole incident, see 1.32-43.

[74] Ibid., 22.35-41.

[75] Ibid., 22.413-416. Observe how Odysseus cites both "the fate of the gods" and the suitors' "own cruel deeds," which are, presumably, "beyond those that are fated" —to use Zeus' expression.

[76] Ibid., 1.76-77 and 5.41-42.

[77] For Athena's discussion with Zeus, see ibid., 24.472-486.

[78] Ibid., 13.312.

[79] The Greek for "much-able," *polumēchanos*, may also be given as "ever-ready, resourceful, full of resources, inventive" or "much-contriving."

[80] Ibid., 11.473-475.

[81] Ibid., 13.291-295.

[82] Ibid., 9.366, 369, 408. Their response? "If you're alone and nobody is harming you, then it must be some sickness from almighty Zeus that you cannot avoid" (9.410-411).

[83] Ibid., 20.20-21.

[84] Ibid., 8.329-332.

[85] Ibid., 19.203.

[86] Ibid., 1.169-170, 174-176. They recur 15 and 7 times respectively.

[87] Ibid., 14.361-364. For Penelope, see ibid., 19.268 ff.

[88] Ibid., 19.215-219. After Odysseus describes the clothing, Homer reveals that Penelope "recognized the certain signs that Odysseus pointed out" (19.250).

[89] Ibid., 1.207, 215-216.

[90] Ibid., 1.89, 24.515. The word *aretē* may be given as "excellence," as we do in the text. But translators often give "valor" for *aretē*. The reason is that the particular excellence of a man *as man* is valor or courage. In fact, a later Greek word for courage (*andreia*) is related to the Greek word for man (*anēr*).

[91] *Odyssey* 1.321-324, 382. See also 19.268-269 for a similar astonishment at Telemachus' boldness.

[92] See ibid., 17.63-64.

[93] Ibid., 21.348-355.

[94] The Greek term *olbios*, given here as "happy prosperity," is an adjective that primarily means "happy" or "blessed"; it is a state of happiness that results from abundance. For an extended discussion, see Tim J. Young, *A Hero's Wish*, 63-65.

[95] Ibid., 11.119-137.

[96] It is a passing that contrasts with Achilles' own in battle before Troy —Achilles who chooses death and glory in battle instead of returning home to a long life without glory, and, presumably, a peaceful death. See *Iliad* 9.412-416.

THE *ODYSSEY*
TRANSLATED AND SUMMARIZED PASSAGES

BOOK 1

THE GODS IN ASSEMBLY
ATHENA AND TELEMACHUS

IN BRIEF: *The action opens with the "man" Odysseus struggling to return home from Troy. He's trapped and depressed on Calypso's island. Many of the Achaeans have returned; many have not—the ones who are now dead. Although men typically blame the gods for such ill fortune, Zeus, in assembly with the other gods, declares their destruction is the result of their own foolish recklessness. Such is the case with Aegisthus, who wooed Agamemnon's wife contrary to the advice of Zeus. Thanks to Athena's prodding, the conversation turns to how Odysseus will return home from Calypso's island, Ogygia. Once a decision is reached, Athena flies down to Ithaca disguised as Mentes to motivate Telemachus, the son of Odysseus, to act. There she encounters the suitors, who want Penelope and her wealth now that her husband, Odysseus, is presumably dead. Athena-Mentes speaks with Telemachus. Once she departs, Telemachus boldly calls for an assembly.*

MAN—TELL ME, Muse, of the versatile man of many adventures, who wandered much after he had sacked the holy town of Troy. He visited many cities and knew the mind and thoughts of many men. When he was out to sea, he suffered much pain in his spirit in the attempt to save his own life and win his comrades their return home. Whatever he did, though, he could not save his men, for they were destroyed through their own recklessness by eating the cattle of Helios, the sun god Hyperion. The fools! So the god snatched away the day of their return. [10] From whatever source you may know these things, goddess, daughter of Zeus, speak to us of these.

So then, all the rest of them, the ones who had escaped utter destruction, were at home having fled both the dangers of the war and the sea. That man alone, though he was longing to return home and for his wife, was detained by the queenly goddess Calypso, who kept him in her hollow caves and wanted to marry him. But as the years revolved one after the other, there came a day when the gods all agreed it was his destined time to return home to Ithaca. Yet even then his troubles were not over. When home among his dear people, he suffered more. Nevertheless, all the gods had now begun to pity him—[20] all except for Poseidon, who still hotly raged against him without ceasing until godlike Odysseus came to his own land.

Now Poseidon had gone off to the Ethiopians, who are at the world's end and live far apart from other men. They are divided in two. Half of them live where the Sun sets, and the other half live where he rises. He had gone to them to accept a hecatomb of bulls and rams. And seated, he was delighting himself at the feast.

The other gods were assembled together in the great halls of Olympian Zeus. And among them, the father of men and gods spoke first. He had in mind the nobleman Aegisthus, [30] who had been killed by far-famed Orestes, the son of Agamemnon. And so, thinking about this, he addressed the other immortals:

"How shameful it is that the mortals even now blame the gods! From us, they say, come all sorts of bad things. But it is through their own recklessness that they have sorrows beyond those that are fated. Look at Aegisthus! Beyond fate he felt like he had to make love to Agamemnon's wife, and then kill Agamemnon upon his re-turn home. He did this even though he knew it would mean his own utter destruction! Aegisthus knew he would die because I sent Hermes, the watchful slayer of Argus, to warn him that he should neither woo Agamemnon's wife nor slay the man. [40] Hermes ex-plained that Orestes would surely make Aegisthus pay for Aga-memnon's death when he reached his prime and longed for his homeland. That's what Hermes said. But his good intentions to-ward the man didn't convince Aegisthus. And so now he's paid the price in full."

Then the goddess, bright-eyed Athena, said in turn, "Father of us all, the son of Cronus, highest ruler—it seems to me that Aegisthus, who is now dead, earned his destruction. Given what he did, it was fitting. Anyone who does what he did deserves the same. But Aegisthus is neither here nor there. No, my heart is torn in two over the fate of wise Odysseus, that ill-fated man. He's suffering pain far from all his loved ones [50], trapped on an island in the middle of the sea. It's an island covered with forest, and a goddess lives there, the daughter of destruction-minded Atlas, who knowingly stands in the depths and carries the great columns that separate the sky from the earth. This daughter of Atlas detains Odysseus, wretched and weeping, and makes him forget Ithaca by means of soft attractions, wheedling flattery, and beguiling enchantments. Regardless, he's tired of life with her and wants to die. He can think of nothing more than how to return—even if only to see the smoke rising up from his own land. Yet now, Olympian god, [60] you do not think about these things in your dear heart. Didn't Odysseus delight you with many sacrifices by the Argive ships when he was in the wide land of Troy? Why do you hate him so much, Zeus?"

In reply, cloud-gathering Zeus said, "My child, what's this word that has flown past the wall of your teeth? How can I forget godlike Odysseus? He surpasses all mortals in his mind, and no man offers more sacrifices to the immortal gods, who possess the wide sky above. No, it's not me. Rather, earth-carrying Poseidon obstinately rages against Odysseus because he blinded the Cyclops—he blinded the eye of [70] godlike Polyphemus, whose strength is the greatest among all the Cyclopes. The nymph Thoōsa, the daughter of Phorkys who rules over the barren sea, gave birth to Polyphemus when she lay in love with Poseidon in the hollow caves. Therefore, even though the Earth-shaker Poseidon will not slay Odysseus, he leads him far astray from his homeland. But come, let us all consider his return home, how he will go. And Poseidon must let go of his anger. For if we are all together, then he won't have the power to stand alone in strife with all the immortal gods."

[80] Then the goddess, bright-eyed Athena, said in turn, "Father of us all, the son of Cronus, highest ruler—if much-thinking Odysseus' return home is now pleasing to the blessed gods, then we should encourage the messenger Hermes, the slayer of Argus, to quickly go the

island of Ogygia to tell fair-headed Calypso our inviolable plan about stouthearted Odysseus' return, that he may go. Meanwhile, I will go to Ithaca in order to stir up his son Telemachus and put courage into his heart. [90] He will then call the long-haired Achaeans to an assembly to renounce all his mother Penelope's suitors—the same ones who keep on slaughtering and eating up all his wooly sheep and lumbering cattle. I will also conduct him to Sparta and to sandy Pylos, to see if he can learn anything about his dear father's return—if somewhere he hears anything—and so that he will have noble glory among men."

96-157 Finishing her speech, Athena flies down to Ithaca and appears in the doorway of Odysseus' house in the guise of Mentes, the leader of the Taphians. Holding a spear, she sees all the "arrogant suitors" delighting in the checkers-like game of pessos, while the various servants and other men are mixing the wine and carving the meat.

Deep in thought about his lost father Odysseus, daydreaming about his glorious return, Telemachus spots Athena-Mentes and rushes out to meet her in the doorway, feeling ashamed that a guest was made to wait for so long. Greeting her, Telemachus promises help once she's had wine and food. Inside, he sits Athena-Mentes away from where the suitors usually recline.

After some time, the suitors come in and begin to feast and enjoy themselves. Eventually, the bard Phemius plays the lyre and sings at their command, and Telemachus speaks quietly to his guest so the suitors cannot hear him.

158-220 "Dear stranger, I trust that you will not be offended by what I'm going to say. A bard is cheap entertainment for those who don't pay for him. [160] All this—*the drinking, the feasting,* the lyre playing and singing, the consumption of another man's riches—is done at the expense of one whose bones lie rotting in some wilderness or grinding to powder in the surf. But if these men saw my father return to Ithaca, they would pray for longer legs and speed than to be richer in gold and fine clothing. But now he has been killed by some evil fate. We no longer feel any hope or comfort when we hear some man say that he's coming home. No, the day of his return has been lost forever. But come, tell me this, and recount it accurately. [170] Who are you among men and where do you come from? Tell me about your city and parents. And what kind of ship you came in. And what course the sailors took to bring you here to Ithaca. And who are these sailors—what land do they boast is their own? I ask because I don't imagine you walked here. And declare to me the truth of this so that I may know it well: is this your first visit to our house, or are you my father's guest-friend? I ask because in the past a great number of men visited our house since my father travelled much and stayed with many other men."

The goddess, bright-eyed Athena, said to him, "I'll truly give you all you want to know. [180] I boast that I am Mentes, the son of battle-minded Anchialus, and I rule over the oar-loving Taphians. I have come here with my ship and crew on a voyage over the wine-faced sea to men of a strange tongue. We are bound for Temese with a cargo of iron, and we hope to bring back copper. As for my ship, it is anchored away from the city, in the harbor of Rheithron, under the wooded mountain Neion.

"Our fathers were friends before us, as old Laertes will tell you if you will go and ask him. They say, however, that he never goes to the city now [190] and lives far away in the fields, suffering misery, with an old woman to look after and get his dinner for him when he comes in tired from the vineyard.

"I have come because some men told me your father was at home again among his people. Nevertheless, it seems the gods are still keeping him back, putting obstacles in his way. I don't believe godlike Odysseus is dead somewhere along the paths of the earth. No, I imagine he is alive on some island in the middle of the wide sea. It's likely he's detained there, held by dangerous men—by wild and uncivilized men. [200] Look, I am no seer. And I know very little about bird signs. But I'll speak to you as the immortals give it to me, and I believe it will happen this way. Your dear father will not be away from his homeland for much longer. For your father is a man of many resources and abilities. Even if he were held in chains of iron, he would find some way to get home again.

"But come, tell me this, and recount it accurately: are you, so tall as you are, truly the son of Odysseus? It is a wonder to see how much you are like him—your head and face and your fine-looking eyes. I know because we were close friends [210] before he embarked for Troy with the rest of the Argives, the best of them, in their hollow ships. But since then, we haven't seen each other."

In turn, mindful Telemachus answered her, "Well then, stranger, I'll explain to you everything as it is. My mother tells me that I am Odysseus' son. But me—I don't know. For what man has ever known his male ancestors with certainty? Whatever the case, I wish I had been the son of a blessed man, an advantaged man who was surrounded by his wealth and possessions when old age came to him. But now Odysseus has come to be unhappy among mortal men. [220] And this, they say, is the one who fathered me. I tell you this only because you asked."

221-305 *Athena-Mentes assures Telemachus that his is not an unknown and "nameless" family line. Then she asks him to explain the suitors' unseemly feasting—as it does not appear to fall under the usual categories of celebration, a festal banquet, or a feast to mark a wedding. She observes the suitors' obnoxious, overbearing behavior. It is shameful—surely to arouse wrath, she remarks.*

Telemachus groans and wishes his father had been honored by the Achaeans with a great burial mound and glory. Rather, he suspects the Harpies have caused him to vanish. So it is that the best of men who rule the land and islands surrounding Ithaca woo Penelope, his mother, as if Odysseus were dead. These are the suitors. But she will not tell one of them yes or no, and so they consume the wealth of the house.

Athena-Mentes angrily wishes that Odysseus might come and forcefully drive the suitors away with spear and shield in hand. Whether he will or not, however, is up to the gods. She then advises Telemachus to call an assembly to order the suitors to leave. As for Telemachus, when the assembly breaks up, he should go to the mainland by boat to seek news of his father. If you hear he is alive, she directs, give him another year. If dead, then give your mother over to marriage, offer him proper funeral rites, and consider how to slay the suitors as a man might do and as Orestes has done.

306-313 In turn mindful Telemachus answered her, "Stranger, it has been very kind of you to talk to me in this way, as a father to his son. I will forget nothing and do all you tell me. But come now and remain in my house even though you are in a hurry to be on your way. [310] Stay so that you may refresh yourself with a bath and satisfy your dear heart. I will then give you a present so that you may go to your ship rejoicing. I will give you one of great beauty and value—a treasure such as only dear guest-friends give to guest-friends."

314-318 *Athena tells him to keep the gift until she returns. Then she flies away.*

319-324 That is what bright-eyed Athena said. And with these words [320] she flew away like a bird into the air. But she instilled strength and courage into Telemachus' spirit and caused him to think more than ever about his father. He felt the change and was astonished. And suddenly it became clear to him that the stranger was a god. Thus emboldened, he went straight to where the suitors were sitting, a godlike man.

325-387 *The bard Phemius is performing for the suitors, singing about the heroes returning from Troy. Penelope comes down to listen, weeping. She asks Phemius to sing a different song since this one reminds her of Odysseus. Seeing her, Telemachus directs his mother to return upstairs to her own work at the loom, and to leave speechmaking to the men—namely, to him. She leaves, admiring her son, while many of the suitors wish they could go to bed with her. Before anyone goes to sleep, though, Telemachus, angry that the suitors are eating up his wealth and livelihood without compensation, orders them to disperse and meet in the assembly place in the morning. They marvel at his new confidence. The suitor Antinous informs Telemachus that he hopes Zeus never makes Telemachus the leading ruler of Ithaca, as his father Odysseus was.*

388-398 In turn mindful Telemachus answered him, "Antinous, I trust that you will not be offended by what I'm going to say. [390] I would willingly wish to be the chief ruler—if Zeus, at any rate, granted it to me. Are you truly saying that having such power is the worst thing that can happen to a man? Let me tell you: it is no bad thing to be the leading ruler. With it your house suddenly becomes wealthy and you yourself are honored. Even so, there are many other rulers, young and old, among the Achaeans in sea-girt Ithaca. Perhaps one of these men will carry the title now that godlike Odysseus is dead. Whatever happens, I know this: I will rule over our house and all the slaves taken in war that godlike Odysseus carried off as booty.

399-442 *Eurymachus, the son of Polybus, suggests the men of Ithaca will help defend Telemachus' property against any man wishing to take any of it by force. And yes, he should be lord over his own house. He then asks Telemachus about the stranger who has vanished. Did he say anything about your father's return? Telemachus tells Eurymachus who he was — that his name was Mentes. But inwardly he knows the stranger was Athena.*

After dancing, listening to song, and taking further delight, the suitors eventually leave, and Telemachus retires to his bedchamber with the help of his beloved nurse Eurycleia, whom Telemachus' grandfather Laertes had purchased for twenty oxen, and prized.

443-444 So then, all through the night, and covered with a lamb's wool throw, Telemachus deliberated in his mind about the way Athena had shown him.

BOOK 2

THE ASSEMBLY AT ITHACA
TELEMACHUS STANDS UP

IN BRIEF: *Old and wise Aegyptius wonders why the assembly has been called and who called for it. Telemachus rises to explain why he has called them together. He accuses the suitors of improper behavior, of wasting his wealth. The suitor Antinous in turn blames Penelope for tricking the suitors and putting them off with the burial shroud she was making for Laertes. She must marry one of them, he demands. Telemachus prays for revenge. In response, Zeus sends two eagles to foretell the suitors' destruction. The birdwatcher Halitherses stands to confirm the bird sign and states that Odysseus is nearby and ready to slaughter the suitors. The suitor Eurymachus expresses skepticism. Telemachus asks for a ship to go and search for information regarding his father. Mentor stands to rebuke the suitors and the others who have let the suitors behave as they do. Odysseus will return, he asserts. The suitor Leiocritus declares they'll fight Odysseus if he returns. Then he breaks up the assembly. Telemachus prays to Athena, who appears as Mentor. She gathers a ship and men for the young man while he gathers provisions. Finally, they set sail for the mainland to gather news about his father.*

WHEN THE EARLY-BORN rosy-fingered Dawn appeared, the dear son of Odysseus stirred from his bed and put on his clothes. He hung his sharp sword from his shoulder, tied his fair sandals around his strong feet, and stepped from his bedroom looking like a god. Right away he sent the heralds around to call the long-haired Achaeans together in assembly. And they gathered quickly. Now when they were already together, [10] Telemachus went to the place of assembly holding a bronze-tipped spear in his hand and accompanied by two swift-footed dogs—so he wasn't alone. Not only that but Athena charmed him so that the people were impressed by the way he looked. Indeed, the old men drew back in his presence as he sat down in his father's chair.

15-24 Old and wise Aegyptius rises to speak first. Homer tells us that his son Antiphus went to Troy and was eaten by the Cyclops on the return home. Another son, Eurynomus, is among the suitors. Two others farm. Aegyptius wonders why the assembly has been called.

25-34 "Listen to me now, men of Ithaca, listen to what I will say. We Ithacans haven't held an assembly since godlike Odysseus embarked in his hollow ships. Who, then, has called us together? Is it one of the younger men who feels the need? Or perhaps it is one of the older men, one who was born long ago? [30] Has he heard some rumor about the army's return—some word he can report with certainty since he learned of it first? Or is it some public matter he needs to declare and discuss? A noble and brave man he seems to me, a blessed man. May Zeus accomplish some good for him, whatever is his heart's desire."

35-44 Telemachus rejoices at Aegyptius' speech. Then he rises to speak in order to explain his need.

45-67 "The need is mine, for two evils have fallen upon my house. The first is the loss of my noble father. Among all of you, he was the chief ruler and was as gentle and kind as a father is to his children. And now there is a much bigger problem, one that threatens to totally destroy my whole household and deplete everything I have and rely on to live . . . [50-54] . . . The suitors come to our house every single day. And while here they sacrifice our oxen, sheep, and fat goats in order to hold feasts for many people. And they drink our sparkling wine recklessly without good reason. Consequently, much of what we have is being used up. Wasted! And no man such as Odysseus will stand up to defend our house from ruin. [60] We men of the household don't have what it takes to defend our house. No, our plight is sad—we've never learned the ways of battle. I myself would defend the household if I were strong enough. . . . You yourselves should feel indignant—you should feel ashamed before the neighboring men who live around us."

68-84 Telemachus warns them to fear the gods and begs to be left alone to mourn his missing father. After speaking, he dashes the scepter on the hard ground. The people pity him. Antinous alone stands to make an angry response.

85-96 "Telemachus, your speech has gone too far! Your feelings of rage are out of line, uncontrolled! What are these words you have marshalled to shame us? You wish to blame us, the Achaean suitors of your mother Penelope? Well, we suitors are not to blame! Rather, your dear mother who is full of tricks is behind everything we do.

"For the past three years, and nearly four, [90] she has been driving us out of our minds with false hope. She encourages each one of us with messages and promises without meaning a word of what she says. And then there was the clever trick she played on us! She set up a great loom in her room and began to weave an enormous cloth. 'My young suitors,' she said, 'godlike Odysseus is indeed dead. Still, do not press me to marry again immediately. Wait until I have finished this burial shroud for the hero Laertes, so that he will have one when [100] the destructive fate of death takes him down. If I don't make him one, the Achaean women will shame me. They'll express astonishment that a man of so many possessions and much wealth went down to death without a burial shroud.' That's what she said, and our manly spirits were persuaded. And from that day forward she would weave on her great loom during the day and by torchlight unravel what she had done at night. She fooled us in this way for three years. Yet as the seasons passed and the fourth year came on, one of the women who clearly knew what she was doing told us, and we caught her in the act of undoing her work. [110] And so we compelled her to finish. She had to.

"The suitors, therefore, make this answer to your speech and accusations so that you and all the other Achaeans may know our position well. Send your mother away from your house. Command

her to marry the suitor her father bids her to marry and the one that
is pleasing to her."

*115-160 Antinous goes on to explain that they have never heard of any
woman like Penelope—neither Tyro, Alcmene, nor Mycene. Still, it wasn't
a good move to deceive the suitors in this manner. They will not leave until
she marries one of them—"one of the Achaeans."*

*In reply, Telemachus complains that he can't force Penelope to leave or
marry. And if they must seek his mother's hand, they should do it in their
own homes. As for Telemachus, he prays that Zeus will grant him revenge,
that the suitors will be destroyed unavenged in his house.*

*In response to his prayer, Zeus sends two eagles as omens. Foretelling
the suitors' destruction, they fly above the assembly and tear at each other.
Seeing this heavenly sign, Halitherses, the best of the birdwatchers and read-
ers of omens, addresses the assembly.*

161-185 "Listen to me, men of Ithaca, so that I may speak to you.
And you suitors, what I declare is especially for you since I'm aware
of great pain and suffering coming your way. Odysseus is not going
to be away from his dear ones for much longer. No, even now he is
nearby and ready to slaughter and kill all the suitors. And this will
be an evil for the rest of us who live in far-seen Ithaca.

"Let us consider this matter, then, and put a stop to this wicked-
ness before he comes. Let the suitors do so freely. It will be better
for them, [170] for I am not prophesying without knowledge or
without experience. Everything I foretold about the Argives when
they launched for Troy, and about Odysseus of many counsels, has
happened. I said that after suffering much evil and losing all his
comrades, he would come home again in the twentieth year, and
that no one would know him. Now all this is happening."

In turn Eurymachus, the child of Polybus, answered him, "Go
home now old man to prophesy to your own children so that they
won't suffer evil. [180] Anyway, I'm much better than you at proph-
esying. Birds are always flying around in the sunshine somewhere
or other, and so they can't all be fateful. No, Odysseus has perished
in a faraway land. It's too bad you're not also dead—then you

wouldn't be going on about your prophesies and backing Telemachus' anger."

186-207 Eurymachus goes on to tell Halitherses to leave them alone or they will fine him. Furthermore, he advises Telemachus to marry off his mother. Until then, they will compete for her in his house.

208-223 Then mindful Telemachus said to him, "Eurymachus and you other noble suitors, [210] I will say no more, nor will I entreat you further—for the gods and all the Achaeans now know what is going on. Here's what I need, though. Give me a ship and a crew of twenty men to take me abroad, and I will go to Sparta and to sandy Pylos to see if I can find out anything about my father, who has so long been missing. Some mortal man may tell me something, or I may hear some report from Zeus, who often produces glory for human beings. If I hear that he is alive and returning home, then, even though I am worn out, I will endure for another year. [220] If, on the other hand, I hear of his death, I will return at once, appropriately celebrate his funeral rites, pile up a mound to his memory, and make my mother marry again."

224-239 Telemachus sits down, and Mentor, Odysseus' comrade and the man to whom he had given charge of his house, stands to rebuke the suitors. He asks if they behave this way to repay Odysseus' kindness—for Odysseus was always a good ruler. Well, he declares, they do so at their own peril considering Odysseus will return. He turns to the other people and asks them why they let the suitors behave as they do.

239-241 "I am indignant with the rest of you! You all sit there in silence without saying a word to stop the suitors, even though you are many and they are few."

242-245 The suitor Leiocritus responds by declaring that even if Odysseus returns, he won't be able to stand up to the suitors and drive them from his own house.

246-251 "Even if Odysseus himself came upon the noble suitors feasting in his own house, and even if he eagerly desired to drive them out of his great hall, his own wife would take no joy in his coming no matter how much she missed and needed him. [250] Rather, he'd meet up with a shameful death if he fought against us who so clearly outnumber him."

252-311 *With this, Leiocritus breaks up the assembly, suggesting Halitherses and Mentor should help Telemachus prepare for his journey even though he doubts it will ever happen.*

After praying to Athena, Telemachus encounters her disguised as Mentor by the seashore. She praises his likely might—like his father in accomplishing his desires in both word and deed. Still, she says, only a small number of sons are the same as their fathers. Most are worse, and only a few are better. Telemachus likely has the good qualities of his father. Therefore, he'll be able to successfully make the voyage. She tells him to forget about the suitors who are unaware of the "death and black fate" that approach them. They will all be destroyed in a single day, she says. Mentor promises Telemachus a ship and a crew of twenty men and advises him to prepare for the voyage ahead.

Telemachus returns to his house where Antinous invites him to relax and feast. The son of Odysseus reveals that he cannot possibly enjoy a feast in their company. No, he will go as he promised and figure out a way to make the suitors pay for taking his many possessions.

312-317 "Was it not enough that you suitors wasted so much of my good property and wealth while I was still a boy? But now that I'm older and wiser,—I've learned more by listening to what others say—, and now that my spirit grows stronger within me, I'll try to bring harm and death to you either from Pylos or from the people here in this land."

318-324 *Hearing this, some of the suitors mock him.*

325-330 "It's certain—Telemachus is planning to kill us! He'll fetch some allies from sandy Pylos, or possibly from Sparta, since now he's really, horribly set on doing it! Or maybe he wishes to go to Ephyre, that fertile land, in order to bring back life-destroying poisons. [330] He'll toss these in the wine bowl and kill us all!"

331-419 *Another suitor mockingly suggests that Telemachus will wander like his father and die. He proposes that they could divide his things and one could marry his mother and keep the house.*

While they go on, Telemachus prepares the stores of wine and grain for the ship with the help of Eurycleia, the nurse who helped to rear him. He tells her about his journey to the mainland. Hearing this, she shrieks but promises to keep the secret of his launch and journey from his mother. She is afraid the suitors will trick him, kill him, and divide all his possessions. Telemachus assures her that the plan has divine sanction. He further asks her not to tell Penelope until the twelfth day after he has gone. She swears an oath.

Meanwhile, "appearing like Telemachus," Athena gathers a crew of men and secures Noemon's ship. Later she causes the suitors to sleep so that Telemachus may join the others in the ship. They pack the boat with the earlier prepared stores, and, finally, they sail.

420-434 Bright-eyed Athena sent them a fair wind, strong-blowing Zephyrus, the West Wind. And he roared across the wine-faced sea. Telemachus ordered the men to take hold of the ropes and raise the sail. They did as he told them—they set the mast in its socket in the cross plank, raised it, and made it secure with lines running from the mast all around. Then they raised the white sails aloft with ropes of twisted oxhide. As the sail bellied out with the wind, the ship flew through the deep blue water, and the foam hissed against her bows as she sped onward.

Then, when everything was set in the swift black ship, they filled the wine bowls to the brim and poured out libations to the immortal and everlasting gods—and most of all to the bright-eyed child of Zeus.

So it was that all night long until the dawn the ship tore through the waves along its journey to sandy Pylos.

BOOK 3

TELEMACHUS WITH NESTOR IN PYLOS
THE YOUNG MAN LEARNS TO SPEAK

IN BRIEF: *First stop, Pylos. With the encouragement of Athena-Mentor, Telemachus meets up with Nestor, who hosts him, telling him about the great suffering the Achaeans endured at Troy, and about the successful and unsuccessful homecomings of the many heroes. He relates how Agamemnon was murdered by Aegisthus, and how Orestes took revenge and killed his father's murderers. He tells of Menelaus' journey to Egypt and of all the gold he gathered there. After an overnight stay, Telemachus departs by chariot with Nestor's son Peisistratus to visit Menelaus in Sparta.*

B UT AS THE sun was swiftly rising up from the beautiful sea into a copper-colored sky in order to give light to the immortals and to mortal men who live among wheat-bearing fields, Telemachus and his crew came to Pylos, the well-built city of Neleus.

5-13 *Mooring on the sandy beach of Pylos, the ship arrives as some 4,500 Pylians are making sacrifice to Poseidon and feasting on the shore. Athena disguised as Mentor leads the way to them. She speaks to Telemachus to give him nerve in his mission.*

14-28 "Telemachus, you don't need to feel undue shame, not even a small amount. You've sailed across the sea for this reason—to discover news about your father. You want to learn where the earth covers him over and how he came to his destined end. But come now. Go straight up to horse-taming Nestor. Let's see what bit of counsel he has tucked away in his heart and mind. Go up yourself and ask him to speak truthfully to you. [20] He won't tell you a lie—no, he's a very wise and prudent man."

In turn mindful Telemachus answered her, "Mentor, how should I go up to him? How should I greet him? I'm not used to speaking shrewdly with others. And isn't it shameful for a young man to pester an old man with questions?"

But the bright-eyed goddess Athena said to him, "Here's what will happen, Telemachus. Some things you'll think up by yourself in your own mind. Others will be provided by some god. Either way, I imagine that the gods have been with you from the time of your birth until now."

29-68 Athena-Mentor and Telemachus make their way toward Nestor. When they see the strangers, Nestor and his sons Peisistratus and Thrasymedes, among others, welcome them, sitting them on fleece throws and giving them roasted meat and wine. Peisistratus first gives the cup to Athena-Mentor because he is older. He commands her to pour out a libation and pray to the Earth-shaker—since, he declares, "all men need the gods." Athena rejoices at his wisdom and observance of custom. Praying, she asks Poseidon to bless Nestor and his sons with glory, and to reward all the people for the hecatomb sacrifice. She finishes by asking for the successful completion of their journey. Homer finishes by declaring, "Like this she prayed, but she herself was making everything happen." After her prayer, Telemachus pours out a libation and prays, and they all drink wine and eat roasted meat there on the seashore.

67-74 When they had set aside the desire for drink and food, the Gerenian horseman Nestor was the first among them to offer words. "Now that we are finished with that, it is a good time to seek out and ask [70] the strangers what men they are, since they've had their fill and delight of food. So strangers—guests and friends— who are you? Where do you come from, sailing over the watery ways? Are you out on business—on some trading voyage? Or do you aimlessly wander, as pirates roam the seas, risking their lives and bringing misfortune to people in another land?"

75-101 Telemachus replies with courage supplied by Athena. After explaining that they sailed from Ithaca, he asks about his missing father, who,

*he declares, was brought into the world by his mother "to a miserable life."
Still, he says that he has heard that his father fought by the side of Nestor
when the Achaeans sacked Troy, "where you Achaeans suffered woeful
misery." He asks Nestor if he can tell him anything at all, bidding him to
speak truthfully.*

102-114 Then the Gerenian horseman Nestor answered him,
"Friend, you remind me of the misery we endured in that land, we
the irrepressible sons of the Achaeans in battle might. I recall what
we suffered while roving after booty with our ships upon the misty
sea, we who were led along by Achilles, and while we fought
around the great city of lord Priam. How many of our best men fell
there! Warlike Ajax lies there dead—and Achilles, [110] and Patroc-
lus, a counselor equal to the gods. And there lies my own dear son,
Antilochus. He was strong and blameless, a man quick at running,
when compared to others, and a fighter. We suffered much more—
what mortal man could possibly describe all the harm we suf-
fered?"

115-192 *Nestor claims that not even five or six years would be enough
time to recount all the suffering. They fought for nine years and finally
took Troy. He explains how Odysseus was by far the best in counsel, and
how he himself was always one in mind with him. He informs Telemachus
how similar he is in speech to his father—if indeed he is his son, he says.*

*Nestor goes on to tell the story of how Zeus caused a sorrowful return
for the Achaeans thanks to their lack of intelligence and failure to observe
custom. "Many of them pursued an evil fate that arose because of the mur-
derous wrath of the bright-eyed daughter of the mighty father when she
put strife between the two leading brothers." Just as the Achaeans were
ready to return home, Agamemnon and Menelaus, drunk with wine, fool-
ishly and without order called for an assembly as the sun was setting.
Menelaus said he wanted to depart right then. Agamemnon didn't agree.
Instead, he wished to set sail after offering hecatombs to appease Athena.
Nestor relays that they traded grievous words with each other. In the end,
half of the Achaeans—Nestor among them—sailed off with Menelaus, and
half remained with Agamemnon. Then, as if this weren't unfortunate*

enough, the first half split in strife again on the island of Tenedos, thanks to Zeus the cruel and merciless god. Half of them, including Odysseus, returned to Agamemnon. The other half followed Nestor and sailed on quickly, knowing that a god was planning evil for them. Heeding a sign from a god, they sailed directly from Lesbos to Euboea, and from there to Argos, where they left behind Diomedes and his men. As for Nestor himself, he continued on to Pylos.

Otherwise, Nestor reports that the Myrmidons, with their leader Neoptolemus, the son of Achilles, Philoctetes, the son of Poias, and Idomeneus, with his Cretans, returned home safely. He finishes by telling Telemachus about Agamemnon.

193-238 "Even though you live far away, surely you all have heard how Agamemnon, the son of Atreus, came home and how Aegisthus plotted a pathetic end for him—a sad, sad destruction. But he paid the gloomy price for it! How good it is, when a man is dead and gone, for him to have left a son behind. I say this because Agamemnon's son Orestes took revenge. He made that father-killer—the scheming man Aegisthus—pay the price because he murdered his own glorious father. And you, friend, since it's clear that you are noble looking and tall, [200] be brave so that men to come may speak well of you."

In turn mindful Telemachus answered him, "Nestor, son of Neleus, great glory of the Achaeans, it is true. Orestes made that man pay by taking revenge. And for that, the Achaeans will spread his glory and fame far and wide, singing about his great deed in the time to come. If only the gods would give me enough power to make the injurious suitors pay for their transgressions—those arrogant men who recklessly plot against me. But the gods haven't planned this kind of happiness for me—for my father or for me. Nevertheless, I must now endure."

[210] Then the Gerenian horseman Nestor answered him, "Friend, since you have spoken about it and have reminded me of all this, they say that there are many suitors who have disregarded your will and caused harm to you in your own halls—and all because of your mother. Tell me, have you given them permission to

take over your house? Or do the people—you know, all those throughout the land—do they detest you, following after the voice of some god? But who knows? Odysseus may come home one of these days and make them pay for all their willful behavior. Maybe he'll do it by himself or maybe he'll come with all the Achaeans. If only bright-eyed Athena would choose to love and befriend you as she did Odysseus [220] in the land of the Trojans where we Achaeans suffered all sorts of pain—for I've never seen a god show affection as I did when Athena stood by that man. If she befriended you like that and cared for you from deep within her spirit, then all those men would totally forget about your mother and a wedding."

In turn mindful Telemachus answered him, "Old man, I doubt that what you've said will ever happen. No, your word is all too good. I'm amazed. I have no hope that this will happen, not even if the gods want it to happen."

The bright-eyed goddess Athena called on him, [230] "Telemachus! What's this word that has flown past the wall of your teeth? As long as the desire were there, it would be easy for a god to rescue a man, even if he were in a faraway land. As for me, I wouldn't care how much I suffered before getting home as long as I were safe on the day of my return. I'd prefer this over getting home quickly only to be slaughtered by my own hearth as Agamemnon was drawn in, deceived, and destroyed by Aegisthus and his wife. Still, death that is common to all men is certain. Not even the gods have the power to defend a loved man against it when the destructive fate of death finally drops a man to the dust."

239-312 *Telemachus tells Athena-Mentor to stop speaking in this way. He asserts that his father has already died and will not return home. Then he asks wise Nestor about Agamemnon's end and what happened to Menelaus.*

Nestor explains how Aegisthus came to seduce Clytemnestra. She initially held him off thanks to her own noble heart and the bard assigned to guard her. But fated by the gods, Aegisthus murdered the bard by leaving him on a desert island, and so Clytemnestra willingly moved in with Aegisthus. In the end, Aegisthus killed Agamemnon upon his return home.

As for Menelaus, after offering proper burial rites on Sunium, the cape of Athens, for Phrontis, the son of Onetor and the most excellent steersmen in a storm, Zeus blew him and his men southward from Cape Malea on the Peloponnese. Half drifted on the mountainous waves to Crete and escaped destruction even though their ships were lost on the reef. The other half—five ships—went on to Egypt with Menelaus. There he gathered much gold and other wealth among the Egyptians. During this very long time Agamemnon returned to Mycenae and was murdered by Aegisthus, who ruled until Agamemnon's son Orestes came in the eighth year of his reign and took revenge. Nestor recalls what happened.

307-318 "Orestes came from Athens and killed the murderer of his father, the cheating trickster Aegisthus, the man who had slaughtered his glorious father. The slaughter complete, Orestes held a funeral feast for the Argives [310] over his hateful mother and the now-impotent Aegisthus. Menelaus, good at the battle cry, came home that very day, bringing with him much wealth, as much cargo as his ships could carry.

"And you, friend, take my advice. Do not wander about for long so far from home. Don't leave your possessions in your house with those arrogant men, or they may divide all your property and gobble up all your wealth. If that happens, then your venturing out will have been pointless. Instead, I call on you and direct you to go visit Menelaus—who has recently come home from abroad."

319-370 *Nestor assures Telemachus that Menelaus will tell him the truth of what he knows rather than a lie, for Menelaus is prudent. Finally, the old man offers a chariot for the journey to Sparta and the escort of his sons.*

As the sun sets, Athena-Mentor recommends they finish the feast with proper libations and then go to sleep. Nestor declares that he cannot let them sleep in the ship when he can easily accommodate them in his house with all he has. He's no poor man, he says. Athena-Mentor agrees that Telemachus should go to Nestor's house and then speed on to Menelaus in the morning. As for her, she will return to the ship and to the young men, and in the morning she will sail on while Telemachus travels to Sparta.

371-385 After bright-eyed Athena said this, she flew away in the form of a sea-eagle, the osprey, and all marveled as they beheld it.

Nestor was astonished and took Telemachus by the hand. "My friend," he said, "I don't think you'll turn out to be a cowardly man, one without battle strength, since the gods escort you in this way while you are still young. Of all the gods and goddesses who have their homes on Olympus, this could have been no other than the daughter of Zeus, most glorious Tritogeneia, the same goddess who honored your noble father among the Argives. [380] Be gracious queen, and grant noble glory to me, my children, and my highly regarded wife. In return, I will offer you in sacrifice a year-old broad-browed heifer, unbroken, one that no man has ever brought under the yoke. I will cover her horns with gold and will offer her up to you in sacrifice." That's what he spoke in prayer, and Pallas Athena heard him.

386-489 *When they finally come to his beautiful house, Nestor serves eleven-year-old wine. They pour out libations and pray to Athena. Then they all sleep — Telemachus with Peisistratus and Nestor deep within the house.*

In the morning Telemachus gathers with Nestor and Nestor's sons — Echephron, Stratius, Perseus, Aretus, Thrasymedes, and Peisistratus — in assembly. Nestor gives various orders. And after everyone comes together again, they sacrifice the promised bull with gold-covered horns to Athena. Washing their hands with water, they sprinkle barley grain and toss tufts of the bull's hair into the fire. Then Thrasymedes cuts the hind side of the bull's neck in order to slaughter it, and the women, led by Nestor's wife Eurydice and his daughters and daughters-in-law, ululate in honor of Athena. Next, the men raise the bull's head and Peisistratus cuts its throat, draining the animal of its dark blood. Finally, they cut up the body, wrap the thighs in fat, wholly burning them, and roast the rest of the bull over the fire.

While the meat is roasting, Nestor's youngest daughter Polycaste bathes Telemachus, anoints him with fragrant olive oil, and clothes him with a fine tunic. Sitting down next to Nestor, Telemachus now looks like the immortals.

The party feasts on roasted meat and drinks wine. When they're all satisfied, Nestor commands his sons to prepare a chariot so that Telemachus may continue on his journey. They do, and a house-woman packs bread and wine onboard. So it is that Telemachus and Peisistratus, the son of Nestor driving, ride off from Pylos in a chariot pulled by swift horses. They travel all day long across the plain, coming to the house of Diocles, the son of Ortilochus, just as the sun is setting and darkness is covering the earth.

490-497 Telemachus and Peisistratus spent the night there, and Diocles set before them the gifts of hospitality shown to guest-friends.

When the early-born rosy-fingered Dawn appeared, they again yoked their horses and drove out from the gateway and the echoing portico. Peisistratus lashed the horses on, and they flew forward willingly. Very soon they came to the wheat-bearing plain, and travelling on, they reached the end of their journey, so quickly did the swift horses carry them forward. As they came to their destination, the sun sank, and all the pathways grew dark.

BOOK 4

TELEMACHUS WITH MENELAUS IN SPARTA
THE SUITORS PLOT TO AMBUSH THE YOUNG MAN

IN BRIEF: *Menelaus and Helen host Telemachus in Sparta. During a feast, they recall all the tragedy of the past. Menelaus doubts whether the wealth he has gathered is worth all the suffering he and the others endured at Troy and afterward. He mournfully speaks of his brother Agamemnon's murder, and about how he grieves for his good friend Odysseus. Hearing this, Telemachus weeps and is revealed as Odysseus' son. They all weep. After telling Menelaus about the suitors' behavior, Telemachus asks him if he has any news of his father. Promising the full truth, Menelaus tells of his time stuck in Egypt and his eventual getaway thanks to the help of Proteus, the old man of the sea. As for Odysseus, he explains that Proteus told him he was trapped with the nymph Calypso on her island. Meanwhile, the suitors conspire to kill Telemachus by means of an ambush at sea. Penelope hears of the plot and swoons.*

TELEMACHUS AND PEISISTRATUS came to the low-lying valley of Lacedaemon, full of hollows, where they drove straight to the of house of glorious Menelaus. They found him there feasting with his many clansmen in honor of his son's wedding and also that of his blameless daughter, whom he was sending off to the son of Achilles, the breaker of men's ranks.

6-58 Menelaus' attendant Eteoneus informs him that two men have arrived. He says they look like the offspring of Zeus. He asks Menelaus if they should host the two or send them on to another house. Menelaus answers by reminding Eteoneus of all the times men hosted them on their way home from Troy. The answer is clear. Consequently, Eteoneus and a few other men unyoke the horses, feed them, and invite Telemachus and

Peisistratus into the shining house that awes them. Inside, female slaves bathe and anoint them and dress them in fresh tunics. Finally, after washing their hands in order to feast with the meat and wine set before them, Menelaus addresses them.

59-64 Yellow-haired Menelaus greeted them and said, [60] "Take hold of the food, men, and enjoy it. And when you are finished with the meal, we'll ask you who among men you are—for your father's lineage has not been lost in you, but you are the kind of men that come from scepter-bearing kings fostered by Zeus. Common men do not bring sons into the world such as you are.

65-75 *The two guest-friends feast on bread and meat and drink wine. Once they are satisfied, Telemachus quietly whispers his amazement at Menelaus' house, decorated as it is with gold, silver, amber, and precious ivory. He judges it must be like Zeus' house, with its unfathomable wealth.*

76-122 Yellow-haired Menelaus overheard Telemachus as he spoke and addressed them with winged words: "My dear sons, no mortal man can strive with Zeus since his house, possessions, and everything about him is immortal. [80] But among mortal men, there may be another who can compete with me and my possessions—or there may not be such a man.

"Whatever the case, I have wandered and suffered much over eight years to bring these riches home in my ships. I wandered over Cyprus, Phoenicia, and the land of Egypt. I visited the Ethiopians, the Sidonians, and the Erembians. I came to Libya where the lambs grow horns as soon as they are born and where the sheep bear their young three times per year. And whether he is a lord or a shepherd in that land, every man has plenty of cheese, meat, and sweet milk, for the ewes give their milk throughout the year. No one goes without.

[90] "But while I was roaming about and gathering great riches among these people, another man secretly murdered my brother, unexpectedly, with his damnable wife's help—it was *her* treachery, *her* deceptive plan. Consequently, I have no pleasure in being lord of all this wealth, all these things.

"Whoever your parents are, they must have told you the story. I have suffered much. . . . If only I had stayed home! I wish that I had only a third of my possessions and that all those who perished on the plain of Troy, far from horse-nourishing Argos, were still safe and alive. [100] It is for all these men that I lament and mourn as I sit here in my house. At times I delight my heart in weeping for them. Then I stop—for crying suddenly becomes a bitterly cold form of satisfaction.

"There's one man I grieve for more than all the others. I can't think of him without loathing both food and sleep, so miserable I am at the thought of him. The reason is that no other man of all the Achaeans toiled as he did or took on so much. And what did Odysseus get in the end? It seems his destiny was nothing but distress and trouble. And mine? I feel insufferable and everlasting pain for that man since he has been gone a long time and we don't know [110] whether he is alive or dead. I imagine that his father, the old man Laertes, and his thoughtful wife, Penelope, and his son, Telemachus, whom he left behind an infant in his house, lament him."

That's what Menelaus said, and the heart of Telemachus yearned to weep as he thought about his father. Tears fell from his eyes to the ground when he heard his father's name. To cover, he raised his purple-stained cloak over his eyes with both hands.

When Menelaus observed this, he considered in his heart and spirit whether he should permit Telemachus to identify his own father or whether he should bring it up and ask him about him. [120] While he was pondering what course to take in his heart and spirit, Helen came down from her sweet-smelling high-roofed room, looking as lovely as Artemis of the golden distaff.

123-167 *After sitting down upon a chair covered with soft wool, Helen begins to question her husband about the two guests. She whispers that one looks like Odysseus—so much so that she's amazed. Menelaus agrees, saying that he looks like him in his feet, hands, head and hair, and the way he darts his eyes about. He tells her how the young man hid his tears with his cloak. Hearing them, Peisistratus confirms the identification. He is in fact Telemachus, he says, the son of Odysseus. He then explains their*

mission and how his prudent friend is afraid to speak recklessly to Mene-
laus. Still, Telemachus needs his help since a son lacks a defender when his
father is gone.

168-188 In reply yellow-haired Menelaus said, "It's incredible! The
son of that very dear man has come to my house—[170] the man
who suffered so much hardship enduring so many contests for my
sake. I had always hoped to entertain him here in my home and
love him above all the other Argives when he came back—if far-
seeing Olympian Zeus granted us a safe return in our swift ships
over the salty sea. I would have prepared a city for him in Argos,
and a house for him to dwell in. I would have led him on from Ith-
aca, bidding him to come with all his property and possessions, his
son, and all his people. I would have sacked one of the neighboring
cities that I rule and emptied it of its inhabitants for his sake. Then
we would have joined together often, being together, and nothing
would have separated us, one from the other, in our love and pleas-
ure, [180] until the black cloud of death shrouded us. I suppose,
however, that some god begrudged him this destiny—for this
wretched man alone was not granted his return home."

That's what Menelaus said, and his words stirred in them the
desire to weep. The one born of Zeus, Argive Helen, cried, as did
Telemachus and Menelaus, the son of Atreus. Nor could Peisistra-
tus keep his eyes from filling with tears when he remembered how
his blameless brother Antilochus was killed by the son of bright
Dawn.

189-350 *Peisistratus explains how tears are shed and hair is cut in honor*
of those who have died. They are the fallen man's honor-prize, and so there
is no shame attached to one mortal crying for another whose fate has drawn
him to death. Menelaus praises Peisistratus for his wisdom and declares
his father Nestor happy and fortunate in his marriage and children. He
will grow old in the halls of his house, and after him, his sons will do the
same, full of wisdom and skill in handling a spear.

Diverting their minds from their painful memories and plaintive
mourning, Menelaus suggests they wash their hands and eat. They'll talk

more in the morning, he says. So they do. Asphalion pours water upon their hands, and they begin to eat. Following her own plans, Helen slips a drug into the wine bowl, one that quiets heartache and anger. She learned about it from Polydamna, an Egyptian woman and the wife of Thon.

Then Helen recounts a story about Odysseus. Sometime during the Trojan War, he entered Troy disguised as a beggar and fooled all the Trojans. She alone recognized him. Even so, she swore not to tell anyone because her heart was already set on returning home to Sparta. The truth is she regretted the blind infatuation from Aphrodite that had caused her to forsake her land and child, as well as her wedding bed and excellent husband. Consequently, she was pleased when Odysseus slaughtered many of the Trojan men with his sword.

Menelaus adds his own story. He claims that he has never met a man like Odysseus. He recalls the time during the end of the war when the Achaean heroes were holed up in the great wooden horse before Troy. Helen (then the wife of Paris) and Priam's son Deiphobus, he says, tried to tease them out by imitating their wives' voices and calling each man by name. Many wished to go, including Menelaus and Diomedes, but Odysseus held them back, saving all the Achaeans.

Ah! Telemachus bemoans the fact that his father's heroic action didn't save him. Exhausted, he bids they all go to bed rather than talk. There they will find the relief of sweet sleep. Hearing his wish, Helen orders her slaves to prepare beds for them on the porch—purple blankets and woolen throws. There they rest while Menelaus and Helen sleep deep within the house.

In the morning, Menelaus asks Telemachus what his need is—why he has come. Is it the people's business or your own? he asks. Telemachus tells him about the oppressive suitors, who are devouring his household's wealth, and asks if he has any news of his father, who was born to suffer pain, he declares. He begs him to speak the truth rather than comforting words motivated by pity.

Hearing about the suitors, Menelaus is angry. He prays that Odysseus may return to kill them quickly—like a lion—that they may be wed to death rather than the woman they desire. Then he promises the truth to Telemachus, the very words of the old man of the sea.

351-369 "Even though I was eager to return home when I was in

Egypt, the gods detained me there since my hecatombs were not complete—and the gods are very strict about their commands.

"Now there is an island in the stormy sea some distance from Egypt. Men call it Pharos. It's about as far as a hollow ship can sail in a day with the help of a whistling wind blowing from behind. The island has a harbor that's good for mooring well-balanced ships, from which the vessels can launch again into the sea when they have drawn black water from the deepest wells.

"[360] It was there on that island that the gods kept me for twenty days. Never were there fair winds—nothing blowing seaward. No winds appeared for our ships that would escort them over the broad back of the sea. We would have run out of provisions and my men would have starved if a goddess had not taken pity on me and saved me. She was Eidothea, the daughter of mighty Proteus, the old man of the sea. I deeply moved her spirit.

"She came to me one day when I was alone, apart from my comrades, who were always wandering around the island fishing with curved hooks—for hunger oppressed their bellies."

371-467 *Menelaus explains to her how they are trapped on the island and asks her to reveal which of the gods is upset and how he can leave. In response, Eidothea commands him to take hold of her divine father, the old man of the sea, by stealth when he is resting among his seals. She promises that he will tell the stranded man everything he needs to know.*

In the morning, Menelaus follows her instructions, and by means of trickery he takes hold of the old man. Though Proteus shape-shifts in order to escape, taking on the form of a lion, a serpent, a leopard, a boar, a waterfall, and a tree full of leaves—Menelaus holds him tightly until the old man is ready to talk. Finally, he is able to ask the old man the questions he wants him to answer.

468-480 "'Tell me—for the gods know all things—which one of the immortals keeps me here and bars my way home? [470] And tell me of my return, how I will go over the fish-filled sea.'

"That's what I said. And in response, Proteus said to me at once, 'But you should have made noble sacrifices to Zeus and the other gods before loading onto your ships. Then you would have quickly come to your fatherland, sailing over the wine-faced sea. For it is not your fate to see your friends nor to reach your well-built house or the land of your fathers until you have gone again to the waters of Egypt, to the river fallen from Zeus, and have offered sacred hecatombs to the immortal gods, who possess the wide sky. [480] At that time the gods will grant you the voyage you eagerly desire.'"

481-555 Menelaus promises to do as told. Then he asks about the other Achaean leaders. Who made it home? Who died along the way?

The old man begrudgingly reveals what happened—how Ajax, the son of Oileus, perished thanks to Athena's hatred for him and Poseidon's ire at his "bigtime blindness" and "arrogant speech" against the gods. (Ajax boasted that he had "escaped the great gulf of the sea in spite of the gods.") He next describes how Aegisthus murdered Agamemnon with the help of twenty men in ambush.

Learning this for the first time, Menelaus weeps for his brother and wishes to die and to no longer see the sunshine." The old man of the sea counsels him to stop his useless weeping. "It won't accomplish anything for you," he says. Rather than crying, he advises him to return home to avenge his brother—unless Orestes, of course, has already done so. The advice makes Menelaus feel better. Finally, he asks about a third man—one who yet lives even though he is still detained somewhere upon the wide sea.

556-569 "It is the son of Laertes, whose home is in Ithaca. I saw him on an island, big tears pouring from his eyes, in the halls of the nymph Calypso. She holds him there by force. He has no power to reach his homeland since he has no oar-equipped ships nor comrades [560] to escort him over the broad back of the sea.

"As for you, god-nourished Menelaus, it is not decreed for you to die and meet your destined doom in horse-nourishing Argos. Rather, the immortals will escort you to the Elysian plain and to the limits of the earth, where yellow-haired Rhadamanthus is. Here, life is the easiest for men. There's no falling snow or much of winter or thunderstorms. But a clear West Wind always blows—sent up by Ocean to cool and refresh the men there. You will not die because you hold Helen as your wife and so are the son-in-law of Zeus."

570-584 With this, Proteus vanishes into the sea. The following morning Menelaus sails with his men to Egypt's great river where they offer well-made hecatombs and pile up a mound for his brother Agamemnon "so that his glory might be inextinguishable."

585-586 "Finishing these things, I turned to go, and the immortals gave me a fair wind, swiftly sending me on to my dear homeland."

587-624 Menelaus invites Telemachus to stay with him for another eleven or twelve days. He promises him gifts on his departure—horses and a chariot, and a beautiful chalice—if only he will keep Menelaus in mind before the gods. Telemachus tells his host that he must return to Pylos—though he would like to stay, he says. Moreover, he asks him to keep the horses since the terrain of his home island is no good for them. Menelaus promises him instead a well-wrought silver bowl, trimmed with gold, one that was given him by Phaedimus, the king of the Sidonians. They talk and prepare to feast.

625-629 Meanwhile, the suitors were enjoying themselves in front of Odysseus' great home. They were throwing javelins and discuses in an area cleared out and levelled—doing as they had before, weighed down with insolence. There sat Antinous and godlike Eurymachus, the leaders of all the suitors. Standing out in excellence of manly skill, they were the best.

630-695 When Noemon, the son of Phronius, informs Antinous and Eurymachus that Telemachus has actually sailed to sandy Pylos as he threatened to do, they grow angry at his arrogant disrespect for them and gather all the suitors together. Antinous advises they ambush Telemachus as he sails to Ithaca from Pylos. Everyone approves his proposal before heading inside for the evening's festivities. Overhearing their intentions, the herald Medon also returns to the house. Yet instead of joining the suitors in the great hall, he goes to apprise Penelope of their plans. Seeing Medon enter,

Penelope lambasts the suitors' brazen behavior, their wasteful consumption of the livelihood and property of Telemachus, and wonders why they pay evil for all the good Odysseus previously did for them and the people when he was king, doing "no wrong in word or deed" to anyone.

696-705 And again Medon, a man of understanding, spoke to her. "If only that were the worst misfortune, queen. But the suitors are planning another misfortune far greater and far more troublesome—may the son of Cronus never let it happen! [700] The suitors eagerly desire to slay Telemachus with the sharp bronze sword as he's coming home—for he went away to most holy Pylos and divine Lacedaemon to see what he could hear about his father."

That's what Medon said. And right then Penelope's knees were loosened beneath her, and her dear heart was unstrung. And speechlessness seized her for a long time, and her eyes filled with tears.

706-721 *Finally, Penelope asks Medon why Telemachus went to Pylos. He repeats what he has already told her, adding that he doesn't know if some god urged him to go or if it was his own spirit. After Medon leaves, Penelope falls to the floor inconsolable and weeping. Her serving-women rush to relieve her. In turn, she sobs to them.*

722-728 "Hear me, dear ones, for the Olympian has given me grief and distress beyond all those women I grew up with. Before this I lost a good husband, lion-spirited, who surpassed the Danaans in manly excellences of all sorts—all the noble excellences—whose glory is far spread through Hellas and mid-Argos. And now my loveable son has been snatched up and carried away from our halls by a furious storm without any report whatsoever."

729-749 *Penelope rebukes the serving-women for not telling her about Telemachus' expedition, and then she orders them to have Dolius, her aged servant and groundsman, inform Odysseus' father Laertes so that he might consider a plan. Observing Penelope's concern, the one who reared Odysseus, his nurse Eurycleia, speaks up and admits her complicity in*

Telemachus' voyage. She explains why she kept silent — that he swore her to silence so that his mother would not miss him too much and ruin her beautiful skin with weeping.

750-757 "But now go and bathe yourself in fresh water, and put on fresh clothes to cover your body. And afterward, go to your bedroom upstairs with the other women, your handmaids, and pray to Athena, the daughter of aegis-bearing Zeus — for then she may save Telemachus from death. But do not trouble the old man with misfortune, for he's had enough of his own. Either way, I don't think the line of Laertes, the son of Arceisius, is entirely hated by the blessed gods. No, at the very least one will survive to hold on to the high-roofed house and its rich and fertile fields that surround it both near and far."

758-803 *Eurycleia's remarks "lulled to sleep Penelope's weeping." Consequently, she goes to bathe and pray to Athena for her son's safe return, that the suitors will not harm him. As she does, and as the goddess hears her, the suitors downstairs brag about what they're going to do. They choose twenty of the best men for the ambush and leave for the shore. While they drag the ship into the water and drift into the sea, Penelope fears for the worst, that her son will perish at the suitors' hands. Finally, she falls asleep, and Athena sends a dream-image to her in the form of her sister Iphthime. Slipping into the bedroom through the strap-hole, the image stands above her and addresses her.*

804-807 "Are you asleep, Penelope, dear one with a sorrowing heart? May it not be — for the gods who live at ease don't want you to cry or to be distressed since your son is destined to return. In no way has he transgressed against the gods."

808-829 *Penelope answers her in her dreams. She tells her sister of all her sorrow — over Odysseus, Telemachus, and the suitors' plotting. Iphthime tells her to be courageous and not to fear too much for Telemachus. She promises her that Athena is with him — that indeed she has sent her to speak with Penelope.*

830-847 Again, thoughtful Penelope, ever cautious, spoke to her. "If you are truly a god and have come here upon a divine mission, then come and tell me at length about that miserable man, whether he still lives and sees the light of the sun or whether he's already dead inside the house of Hades."

In reply, the dimly seen dream-image said to her, "Of him I will not speak at length, whether he is living or dead. It is evil to speak words that are as empty as the wind."

Saying this, the dream-image slipped through the strap-hole that fastened the door and off into the blowing wind. At this, Icarius' daughter Penelope woke up suddenly. [840] Her dear heart felt warm at the clear dream that was sent to her in the dead of night.

Meanwhile, the suitors embarked on the ship and sailed along their watery path, anxiously considering in their minds Telemachus' murder.

Now, there is a fairly small and rocky island in the middle of the sea. It's called Asteris, the Star, and it sits between Ithaca and rugged Samos. The island has a double harbor where ships can anchor. It was there that the Achaeans waited in ambush.

BOOK 5

ODYSSEUS SAILS TO SCHERIA (THE PHAEACIANS)
THE PLOTTING OF THE GODS

IN BRIEF: *The gods assemble and decide what to do with Odysseus. Hermes carries out their plan by telling Calypso that she must let him leave her island home. After initially protesting, she does. Odysseus sails off on a raft. All is well for seventeen days until Poseidon spots him and angrily raises a dark storm. The sea nymph Ino advises and saves Odysseus. Although the going is rough, he makes it to Scheria, the island of the Phaeacians, and falls asleep beneath a pair of shrubs.*

N OW DAWN AROSE from her bed beside noble Tithonos to carry light to the immortals and the mortals. And the gods met in council. Among them was high-thundering Zeus, whose power is greatest. Athena began to tell them about the many sorrows of Odysseus, for she was bothered by his stay at the dwelling of the nymph Calypso.

"Father Zeus and all you other blessed gods who live forever, I hope there will never be such a thing as a kind and well-disposed scepter-bearing king anymore, nor one who knows what is right and reigns fairly. [10] No—I hope they will all be harsh and unjust. I hope this because every last one of his people has forgotten Odysseus, the man who ruled them gently as though he were their father. Ah, but there he is lying in great pain upon the island where the nymph Calypso dwells. Keeping him there by force, she will not let him go, and so he does not have the power to return home to the land of his fathers."

16-28 Athena reminds Zeus that Odysseus has no way to get home, and now the suitors are waiting in ambush to slay Telemachus.

Hearing her, Zeus is shocked by Athena's hope for future rulers. He tells her to bring Telemachus home by her own wisdom and reminds her of her plan to see Odysseus home so that he will get his revenge. He then turns to his son Hermes and orders him to take a message to Calypso.

29-43 "Hermes, since you in all other things are my messenger, [30] go and tell the beautiful-haired nymph my infallible plan—that stouthearted Odysseus may now return home. He may go without the escort of the gods or of mortal men. But upon a well-fastened raft, and after suffering miserable woe, he may come to fertile Scheria, the land of the Phaeacians, who were born the near kin of the gods, on the twentieth day. These people will wholeheartedly honor him as if he were a god, and they will send him in a ship to his dear fatherland. They will do this after giving him loads of bronze and gold and clothing—more than Odysseus would have ever squeezed and taken from Troy itself [40] had he returned unharmed with his allotted share of plunder. Just as I have explained, then, it is his fate to see those who are dear to him, to come to his high-roofed house in his own fatherland."

That's what Zeus said. And the messenger of Zeus, the slayer of Argus, did not disobey.

44-84 *Hermes speeds off. Like a low-flying seabird he flies over the water to Calypso's distant island and cave. Arriving at her home, he marvels at its lush vegetation, the various trees and grape vines heavy with clusters, and the many kinds of birds. There is a great fire burning on the hearth, and nearby the nymph is weaving upon a great loom, singing. When he enters her cave dwelling, Calypso immediately recognizes him, "for the immortal gods are not unknown to one another" no matter how far apart they may dwell.*

85-90 And now Calypso, the heavenly goddess, questioned Hermes after seating him on a radiant and shining chair. "Tell me, Hermes of the golden wand, why have you come? I revere you and hold you dear, but you haven't visited often before now. So, tell me what is on your mind. My spirit commands me to accomplish it [90] if I have the power to do it and if it is something that can be done."

91-115 Before hearing his reply, Calypso offers him the usual refreshment given to guests. Rather than bread and wine, however, she sets a full table of ambrosia before him and pours out cups of nectar—the food and drink of the gods. Once he eats and is satisfied, Hermes explains his mission from Zeus. She must release Odysseus so that he might make his fated journey home to his friends, house, and land.

116-120 Calypso, the divine goddess, shuddered! And speaking with winged words, she said, "You gods are cruel and jealous above all others! You bear a grudge against any goddess that openly goes to bed with a man [120] if she makes him her cherished lover."

121-148 Calypso offers a few examples. Artemis, for instance, slew Dawn's lover Orion, and Zeus evaporated Demeter's man Iasion with a thunderbolt. And now me, she complains—now the gods will take Odysseus from her, a man she saved when his ship sank, and his comrades perished. She loves and cherishes him and hopes to make him immortal and ageless. Still, she will give in to the will of Zeus, she says, as it is impossible to get around it. She will let him go. And more, she will give him good counsel on how best to make his way home.

Hermes reminds her to do as she promised for fear of Zeus' wrath. Then he leaves the island.

149-161 And so the queenly nymph went to greathearted Odysseus [150] after she had heard the message of Zeus. She found him sitting on the shore.

His eyes were never dry from all the tears he shed, and his sweet life drained as he mourned for his return home since the nymph no longer pleased him. He always passed the night by Calypso's side in her hollow cave dwelling. Yet he was unwilling and did it because he had to, whereas she was willing. During the day he sat upon the rocks and the sandy seashore racking his spirit with tears, heart-groans, and grief. With a clear view of the barren sea, he let the tears flow.

Drawing near to Odysseus now, the divine goddess said to him, [160] "Ill-fated man, do not mourn any longer here upon the beach nor let the years of your life waste away. I will now willingly send you off."

162-213 Calypso explains how Odysseus will make a raft and how she will provision him with clothing, water, wine, and food "to restrain his hunger," as well as wind for the sail. Odysseus doubts her good intentions and promises not to go home unless she swears that she is willing to let him leave. Smiling, she swears by Earth, Sky, and the river Styx that she is not plotting to harm him. Rather, she feels compassion for him and will give him her honest counsel. With that, she brings him to her cave dwelling and feeds him the food and drink "that mortal men usually consume," while she feasts on ambrosia and nectar. Finally, once they're both satisfied, she asks him why he must return home even though she would make him immortal if he remained with her. Is his wife truly that remarkable to look at? she asks. Not only that, but she warns him that he must suffer much before reaching his homeland.

214-224 In reply, Odysseus of many counsels said to her, "Queen goddess, do not be angry with me. I myself know that in comparison with you thoughtful Penelope is nothing to look at in form or in stature. This is because she is mortal whereas you are immortal and ageless. Even so, every day [220] I long and wish to go home and see the day of my return. And if a god shipwrecks me again upon the wine-faced sea, then I will endure that too with a spirit in my chest that is able to endure sorrow and misfortune. For I have already suffered very much upon the waves of the sea, and I have toiled even more in battle. If I'm meant to undergo even more suffering than this, then let it happen!"

225-261 The sun sets and the two retire to "delight in love" for the night. The following day Calypso gives Odysseus the equipment necessary for making a raft. After felling twenty trees, he builds the raft like a man well-skilled and knowledgeable in the art of carpentry. He lastly sets the mast and attaches a sail made of cloth provided by Calypso.

262-270 The fourth day came, and Odysseus had finished every-thing. So, on the fifth day divine Calypso sent him from the island after giving him a bath and putting fragrant clothes on him. The goddess also gave him a skin full of dark wine, another large one full of water, and a leather sack full of other provisions for his jour-ney. And she set many other good things in the raft that would sat-isfy his many desires. Finally, she sent him a fair wind, one kindly and warm.

Full of joy, then, godlike Odysseus let the sail unfurl before the wind. [270] And with the rudder he skillfully steered from where he sat.

271-277 Odysseus sails without sleep, steering with the help of the stars.

278-281 He sailed for seventeen days across the sea. On the eighteenth day, there appeared nearest to him the thickly wooded mountains that rise from the [280] land of the Phaeacians. The island looked like a hide-covered shield rising from the misty sea.

282-296 Just as Odysseus is about to reach the island, Poseidon spots him on his way back from feasting with the Ethiopians. And seeing him, he's angry!—still angry with Odysseus over the blinding of his son, Polyphe-mus, and irritated with the gods for changing their plans. Now he vows to deliver the hero over to a full measure of misfortune, even if he is near to Scheria where he is fated to escape all the misery he has known. Conse-quently, Poseidon stirs the sea with his great trident and fosters rushing winds that blow tall waves toward Odysseus' raft. And now a massive wave is rolling straight for him!

297-316 And right then Odysseus' knees were loosened beneath him, and his dear heart was unstrung. Frustrated and angry he spoke to his greathearted spirit:

"Ah me! I am a wretched man! What will happen to me now? [300] I fear that the goddess spoke the infallible truth when she said that I would suffer my fill of pain upon the sea before I came to my homeland. Now it's happening! Look at the many clouds Zeus has scattered in the wide sky. And see him stir the sea. And feel the winds that blast me now. Now I am utterly destroyed! My salvation is gone! Three times—no, four times blessed—were those Danaans who died upon the wide plain of Troy to benefit the sons of Atreus. I wish that I had died and met my allotted destiny on that day when a multitude of Trojans hurled bronze-tipped spears at me [310] as we fought over the body of Achilles, the son of Peleus. Then I would have received my share of funeral gifts and honors, and the Achaeans would have broadcast my fame and glory. But now it is my portion to be conquered by a pathetic death."

Then—while he was yet speaking—a massive wave crashed on him from above, sweeping over him with might and whirling his raft around. He fell far from the raft and sent the rudder flying from his hand.

317-436 Odysseus plunges into the water and is held under thanks to the waves and his heavy clothing. Above him the wind snaps the raft's mast. When he finally reaches the surface, he makes a swimming dash for the raft, seizes it, and hoists himself aboard where he sits in the middle, buffeted by the winds this way and that.

From the depths of the sea, the once human but now immortal nymph Ino observes Odysseus' plight and pities him. She comes up to him and tells him how to save himself. He should strip down, leave the raft, and swim for Scheria, "where you are fated to make your escape." Poseidon's anger will not destroy him, she says. She gives him an immortal veil to tie around his chest. It will preserve his life until he reaches the island of the Phaeacians. After commanding him to return the veil to the sea once ashore, she vanishes.

Odysseus is skeptical. Rather than trusting the nymph, he resolves to stay and endure his pains upon the raft until it breaks up. It's not for long. Just then Poseidon sends a towering wave that shatters the raft. Still, Odysseus hangs on—to one plank of wood. Just barely. As soon as he can, though, he strips off his clothes, ties the veil around his chest, and hurls his body toward the island, willing himself to make it to the shore.

Observing Odysseus' move, Poseidon determines to make his swim hard and full of suffering. Athena, however, has other plans. When Poseidon departs for his glorious house at Aegae, she calms the winds and helps to bring him to the island. Nevertheless, the swim is long and hard. Tossed by the waves and fearing destruction all the way, by fish or sea monster, he swims for two days and nights before finally spotting the island on the third day. And now he's so close that a man could have heard him shout had he been standing there on the shore. Even so, he has to fight the angry surf as it crashes against the cliffs, rocks, and reef. So close, Odysseus dreads being swept out to sea once again. He knows that Poseidon still hates him. Just then, a great wave carries him toward a jagged promontory, rough with rocks and reef. He grabs for a jutting rock, but another wave covers him and threatens to suck him back into the deep sea.

436-453 Then, beyond his fate, wretched Odysseus would have been destroyed if bright-eyed Athena had not given him presence of mind. Emerging from the waves that thundered along the shore, he swam outside, eying the land in the hope of finding [440] a sloping beach or a harbor from the sea.

As he swam, he reached the mouth of a beautifully flowing river—the best place to come ashore. There were no rocks, and the place would shelter him from the breeze.

Feeling the river flowing into the sea, he prayed in his spirit, "Hear me, lord, whoever you are! To you I come, you the fulfillment of all my prayers as I was escaping the sea and Poseidon's abuse. Even the immortal gods revere the wandering man who comes to them. Just so I now come to your flow and your knees after much suffering and toil. [450] But pity me, lord. I pray as your supplant."

That's what Odysseus said. And right away the god stilled his flow and settled the waves, making the sea calm before him, and he brought him safely into the river's mouth.

454-473 *Waterlogged and beat up, Odysseus rests and catches his breath. Once revived, he returns the immortal veil to the sea nymph Ino before anxiously mulling over what to do. He considers staying by the water or going up into the woods. Either way has its dangers. He fears the bitter cold on the one hand and preying animals on the other.*

474-477 As he pondered what to do in this way, this conclusion seemed to him the better one: he walked into the wood that was right by the river's water and found an opening. There he crept under a pair of shrubs sprung from a single spot—the one was wild olive, the other common.

478-490 *Beneath these shrubs, Odysseus is protected from the wind and rain. He makes for himself a bed of leaves and lays down within the pile, thereby keeping warm.*

491-493 In this manner Odysseus hid himself in the leaves. And upon his eyes Athena poured out sleep so that it might cover his eyelids on every side and bring his toilsome troubles to an end.

BOOK 6

ODYSSEUS MEETS NAUSICAA
THE ENCOUNTER BY THE RIVER STREAM

IN BRIEF: *At Athena's prodding in a dream, the princess Nausicaa goes to wash her and her family's clothing in a stream near to where Odysseus is sleeping. When he awakens, he approaches Nausicaa and blesses her. She gives him directions to her house where the Phaeacian king and queen, her father and mother, live. She also tells him what to do once there. They set off for the palace.*

I N THIS WAY did much-enduring godlike Odysseus slumber there, worn out with sleep and trouble. Even so, Athena went to the land and city of the Phaeacians.

4-23 Athena goes to the city to speak to Nausicaa, the beautiful daughter of Alcinous and Arete. Her father is the son of Nausithous, the man who led the Phaeacians to distant Scheria from the land of the Cyclopes—obnoxious men, proud and powerful, who had constantly plundered the Phaeacians. Athena enters into Nausicaa's bedchamber "like a breath of air" and appears to her in the form of her friend, the daughter of Dymas.

24-35 Appearing like her, bright-eyed Athena said, "How did your mother give birth to such a careless one? Your splendid clothes lie there uncared for, even though your wedding day is near at hand when you'll need fine clothes for yourself and you'll want to furnish them to those who may accompany you. It is from such things that a noble reputation rises among humans, [30] and in them that a father and queenly mother rejoice and are glad. But let's go wash them when the light appears at the break of day. I will go with you as your helper so that you may quickly be ready—you won't be a maiden much longer! You're already being courted by all the best men of the Phaeacians in the land.

36-40 Athena finishes by telling Nausicaa to have her father prepare mules and a wagon for her.

41-46 Speaking in this manner, bright-eyed Athena departed for Olympus, where, they say, the abode of the gods stands firm, immovable forever. Neither is it shaken by wind, nor drenched with heavy rain, nor does snow fall there. But a clear sky spreads out cloudless like a great white sail, and the bright sun fills the sky. And there upon Olympus the blessed gods are delighted every day.

47-84 When Nausicaa wakes up, she goes to her father Alcinous and asks him for a wagon to convey the clothes to the river and washing tanks. She's shy about mentioning the reason, the need for clean wedding garments, so she adds that she will wash her father's and brother's clothing as well. He grants her the wagon, which the slaves make ready, while her mother stores food and wine for a feast, and olive oil for bathing in a golden flask. Then, boarding the wagon with her handmaidens, she urges the mules on to the river.

85-101 When they came to the beautiful river's streams, where the washing tanks were always full—for in abundance clear water flowed up from beneath to cleanse even the filthiest clothes—they unhitched the mules from the four-wheeled wagon and let them stray along the eddying stream [90] to nibble on the honey-sweet grass. And from the wagon they took the clothing in their arms and carried it into the deep water. There they stamped the laundry in the pits, vying with one another for speed.

Once they had washed and cleansed the clothing of all the stains, they spread it carefully in rows along the seashore just where the waves washed many small pebbles up on the dry beach. After bathing and anointing themselves richly with olive oil, they took their meal on the riverbank and waited for the clothes to dry in the light of the sun. When Nausicaa and her handmaids were satisfied with food, [100] they threw off their veils in order to play ball. And it was white-armed Nausicaa herself who was first in the dance.

102-110 Dancing, the princess is like Artemis in beauty, standing out amid her handmaidens as Artemis does amid the wood nymphs.

115-121 But when Nausicaa thought about turning toward home once again, and so about yoking the mules and folding up the beautiful clothes, then did the goddess, bright-eyed Athena, form a new plan. She would wake up Odysseus and have him see the sweet looking girl. Then she would lead him to the city of the Phaeacian men.

Just then the princess threw the ball to one of the handmaidens, but she missed her and instead threw it into a deep eddy. Seeing it fall, they shouted aloud. At this, godlike Odysseus awoke, sat up, and considered anxiously in his mind and spirit, "Ah me! To what land of mortals have I come? Are they violent and insolent men? Are they uncivilized and wild, without justice or the proper observance of custom? Or are they hospitable men, loving strangers? And do they themselves fear the gods in their minds?"

122-148 Odysseus thinks the voices may be those of nymphs. Not knowing, he ventures from his resting place to take a look, breaking off a leafy branch to cover his bare genitals. Wary, the need of his belly drives him forward like a hungry lion dangerously breaking into a sheep pen.

When they see Odysseus, the handmaidens flee—all but for Nausicaa. Despite his disfigured looks, she stands opposite him with a courage supplied by Athena.

Meanwhile, Odysseus wonders whether he should approach her and take her knees as a suppliant or stand apart and call out to her to give him clothing and show him the way to her city. Finally, he speaks.

149-161 "I take your knees, O queen. Are you a goddess or are you a mortal? [150] If you are a goddess, one of the gods who possess the wide sky above, then I say that you are most like Artemis, the daughter of mighty Zeus, in your looks, form, and stature. But if you are someone among mortals who live on the earth, then three times blessed are your father and queen mother, and three times blessed are your brothers, too. Surely their spirits forever grow warm with happy thoughts because of you, seeing such a beautiful flower entering the dance. But that one is blessed in his heart above all others who prevails with wedding gifts and leads you home. [160] For with my own eyes, I've never seen a mortal such as you are—whether a man or a woman. Awe holds me as I look at you."

162-169 Odysseus compares Nausicaa to a young tree he once saw on Apollo's altar in Delos. He goes on to explain his trouble from afar.

169-197 "Sorrow that is hard to bear has come upon me. [170] Yesterday, on the twentieth day, I escaped from the wine-faced sea. During all that time, waves and rushing wind carried me away from the island of Ogygia. And now some god has tossed me ashore here so that I may yet surely suffer even more evil. My guess is that the misfortune will not stop yet—not until the gods give me more.

"But pity me, O queen. I have come upon you first after much suffering and toil, and I know nothing about the men who hold the land here or the city. Show me to the city and give me some rag to throw around myself—perhaps the cloth you used to carry the clothing when you came here. [180] And may the gods grant you as much as your heart eagerly desires—a man for a husband, and a house. And may a noble unity of mind and feeling accompany these. For nothing is greater and nothing better than when a man and woman dwell in their household with the same thoughts, feelings, and mind—a huge pain to their enemies and joy to their friends. Their glory is very well known."

In reply, white-armed Nausicaa said, "Stranger, since you do not seem to be a base or senseless man, and since Olympian Zeus himself dispenses fortune and happiness to men, to both the good and the bad as he wills, whether he be a brave man or a coward, noble or base—[190] so I believe that surely he has given misfortune to you. Regardless, you must endure it either way. But now, since you have come to our land and city, you will have whatever any suppliant who has suffered much would need—clothing or anything. I will show you to the city, and I will tell you the name of the people. The Phaeacians hold this land and city, and I am the daughter of greathearted Alcinous, who holds power and strength from the Phaeacians."

198-205 Seeing that her handmaidens are running off for fear of Odysseus, Nausicaa attempts to calm them, assuring them that the distance of Scheria and the care of the gods will defend them against all harm. But more, they have a duty to help the wandering stranger.

206-210 "But this man who has come here is some unhappy wanderer. And now we must take care of him since all strangers and beggars come from Zeus—and a gift, even if small, is valued. So, my handmaidens, give the stranger food and drink, [210] and wash him in the river in a spot sheltered from the wind."

211-320 Nausicaa's handmaidens obey. Yet instead of allowing them to bathe him in the river, Odysseus asks to bathe alone since he's so filthy. He does. And Athena makes him appear taller, stronger, and handsomer than he earlier appeared.

When Nausicaa gazes at him in awe, she declares he is like one of the gods, and she wishes that he might stay and become her husband. She orders her handmaidens to give him refreshment, and so they offer him food and drink. He eagerly eats as one who has not eaten for a long time.

When it is time to go, Nausicaa explains how she will guide Odysseus to the city. While they are still in the countryside and field, they will go together, she says. But once they reach a grove sacred to Athena, they will split up. The grove itself is part of her father's official domain. It's just outside the city—before the city walls and its harbor that holds all the Phaeacian ships (for, as she explains, the Phaeacians are sailors and care only for ships). Nausicaa desires to split up because she doesn't want any of the people gossiping about her walking with a strange man, making up all kinds of stories about marriage and whatnot. Rather, they'll separate at Athena's grove and go one after the other to her father's house. He'll make it to the house with the help of someone within the city. Lastly, Nausicaa gives Odysseus instructions regarding what to do when he actually reaches the house and is within its court. He should approach her mother for help. If she helps him, she says, then he may yet reach his house and homeland.

And now, Nausicaa drives the wagon toward the city and her home while her handmaidens and Odysseus follow on foot.

321-331 As the sun was setting, they came to the glorious grove, sacred to Athena, and godlike Odysseus sat down there. Right away he prayed to the daughter of mighty Zeus:

"Hear me, child of aegis-bearing Zeus. Listen to me, unwearied one. Since you didn't hear me before when I was shipwrecked, when the glorious Earth-shaker Poseidon reduced me to nothing, hear me now. Allow me to come to the Phaeacians as one pitied and held dear."

That's what Odysseus said in prayer, and Pallas Athena heard him. Still, she did not yet appear to him face to face, for she feared and respected her father's brother Poseidon, who vehemently resisted godlike Odysseus until he came to his own land.

BOOK 7

THE HOUSE OF ALCINOUS
ODYSSEUS MEETS ALCINOUS AND ARETE

IN BRIEF: *Thanks to Athena's help, Odysseus comes before Alcinous and Arete. They treat him honorably as a guest-friend. After the hero briefly explains who he is and how much he has suffered, Alcinous offers his daughter Nausicaa to him in marriage. Not wishing to restrain him, however, he also offers him conveyance home in a fast Phaeacian ship.*

IN THIS MANNER, then, much-enduring godlike Odysseus prayed in the sacred grove while the strong mules carried the young girl to the city. When she reached her father's glorious house, Nausicaa stopped before the gateway, and her brothers stood around her like immortals. They unyoked the mules from the wagon and carried the clothing inside. She went into her own bedroom where the old Apeirean woman and maid Eurymedusa lit a fire for her.

9-13 *Eurymedusa had been snatched up on a raid and given to Alcinous, Nausicaa's father. He gave her to serve as Nausicaa's nursemaid. Old, she is still in the young princess' service.*

14-33 And now Odysseus rose to go to the city. But Athena, with affectionate intentions, poured a dense mist around him so that none of the great-spirited Phaeacians would encounter him by chance, question him in some sneering way, and ask him who he was. The goddess, bright-eyed Athena, met him just as he was entering the lovely city. [20] She was disguised as a young girl carrying a water jar. She stood before him, and godlike Odysseus questioned her. "Child, could you not guide me to the house of the man called Alcinous, the one who is the ruler of this people? I ask because I am a stranger from a distant land, a man who has suffered much, and I don't know any of the people here who hold this land and city."

The bright-eyed goddess Athena said to him, "Since you ask me to do so, I will show you the house, father stranger, since my own blameless father lives nearby him. [30] But go in silence—I will walk before you on the path. And do not look at any of the men or ask any questions, for they do not have much tolerance for foreign men, nor do they treat with affection or hold dear that man who comes from a distant place."

34-47 Odysseus follows Athena to Alcinous' palace. He's amazed as they go by the harbor, amazed as he sees the ships therein and all the men going about their work. Thanks to the dense mist, no one sees him as they go. When they arrive, Athena turns to speak to him.

48-54 "Here, father stranger, is the house you asked me to show you. Here you will find the kings fostered by Zeus [50] sitting at table feasting. But go inside and let your spirit not be alarmed. For in the end, the bold and courageous man does better in all things, even if he comes from another place. You will first come upon the lady of the house in the great hall. Arete is her given name."

55-68 Athena tells Odysseus to go straight to Arete, the daughter of Rhexenor. Along with Alcinous, Rhexenor was the son of Nausithous, who was the son of Poseidon and Periboea, the best looking of women and daughter of the Giant Eurymedon. When Apollo struck Rhexenor down, Alcinous wed Arete and honored her like no other woman on earth.

69-82 "In this manner is she wholeheartedly honored [70] by her dear children, and by Alcinous himself, and also by the people who look upon her as though she is a goddess and greet her with many words when she strolls through the city. For she herself possesses a noble mind and settles quarrels if she is well disposed to do so— even among men. If she considers you with affection in her spirit, then there is hope that you will see those who are dear to you and come to your high-roofed house in your own fatherland."

Saying this, bright-eyed Athena left lovely Scheria and flew off over the barren sea. [80] She came to Marathon and to Athens, with its wide streets, and made her way into Erechtheus' strong house. As for Odysseus, he approached Alcinous' glorious house.

83-141 Standing before Alcinous' great house, and gazing in wonder at its opulence, Odysseus sees that it is made of a variety of precious materials—bronze, silver, and gold. The house shines! Two dogs stand guard next to the doorway. Hephaestus made them of silver and gold. They are immortal and ageless. Inside the house are throne-seats luxuriously covered with very finely woven cloth. Here the Phaeacian leaders eat in grand style, for they possess "an abundance" to carry them through the year, year after year. Nearby, youths stand holding lighted torches. Fifty women are scattered about grinding ripe yellow grain and working upon the loom with excellence. Homer explains that just as Phaeacian men are expert sailors, so are Phaeacian women expert weavers. Surrounding the house are orchards, vineyards, and springs given by the gods. The orchards are full of pears, pomegranates, apples, figs, and olives.

After marveling at the abundance, Odysseus finally enters through the doorway and into the great hall. There he sees the Phaeacian chief men and rulers. He passes them all—still within the dense mist provided by Athena—and approaches Alcinous and Arete.

142-152 Then he threw his arms around Arete's knees. Right then the god-given mist scattered from around him, and those sitting there marveled in silence at the sight of the man in the house.

And Odysseus entreated her for protection. "Arete, daughter of godlike Rhexenor, I come to your husband and to your knees after much suffering and toil, and to all these feasting here, too. May the gods grant them a happy and prosperous life, and may each man hand on to his children [150] the wealth in his house and the honors and rights granted by the people. This I ask of you—an escort for me that I may swiftly come home. I ask this because I have been suffering misery far away from my people for a very long time."

153-166 Finishing his request, Odysseus sits down upon the hearth in the

midst of its ashes. Everyone present is astonished. Finally, the hero Eche-
neus advises Alcinous to treat the stranger well as a revered suppliant by
giving him a proper welcome — a chair, wine, and food.

167-177 But when strong and mighty Alcinous heard his plea, he
took Odysseus, the wise and cunning man, by the hand, and he
pulled him up from the hearth and sat him upon a shining chair
next to him — causing his [170] son, manly Laodamas, to stand up,
for since his father loved him very much, he sat next to him. And
one of the handmaids brought water for hand washing in a beauti-
ful vessel made of gold and poured it out over a basin made of sil-
ver so that he could wash his hands. And bringing bread to him,
the well-respected housekeeper set it before him along with much
other food, showing him favor as she was able. So it was that much-
enduring godlike Odysseus ate and drank.

178-185 *As Odysseus eats, the rest drink and pour out libations to Zeus.*
Then Alcinous speaks.

186-198 "Listen, chief men and rulers of the Phaeacians, so that I
may tell you what my spirit within me bids. Now that you have
feasted, go to your houses, and tomorrow at dawn we will call more
of the elders together, [190] and we will entertain the stranger in the
great hall and make fair sacrifices to the gods. After that we will
think about the escort — how with our escort, and without toil or
distress, the stranger may speedily and gladly come to the land of
his fathers, even if he comes from a distant land. In the meantime,
may he not suffer any harm or woe before he sets foot in his own
land. But when he gets home, he will suffer whatever fate that the
grievous Spinners spun out for him with their flaxen thread when
he came to be on the day his mother gave birth to him."

199-210 *Alcinous wonders aloud if Odysseus is actually one of the gods —*
the same gods who feast with them at times because they are closely related,
as are the Cyclopes and wild Giants. Odysseus demurs, clarifying he's not
like the immortals in either bodily frame or stature. He's a mortal man.

211-221 "Whoever you have known among men, the one who has endured the greatest suffering, I liken myself to him in pains and distress. And I could tell of the fill of evil I've endured, the sufferings willed by all the gods together.

"But now permit me to eat, even though I am distressed—for there is nothing more shameful and doglike than one's hateful belly. It calls upon a man to remember it by absolute necessity, even if he is very oppressed and is bearing much grief and misfortune in his heart and mind, as I am now carrying all the sorrow in mine. My belly always insists that [220] I eat and drink, and bids me lay aside all memory of my sorrows and dwell on replenishing itself."

222-316 Odysseus finishes by expressing his simple desire to return home after so much misery. Then, he says, he will be able to die inside his high-roofed house among his own possessions and slaves.

Once the other Phaeacians depart for their own houses, Arete takes the lead in questioning Odysseus, asking where he secured his clothing, for she recognizes it. Odysseus responds by once again stressing how much he has suffered thanks to the gods. Then he tells them about Calypso, the fearful goddess, who lives far away on Ogygia. She has nothing to do with either the gods or men, he explains. He bemoans the bad fortune that led him to her hearth and home after Zeus blasted his ships and all his good comrades perished. He describes how Calypso welcomed him and promised to make him immortal and ageless. Still, after seven years he could not be persuaded to accept her deal. And finally, urged on by Zeus or her own mind, he surmises, she sent him off on a raft in the eighth year. After weeks at sea and great suffering caused by earth-shaking Poseidon, he came to their island and fell asleep by the river. And it was by the river that their daughter found him—the one who looks like a goddess. Odysseus reveals how Nausicaa behaved perfectly by understanding his predicament and giving him bread and wine, even as a good host would, and clothing him— unlike most youths who behave thoughtlessly.

Alcinous is surprised that Nausicaa herself didn't bring Odysseus to their house after he had appealed to her as a suppliant. Odysseus asks him not to be angry with his daughter. And lying, he claims that Nausicaa did offer to lead him, but that he declined since he was afraid that they would respond with anger at the sight of her daughter leading a strange man because, as he judges, "we tribes of men upon the earth are exceedingly jealous." Alcinous responds by asserting that he would not have been angry without good cause—for, he declares, right mindedness and fitting measure is better in all things. He then expresses the same wish that Nausicaa had earlier expressed, that Odysseus would be her husband. If so, he would give Odysseus a house and other property. But only if he desires it, he clarifies. No one will make him stay. Alcinous explains how they will help Odysseus return home.

317-333 "And as for your conveyance home, I will assign the hour for it so that you may be sure of your departure. Let it be tomorrow. Once aboard you will sleep while my men speed you along the calm sea until you reach [320] your homeland and house or whatever place is dear to you. The men will row there even if that place is far beyond Euboea, which is called the most distant land by those among our people who once carried golden haired Rhadamanthus to visit Tityus, the son of Gaia. They reached that land and completed the voyage without trouble, and on the same day they looped back again and went home. But you yourself will judge how my ships and young men are the best in rowing with oars, tossing up much seawater as they go."

That's what Alcinous said. And much-enduring godlike Odysseus rejoiced, [330] and in prayer he said, "Father Zeus, may Alcinous fulfill every word he has spoken. And may the light of his glory and fame never go out through the wheat-bearing land, and may I come to my fatherland."

334-342 *Hearing Odysseus' prayer, Arete has the housemaids give him warm woolen clothing and prepare a bed with purple coverings for him in the portico. With this, they all go off to bed.*

343-347 In this manner much-enduring godlike Odysseus slept there on the bed beneath the echoing portico. But Alcinous slept in the innermost part of his high house, and his wife, the lady of the house, made her bed beside him.

BOOK 8

FEASTING WITH THE PHAEACIANS
SONGS, GAMES, AND SORROW

IN BRIEF: *Alcinous calls an assembly and reveals the plan to sail Odysseus home. He invites the other sceptered kings to a feast. They eat and listen to the blind bard Demodocus. He sings about Odysseus' quarrel with Achilles, and Odysseus quietly weeps. Soon after, the Phaeacians compete in games—Odysseus reluctantly and angrily, after Euryalus insults him. He throws a discus farther than any other man. The Phaeacians dance, accompanied by the bard, who sings about the love affair between Ares and Aphrodite, Hephaestus' wife. They later feast and listen to the bard again. Euryalus makes amends with Odysseus. They all return to the palace to feast again and listen to Demodocus recount the tale of the Trojan horse and the battle in Troy, including Odysseus' fight with Deiphobus. Hearing this, tears fall down Odysseus' cheeks. Alcinous notices and asks him who he really is.*

W HEN THE EARLY-BORN rosy-fingered Dawn appeared, strong and mighty Alcinous stirred from his bed as did god-born Odysseus, the sacker of cities. And now strong and mighty Alcinous led the way to the Phaeacian assembly place, which had been built for them nearby their ships. When the two arrived, they sat down on polished stones that were fitted together side by side. Meanwhile, Pallas Athena went throughout the city in the likeness of Alcinous' wise herald, planning a return home for great-hearted Odysseus.

10-61 Athena calls the Phaeacian men to meet at the assembly place to see a man who is like the immortals. She makes Odysseus bigger so that he might receive a better welcome, the wonder and respect of the Phaeacians.

Once they come together, Alcinous commands the younger men to pre-
pare a black ship for Odysseus' conveyance home and fifty-two of the best
young men to row. Turning to the sceptered kings, he calls on them to join
him at his house for a feast. The young men will join them once the ship is
ready. Lastly, he summons the bard Demodocus to delight them with song.

62-64 And the herald came near to those feasting, leading the trusty
bard. Among men, the Muse loved him and gave him both good
and bad fortune.

65-71 *The good is the gift of song; the bad is blindness. Nevertheless, the*
bard Demodocus is honored with a fine chair, cups of wine, and a lyre.
And everyone eats and drinks.

72-103 When they had set aside the desire for drink and food, the
Muse urged the bard to sing about the glorious deeds of men, a
song whose fame was then as wide as the sky. He sang about Odys-
seus' quarrel with Achilles, the son of Peleus, how they once quar-
reled with violent speech at the gods' abundant feast. . . . [80] . . .
This is the song the famous bard sang.

Meanwhile, Odysseus took hold of his great purple cloak in his
strong hands and drew it around his head, concealing his beautiful
face. He did this because he felt shame before the Phaeacians as tears
poured from his eyes. But when the godlike bard paused in the song,
Odysseus wiped away his tears and drew down the cloak from his
head. And taking up his two-handled cup, he poured out libations to
the gods. [90] But just as he finished, the bard would begin again,
urged on to sing by the best men of the Phaeacians since they enjoyed
the epic story. And again, Odysseus would cover his head and weep.
In this way he hid the pouring tears from all the rest.

Alcinous was the only one that noticed what was going on, for
he sat near to Odysseus and heard his deep-drawn sighs. And to
the Phaeacians, who delight in oars, he said at once, "Listen to me,
Phaeacian chief men and rulers! We've just satisfied our desire for
the generous feast and for the lyre, which always accompanies an
abundant feast. [100] Now let's go and attempt all kinds of contests,

so that when the stranger returns home he may tell his friends how greatly we surpass all other men in boxing, wrestling, jumping, and racing on our feet."

104-157 *The Phaeacian men agree and follow Alcinous to the assembly place. There, all the younger men join in the games. Many step forward, including Euryalus, the equal of Ares. He was the best of the Phaeacians after Laodamas. The three sons of Alcinous also rise to compete, including Laodamas, Halius, and Clytoneus.*

The first competition is the foot race. Clytoneus wins by far. Next, Euryalus triumphs in wrestling, Elatreus with the discus, and Laodamas with his fists in boxing. Then, after sizing the stranger up and judging him to be no weak man—rather, big and strong—Laodamas challenges him to make a trial of himself in one of the contests. For, he says, "there is no greater glory than that which a man has from the accomplishments of his own hands and feet." He urges him on, suggesting that activity will disperse the cares of his spirit. Odysseus responds by declaring that the only thing on his mind is sorrow and his return home. Hearing this, Euryalus decides to tease him.

158-193 "No, indeed, stranger you do not look like one who is very experienced [160] with contests—the many kinds that exist among men. Rather, you look like a man occupied with many-benched ships, the leader of sailing men, who are traders, ever mindful of your cargo, keeping watch over your freights and grasping for gain. No, you don't seem like an athlete."

But with an angry glance from beneath his brows, Odysseus of many counsels said to Euryalus, "Stranger, your words are rude. You seem like a reckless man. It's true that the gods do not give to every man every grace—whether stature, wisdom, or eloquence. For one man is inferior in his looks, [170] but god crowns his words with beauty. Men therefore look on him with delight as he speaks without faltering, respectfully, and with gentle words. That man stands out wherever men are gathered, and as he walks through the city, everyone looks upon him as if he were some god. Then there's the other man—he looks like the immortals, but his speech has no crown of grace. That's what you're like. In appearance you're a standout—the gods couldn't have made another better than you. But your mind is empty! Just now you stirred the spirit within me with your disorderly words without manners. I am not unskilled in games, as you declare. [180] No, I imagine I was among the best, while I could rely on my youth and my arms and hands. Now I am overwhelmed with misery and distress, for I have endured much, cutting through the wars of men and the distressful waves of the sea. Even so, even suffering as much bad fortune as I have suffered, I will attempt the games since your words stung my spirit, stirring me up."

He spoke, and with his cloak still on, he jumped up and took hold of a discus larger than the rest. It was thick, quite a bit heavier than those which the Phaeacians were using for themselves. Whirling around he hurled the discus from his strong hand. [190] The stone flew humming through the air—and down on the ground the Phaeacian long oarsmen, those men famous for their ships, crouched under the rush of the stone. It soared over all the other markers of distance, flying swiftly from his hand.

194-305 *Appearing as a man, Athena marks the discus' landing spot and declares its distance to be far beyond all the other stones. Her judgment makes Odysseus glad. He then challenges all the young men to any contest—to boxing, wrestling, or running. He's very angry, he says. Still, he will not challenge his guest-friend Laodamas. A man would have to be senseless to challenge his own host! He would have to be a worthless nobody! He goes on to boast his own superiority in most games but for archery. He further claims that he can throw a spear farther than a man can shoot an arrow. He only fears being outdone in a footrace thanks to all the suffering he's endured while at sea.*

Now everyone is silent. Alcinous alone speaks up. He first recognizes Euryalus' offense and Odysseus' anger. Then he admits that the Phaeacians are not the best at fighting with their fists or wrestling. They're better at foot racing and the best men on the sea. Moreover, they enjoy feasting, playing the lyre, taking hot baths, and putting on fresh clothes. Even more, they like to dance and will demonstrate for Odysseus how skilled they are at the ball dance. That way, when the stranger returns home, he says, he can report how great they are at sailing, foot racing, singing, and dancing.

After preparing the ground, the youngest boys begin to dance, and Odysseus is truly amazed to see them move to the accompaniment of the lyre and Demodocus' singing. The bard strums the lyre and sings about the love affair between Ares and Aphrodite. He reveals how they slept together secretly, dishonoring Hephaestus' own marriage bed, since Aphrodite was his wife. Discovering the affair thanks to Helios, the divine Sun who sees all, Hephaestus set a trap for them. Then he went off to Lemnos to visit the Sintians. When Ares saw the smith god leaving for the sacred island, he sped over to Hephaestus' house. But when he was sleeping with Aphrodite in love, the trap was sprung, and they were caught naked, bound to the bed. Helios told Hephaestus. In turn Hephaestus spread the news to all the other gods and urged them to come witness what had happened.

306-332 "Father Zeus and all you other blessed gods who live forever, come here so that you might see a laughable deed—though not one that should be endured! This Aphrodite, this daughter of Zeus, forever dishonors me because of my disabled feet and legs, while she loves destructive Ares [310] since he is handsome and has quick feet. I was born disabled—and no other gods are to blame for it than my two parents! It would have been better not to have been born at all!

"But come and you will see where these two have climbed into my bed and are sleeping together in love. As for me, I'm angry at the sight and filled with grief! And yet there's reason to hope that they'll not cling to each other for very long, no matter what they're doing in love. No, very soon they'll not want to sleep together. Still, my trap and the chains will hold them until her father pays me back the many wedding gifts I gave to get that dog-eyed, shameless girl—[320] he has to because, even though his daughter is beautiful, she lacks all self-control of her passions."

That's what Hephaestus said, and the gods gathered together at his bronze-supported house. Earth-carrying Poseidon came, as did the bringer of luck Hermes, and lord Apollo who works from afar.

As for the female goddesses, each one remained at home out of a sense of shame. But the gods, the givers of good things, stood in the doorway. And an unstoppable laughter rose up from among the blessed gods as they beheld the artful skill of inventive Hephaestus. And glancing at the other one would say, "Bad deeds do not thrive. The slow overtakes the swift—[330] just as now Hephaestus, slow as he is, has seized Ares, even though he is the swiftest of the gods who hold Olympus. Lame, he has seized him by craft. Ares must pay the fine for adultery."

333-386 Still, Apollo turns to Hermes and asks him if he would be willing to be trapped like Ares if only he could sleep with Aphrodite. Hermes' declares he would. They all laugh at this—all but for Poseidon, who promises to pay the penalty if Hephaestus sets Ares free. Hesitating, Hephaestus agrees. After their release, Ares flies off to Thrace, and Aphrodite goes to her altar in Cyprus where the Graces bathe and anoint her.

Odysseus delights in the song and story as do all the Phaeacians. By now the younger boys have finished dancing, so the sons of Alcinous Halius and Laodamas expertly perform the ball dance. As they step this way and that to the drumming of other young men, they throw a "beautiful purple ball" high into the air and back and forth to each other. Odysseus turns to Alcinous and expresses his utter amazement, agreeing that, yes, the Phaeacians are the best dancers. In response, Alcinous speaks to his men.

387-389 "Listen to me, you chief men and rulers of the Phaeacians. This stranger seems wise—to really know what he thinks and what he's talking about. But come. Let's give him a guest-gift, the kind that's fitting for a host to give."

390-399 Alcinous directs the others to bring clothing and gold for Odysseus, and, to rectify what had earlier occurred, he orders Euryalus to make up for his rude words.

400-416 And Euryalus answered the king and said, "Mighty Alcinous, most renowned among all people, I will indeed make amends to the stranger, as you command. I will give him this sword made of bronze. Its hilt is silver, and the scabbard that holds it is made of fresh-cut ivory. He will find it to be a possession of great worth."

Saying this, Euryalus put the silver-studded sword into Odysseus' hands. And speaking with winged words he said, "Be glad, father stranger! If any word I uttered was harsh, then may some stormy wind snatch it up and bear it away. [410] May the gods grant that you may see your wife and reach your homeland—since you've been suffering pain far from your loved ones for a long time."

Then Odysseus of many counsels answered him and said, "You too, my friend, rejoice! May the gods give you happiness and fortune for making amends with your words, and may you never miss the sword you give me."

He spoke, and around his shoulders he slung the silver-studded sword.

417-486 *As the sun sets and the Phaeacians return to the palace, the heralds bring the gifts, and Alcinous and Arete generously add a chest full of gifts to the collection. Alcinous gives him a gold cup. Arete advises Odysseus to guard well over the gifts.*

After he seals the chest, Odysseus goes off to bathe in a tub of water that has been warmed over the fire. The handmaidens anoint him with olive oil and dress him. Then, when he's returning to the great hall, Nausicaa sees him and calls on him to remember her when he returns home. He owes her his life, she says. He promises to do so. If he makes it home, he will pray to her as though a god since she kept him alive.

Odysseus enters the hall and reclines next to Alcinous. The servants are "distributing the portions and mixing the wine." A herald walks the bard Demodocus, honored by the people, into the hall. Odysseus adds to his honor by directing the herald to give him a piece of fatty wild boar. They eat and everyone sets aside the desire for drink and food. Then Odysseus turns to Demodocus and praises him.

487-516 "Demodocus, I praise you beyond all mortal men, whether your teacher was the Muse, who is the child of Zeus, or Apollo.

With perfect truth you sing the fate of the Achaeans—[490] all they did and all they suffered, the whole of the miserable Achaean struggle. And you do so as if you yourself were there or you heard the story from a man who was. Move on now and sing the building of the wooden horse, made by Epeius with Athena's help, which god-like Odysseus once led into the upper city—a thing meant to deceive, packed with warriors. They used it to sack Ilium. And if you now tell the story as it was fated by the gods, then I will declare to all men how favorably a god has been toward you by inspiring you with song."

That's what Odysseus said. And stirred by the god, the bard showed his skill in song, [500] beginning the story where some Argives, after setting their shelters on fire, were embarking on the well-benched ships and setting sail, while the others, led by glorious Odysseus, were hidden in the horse in the middle of the Trojan assembly place—since the Trojans themselves had dragged the horse to their citadel.

So there it stood. And seated around it, the people argued for a long time, uncertain what to do. There were three plans that pleased them. They could split the hollow wooden horse down the middle with an axe made of ruthless bronze. Or they could drag it to the city heights and hurl it down upon the rocks. Or last, they could spare the monstrosity and use it to propitiate the gods. [510] So that's what they did, the last, as that's how it was destined to end according to the decree of Fate. They would all be utterly destroyed when the great wooden horse was stationed inside the city. And within its hollow chamber were all the best of the Argives waiting to deliver murder and death to the Trojans.

Demodocus sang about how the sons of the Achaeans left the hollow place of their ambush, poured out from the horse, and sacked the city. And, he sang, each man plundered the city.

517-571 The bard lastly sings about Odysseus' great and victorious fight with Deiphobus. When Odysseus hears this, he breaks down drenching his cheeks with tears. He weeps like a woman who has just witnessed the slaying of her own husband before the city walls. And though he tries to hide

his sorrow from the Phaeacians, Alcinous notices it. He consequently or-
ders Demodocus to stop playing and singing since, he reveals, the stranger
does not delight in it but is full of misery and sorrow. The whole purpose
of the feast, he explains, is to demonstrate affection for the stranger since
strangers and suppliants are equal to brothers.

Turning to Odysseus, then, he calls on him to fully and without guile
reveal his name—since no one, he explains, is born nameless, whether a
base and cowardly man or a noble and brave man. He further bids him to
tell of his mother, father, and the rest of his kinfolk, and where he's
from—his land, people, and city. They need to know what land he comes
from in order to better convey him home.

The last point leads Alcinous to describe the magical Phaeacian ships
that have neither steersmen nor rudders to guide them. Rather, the ships
know the cities of men and follow the thoughts of those onboard through
mist and cloud without fear of destruction. That said, Alcinous relates how
his father Nausithous once told him a story about how Poseidon would one
day wipe out a Phaeacian convoy and pile a mound around the city. Well,
he finishes, the god may or may not accomplish this end as is pleasing to
him.

572-586 "But come—tell me exactly: where have you wandered? To
what lands of men have you come? Tell me about the cities you saw,
the dwellings of men, and the people there. Were they hard to deal
with, wild men living in the fields without justice and lacking the
observance of custom? Tell me also about the ones who were hos-
pitable and love strangers, the ones who are god-fearing in the
thoughts of their minds. And tell me why you weep and lament
when you hear the fated doom of the Argives and Danaans, or
when you hear about Ilium—for the gods caused all this to happen,
spinning out destruction [580] for men so that there would be a
song for those men who do not yet exist. Did some kinsman by mar-
riage fall before the walls of Ilium, some good man such as your
daughter's husband or your wife's father? These are the ones we
care for after our birth families, the ones who share our blood. Or
was it possibly some comrade in arms who pleased you, a noble
man? Such a wise friend is worth just as much as a brother."

BOOK 9

DISASTER ON THE WAY HOME
THE CICONES, THE LOTUS EATERS, AND THE CYCLOPS

IN BRIEF: *Odysseus reveals himself and explains all the suffering he's endured since leaving Troy—the battle against the Cicones; the dreamy lethargy of the Lotus Eaters; the horror of the man-eating Cyclops, Polyphemus. Odysseus wisely escapes the Cyclops by blinding him and using the name, Nobody. In doing so, however, he incurs the wrath of the Cyclops' father, Poseidon.*

IN REPLY, ODYSSEUS of many counsels said to him, "Mighty Alcinous, most renowned among all people, it is a beautiful thing to hear a bard such as this man—his voice sounds like that of the gods! As for me, I declare that there is nothing better or more delightful than when a whole people join in merry festivity together, with the guests sitting side by side listening to the singer, while before them the table is loaded with bread and meats, [10] and the cupbearer draws wine from the mixing bowl and pours it into all the goblets. In my mind, this seems to be the most beautiful thing.

"Now, however, since you have turned to ask the story of my sorrows and of all the wretched trouble I have known so that I may groan about and lament the past all the more, I wonder where to begin or how to go on telling the story, for the heavenly gods have given me much distress. First, I will tell you my name so that you too may know it. And one day, if I escape this ruthless sorrow, may you be my guests and I your host in the house where I dwell, even though it is far away. As for my name, I am Odysseus, the son of Laertes. And for all manner of tricks and stratagems, [20] I am well-known among men—so much so that my glory rises into the sky and to the heavens above. I live in far-seen Ithaca where there is a high mountain called Neriton that juts out from the sea. It is covered with forests of trees that sway in the wind. Around Ithaca is a group of islands very near to one another—Dulichium, Same, and the wooded island called Zacynthus. Ithaca itself stretches out low along the sea, westward toward the darkness. The others stretch eastward toward the dawn and the rising of the sun. Ithaca is a rugged land but a good one for rearing children. Nothing is sweeter than to see one's own land.

"As for what happened, the divine goddess Calypso kept me with her [30] in her hollow cave, longing for me to be her husband. So too did Aeaean Circe, full of deception, retain me in her great hall, eagerly wanting me to marry her. But neither goddess could persuade the spirit in my chest, for there is nothing sweeter to a man than his own homeland and his parents. However rich a home he may have in a faraway land, if it is distant from his mother or father, he does not want it.

"But come, I will tell you of my grievous homecoming, full of many troubles that Zeus permitted while I was venturing home from Troy. The wind took me from Ilium and carried me to the land of the Cicones, [40] to Ismarus. There I sacked the city, bringing destruction to all the men. As for the women, we seized them and took them from the city along with much property and wealth that we later divided equally so that no man was cheated."

43-81 *Odysseus advises fleeing from the land of the Cicones. But the men want to relax while eating and drinking the plenty they had stolen. While they are feasting, however, the Cicones gather their neighbors and attack. In the end, Odysseus and his men are routed, and many are killed, six from each ship. The rest, who "escaped death and fate," sail on, sad at heart. Their problems are not at end, though. Instead, Zeus raises a great storm that blows them in darkness, blindly. After rowing ashore and staying there for a few days, they once again attempt to sail home on the third day. But a great North Wind, the god Boreas, blows them off course just as they are rounding Cape Malea off the Peloponnese. For nine days, the wind blows them south over the fish-filled sea, past the island of Cythera and beyond.*

82-115 "But on the tenth day we went ashore in the land of the Lotus-eaters. These men eat a food that is like flowers. . . . [85-87] I sent some comrades out to go and learn what sort of men who live by bread dwelled in the land. [90] I sent two—and a third as herald with them. These left without delay to go and mix with the Lotus-eaters.

"The Lotus-eaters had no intention to bring ruin to our comrades when they gave them the lotus to eat. But whatever man ate the sweet fruit of the lotus, he no longer wished to bring back a report to the ship, nor did he wish to return home. No—his only desire was to stay among the Lotus-eating men, feeding on lotus and forgetting his return.

"So by force I brought these men weeping back to the ships. And dragging them under the hollow ships' benches, I bound them with fetters. [100] And I urged on my other faithful comrades to move quickly and load into the swift ships so that no other man would eat the lotus and forget his return home. Quickly, then, they climbed aboard, took places at the rowing benches, one after another, and they dug into the foamy gray sea with their oars.

"From then on we sailed forward with distressed hearts until we came to the land of the Cyclopes. They are an arrogant and lawless people who rely solely upon the immortal gods, and thus they do not sow any plants with their own hands, nor do they till the earth. Even so, all these plants spring up unsown and without plowing— [110] wheat, barley, and grapevines bearing wine in their heavy clusters—since Zeus' rain makes them grow. There are no counsel-giving assemblies among them, nor do they have any established laws or customs. Instead, they live at the top of lofty hills in hollow caves, and each Cyclops declares what is right for his children and his wives, and pays little attention to the rest of them."

116-186 *Odysseus goes on to discuss an island off the land of the Cyclopes, who, incidentally, do not possess ships as other men do. He describes the island's hillsides and meadows, its woods, vines, and springs, and the many wild goats that live there. There's also a protected harbor, Odysseus says, where he and his men finally beach the ships and fall asleep.*

Rising the following morning, Odysseus and his men hunt wild goats and kill enough for each ship, twelve total, to have nine. For the remainder of the day, they eat roasted meat and drink a sweet red wine they plundered from the Cicones. Toward dusk they spot smoke rising up from evening fires in the land of the Cyclopes, and they hear voices. Consequently, when dawn comes, Odysseus takes the men from his own ship to learn about the Cyclopes, to see if they are "violent and wild men without custom, or if they love strangers and fear the gods in their minds." Reaching the land of the Cyclopes, they see a high cave that has sheep and goat pens surrounding it and a courtyard made of stones and pine trees.

187-192 "There slept a gigantic man, monstrous in form, who drove his sheep alone and far away—he did not deal with others, but far apart he followed his own lawless and wicked ways. [190] Thus it happened that he became a marvel to behold, a monster, not like a man who eats bread, but like a wood-covered peak on a lofty mountain, one jutting out that appears alone and apart from the others."

193-235 *Odysseus selects a handful of his men, twelve, to go with him to explore the Cyclops' cave. He takes with him a large goatskin of very fine and potent wine, and other provisions. He received the wine from Maro, a priest of Apollo, as a gift for not harming him or his family when Odysseus and his men were sacking the Cicones.*

When they reach the cave, the Cyclops is not there. He's out with his sheep. Odysseus enters the cave with his comrades. Amazed at the Cyclops' stores, the men all wish to take hold of the cheeses there, as well as a number of goats and lambs, and flee to the ship. Not Odysseus. Rather, as he puts it, he wants "to behold the man himself in order to see if he would grant to me those gifts rightfully belonging to a stranger." Speaking to the Phaeacians, Odysseus concludes, "He appeared, but he was not destined to be a delight to my comrades."

Following Odysseus' desire, he and his men remain in the cave. While waiting for their host-to-be, they make a fire, sacrifice to the gods, and eat some of the cheese. Finally, the Cyclops enters the cave, carrying a huge bundle of wood for a fire.

236-306 "Terrified, we crept into the innermost part of the cavern. But into the wide cave the Cyclops drove his fat sheep, the ones that he would milk. As for the males, both rams and he-goats, he left them outside in the wide courtyard. [240] And now, lifting it high into the air, he set in place an enormous door-stone. It was a very heavy thing. Mammoth. Not even twenty-two solidly constructed four-wheel carts could hold the stone up from the surface of the earth—that's what this massive rock was like that he placed in the entryway.

"Sitting down, he then milked the ewes and bleating goats, all in due order. And beneath them he ushered the youngest ones. Once done, he curdled half the white milk, gathered it in wicker baskets, and set it to the side. He left the other half standing in the pails, ready for him to take and drink, and ready also for his supper.

[250] "But after he had worked hard and quickly at these tasks, he kindled a fire. It was then that he spotted us. And questioning us, he asked, 'Strangers, who are you? Where do you come from, sailing over the watery ways? Are you out on business—on some trading voyage? Or do you aimlessly wander, as pirates roam the seas, risking their lives and bringing misfortune to people in another land?'

"As he spoke, our dear hearts were shattered within, fearful of his booming voice and of the monstrous giant himself. Even so, I answered him and said, 'We are Achaeans. We've come from Troy driven [260] from our path across the great depth of the sea by all sorts of winds. We were moving toward home, but by this way and other paths we have come to this place. So it was that Zeus was willing to plan it. We boast ourselves to be the people of Agamemnon, the son of Atreus, whose fame and glory is now the greatest under heaven since he sacked a great city and slaughtered so many men.

"'But hitting upon this place, we come before your knees to ask that you will offer us hospitality, and that in other ways you will give us the customary gifts due to strangers. Mighty one, you should respect the gods. We are your suppliants, [270] and Zeus is the protector and avenger of the suppliant and the stranger. Zeus is the stranger's god, who guards the revered stranger.'

"That's what I said, and at once the Cyclops ruthlessly answered me from his pitiless spirit. 'You're a fool, stranger, or you have come from far away if you're urging me to fear the gods or shrink before them. The Cyclopes don't trouble themselves with aegis-bearing Zeus or the blessed gods since we are much better than they are. I wouldn't spare you or your comrades just to escape the wrath of Zeus—not unless my own heart urged me to do so. [280] But tell me so that I may learn where you left your well-built ship when you came here. Was it at the far shore, or the one nearby?'

"That's what the Cyclops said, testing me. Yet he could not escape my notice—not a knowing man like me. And so, as I did before, I replied with deceptive words meant to trick him.

"'Poseidon the Earth-shaker shattered my ship, driving her against the rocks where the land comes to an end, throwing her against the cliffs. The wind carried her in from the sea. Nevertheless, with these men here I escaped utter destruction.'

"That's what I said. But ruthlessly, the Cyclops didn't reply from his pitiless spirit. Rather, darting up, he threw out his hands to grab at my companions. He took hold of two and dashed them upon the ground as if they had been puppies. [290] And their brains ran out over the floor and wet the earth. Then, butchering them limb from limb, he prepared his evening meal and ate as a mountain lion does, leaving nothing—neither entrails nor flesh nor marrow nor bones. Seeing these reckless deeds, we raised our hands up to Zeus and wailed, feeling powerless to do anything at all.

"But when the Cyclops had filled his cavernous belly by eating human flesh and drinking milk unmixed with water, he stretched himself out among the sheep and went to bed in the cave. It was then that I deliberated within my great-hearted spirit and came up with this plan: [300] I would creep near to him, and drawing my sharp sword from its scabbard by my side, I would stab him in the chest where the midriff holds the liver, feeling the place out with my hand. Yet second thoughts restrained my spirit—for if I had carried out the plan, we would have then and there been wasted by utter destruction. Why? We were not strong enough to push the mighty stone back from the lofty doorway where he had put it.

Consequently, we stayed put, lamenting our situation and awaiting Dawn the divine."

307-335 *In the morning, and after milking his flocks, the Cyclops once again eats two of Odysseus' men. Outraged and full of fear, Odysseus plans revenge, praying that Athena might grant him success and the glory-boast. The idea is to blind the Cyclops by stabbing his one eye. They'll do it with a huge wooden stake that they'll make — one as large as a ship's mast. When the time comes, Odysseus and four others will carry out the plan, five men to hoist the stake and drive it home.*

336-412 "The Cyclops came toward evening, shepherding his flock with beautiful fleece. At once he drove the fat sheep into the wide cave — all of them. And so, he did not leave a single sheep in the wide courtyard outside. I imagine he had some foreboding, or some god urged him to do it.

[340] "Once inside, he lifted the enormous door-stone high into the air and set it in place. Then, sitting down, he milked the ewes and bleating goats, all in due order. And beneath them he ushered the youngest ones. But after he had worked hard and quickly at these tasks, he then took hold of two men and prepared his evening meal.

"Drawing near to the Cyclops and holding in my hands a rustic cup filled with dark wine, I said, 'Here, Cyclops! Drink some wine now that you've had your fill of man-flesh and so that you'll come to know what sort of wine our ship held. I brought it as a drink-offering, hoping you would pity me [350] and send me home. But you're insane! Merciless! It's far too much! How, after this, will any man come to you again from any people since you have behaved inappropriately, far outside the limits of fate?'

"That's what I said, and he took the cup and drained it dry. He was terribly pleased as he drank the sweet wine, and so for a second time he begged me for some. 'Be generous and give me another cup. And now, at once, tell me your name so that I may give you guest-gifts that will make you glad. For even though the Cyclopes' wheat-giving fields produce wine made of fine grapes, growing large with the help of Zeus' thunderstorms, *this* is a bit of ambrosia and nectar.'

[360] "That's what the Cyclops said, and once again I offered him the shining wine. I brought and gave it to him three times. And three times he thoughtlessly drank it. Even so, when the wine began to overtake the Cyclops' mind and senses, I then addressed him with soothing words: 'Cyclops, you asked me my glorious name, and so I will tell it to you. But just as you promised, you must give me a guest-gift. My name is Nobody. My mother and father call me Nobody, as do the rest of my comrades.'

"That's what I said, and at once the Cyclops ruthlessly answered me from his pitiless spirit. 'Out of all his friends, I will eat Nobody last—[370] and all the others first. This will be my guest-gift for you.'

"Speaking, he leaned over and fell flat on his back. And there he lay with his neck outstretched and bent until sleep that conquers all took hold of him. Then: a stream of wine and chunky flesh-filled vomit rushed from his throat and mouth. Heavy with wine, the Cyclops erupted!

"It was then that I drove the stake under a heap of ashes in order to heat it. And I spoke to my comrades to give them courage so that under the influence of fear no man would hesitate or draw back. And presently, when the olivewood stake—even though it was green—was about to catch fire, and when it was terribly red-hot, [380] I carried it from the fire, while my men stood surrounding me. And a god inspired us with great courage.

"Taking the sharp-tipped olivewood stake in hand, they thrust it into his eye while I twisted it from above. As when a man bores ship beams with a drill, and those below keep the tool in motion with a strap held by the ends, and steadily the drill runs, even so we seized the fire-sharpened stake and turned it around in his eye. As we did so, flowing blood bubbled up by its hot tip. The heat charred the lids around the eye, and even its brow, [390] as the eyeball burned and its roots crackled in the fire. As when a smith dips a great axe or a carpenter's adze into cold water in order to strengthen it, and the water screams like crazy, hissing—for this dipping is the strength of iron—so did the eye hiss around the olive-wood stake.

"Terrible to look on, the giant howled loudly, and the surrounding rocks echoed! As for us, we hurried off in terror while he yanked the blood-covered stake from his eye, and with his hands he hurled it away in a frenzy of pain and agitation. Then he called loudly to the Cyclopes [400] who inhabited the caves around him along the windy heights. Hearing his loud cries, they ran from every side to the cave. And standing there, they asked him what was wrong.

"'What's happening, Polyphemus? Why are you shouting and crying aloud like this in the immortal night? We can't sleep because of you! Is some man driving off your flocks against your will? Or killing you by guile or by strength?'

"And from the cave mighty Polyphemus answered, 'Friends, Nobody is killing me by guile or by strength!'

"In reply, the other Cyclopes harangued him with winged words, saying, [410] 'Well, if you're alone and nobody is harming you, then it must be some sickness from almighty Zeus that you cannot avoid. All you can do is pray to your father, lord Poseidon.'"

413-436 *Finishing their admonition, the other Cyclopes depart while Odysseus laughs inwardly, celebrating the brilliance of his deceptive plan. Meanwhile, Polyphemus sits in pain in the now open entryway hoping to catch anybody daring to leave. Odysseus and his men know better, though. And as the night wanes, Odysseus forms a plan. They'll escape by means of the wooly rams and sheep! Tying themselves to their undersides—one man per three sheep—they'll slip out of the cave in the morning when the Cyclops lets the sheep out to pasture. So, they fasten themselves and await the morning.*

437-463 "When the early-born rosy-fingered Dawn appeared, the male sheep went out to pasture as was their custom, but the un-milked females bleated in their pens [440] since their udders were full to the point of bursting. Oppressed and weakened by evil pain, their master the Cyclops felt over the backs of all the male sheep as they stood up to go outside, but thoughtlessly he didn't notice the men tied beneath the wooly rams.

"The last ram of the flock ambled to the entryway, weighed down by his own wool and by me, the thoughtful and planning one. And feeling him over, mighty Polyphemus said, 'Favorite ram! Why do you leave the cave at the back of the flock? Until now you never lagged behind, but with long strides you're always the first to graze the soft bloom of the grass, [450] and first to reach the flowing river streams, and first to show your longing to return home to the pen when evening comes. Yet now you're the last one out of all the rams. Ah—you must long for your master's eye. Well, when my mind was conquered by wine, an evil man utterly blinded me with his mischievous companions. It was Nobody. And I declare to you that he has not yet escaped destruction. If only you could have thoughts, like mine, and speech, then you could tell me where that man is hiding from my wrath. And then his brain would be smashed throughout the cave and scattered upon the ground— some over here and some over there. And then my heart [460] would recover from the misfortune given me by that wretched man Nobody!'

"Speaking this way, the Cyclops let the ram go, ushering him out the door. When we had gone a little way from the cave and from the courtyard, I first loosened myself from beneath the ram and then my comrades."

464-472 *Driving the sheep with them, and oftentimes glancing back as they go, Odysseus and his men rush down to their ship. The other men are happy to see them but sad for the ones who perished. Still, forbidding them to weep, Odysseus commands them to push off with all haste.*

473-479 "But when I was as far away as I could be so that my voice would carry while shouting, I derisively yelled at the Cyclops in reproach, 'Hey Cyclops! Those men you were going to gobble up in your hollow cave by means of strength and violence—they were not the friends of a weak man! Instead, your evil deeds were destined to rebound and hit you! You're a cruel monster since you did not even fear to eat your own guests in your own house! It's for this reason that Zeus and the other gods have taken revenge!'"

480-501 *Hearing Odysseus' speech, the Cyclops furiously breaks off the top of a nearby mountain and hurls it at his ship. Whoosh! Splash! The massive mountaintop nearly hits! And the downward flow of the sinking mass pulls the ship landward again! Still, Odysseus and his men are able to push off and row away. Once again, however, when they're twice as far offshore, Odysseus angrily turns to yell at the Cyclops—this despite his own comrades' reproof and pleading to the contrary.*

502-505 "Cyclops! If some mortal man asks you about the shameful blinding of your eye, declare to him that Odysseus, the sacker of cities, blinded it! I am the son of Laertes, and my home is in Ithaca!"

506-529 *Hearing Odysseus' true identity, the Cyclops groans while re-calling the prophecy that Telemus, the son of Eurymus, had made. He was a man who had lived as a seer among the Cyclopes. The prophecy was that a man called Odysseus would blind him. But, says Polyphemus, he had al-ways believed he would be a tall, fine looking and mighty man, rather than this powerless nobody that conquered him with wine. The Cyclops then calls on Odysseus to return so that he might give him the proper gifts of hospital-ity, and so that his father Poseidon might escort him home. He then expresses the hope that his father will heal him—he knows none of the other gods will. Odysseus scoffs at the Cyclops, retorting that he would rather take his life from him and speed him on to Hades than see his eye restored! The Cyclops raises his hands "to the starry sky" in order to pray to Poseidon. But instead of asking for the repair of his eye, he calls down harm upon Odysseus.*

530-535 "May Odysseus, the sacker of cities, the son of Laertes who has his dwelling place in Ithaca, never make it home. But if it is his fate to see those who are dear to him and to come to his high-roofed house in his own fatherland, then may he arrive after a long time and in horrible shape, after all his comrades are destroyed. And may he arrive in a ship that belongs to another man and discover woe and suffering in his house."

536-564 *Poseidon hears Polyphemus. And finishing his prayer, the Cyclops tosses yet another even greater stone at Odysseus' ship. It lands short—and the splashing wave drives the ship to the island opposite the Cyclopes' land. There the other men and ships are waiting for their leader and other comrades.*

When they reach the shore, Odysseus and his men divide the sheep they've taken from the Cyclops. Each ship receives an equal number. As a bonus, his men give their leader the wooly ram that saved him. Odysseus sacrifices the ram to Zeus, but the ruler of all does not bother himself with the offering. "Rather he was thinking about how he would utterly destroy" the rest of Odysseus' ships and faithful comrades.

They feast for the remainder of the day on an unspeakable quantity of meat and sweet wine. In the morning, they prepare the ships and embark to make their way home.

565-566 "From there we sailed on with aching hearts. Glad to have escaped death, we mourned the loss of our dear comrades."

BOOK 10

A YEAR WITH CIRCE
AEOLUS, THE LAESTRYGONIANS, AND CIRCE

IN BRIEF: *Odysseus and his men nearly reach Ithaca and home after a prolonged stay with Aeolus and his family, but Odysseus' men open the bag of winds that drive them off again. They next meet up with the monstrous man-eating Laestrygonians, who kill and eat many of them, destroying all the ships but one. They sail to Circe's island. The goddess turns half of his men into pigs with a magical potion. Nevertheless, Odysseus, with the help of Hermes, forces her to return their manly form, and they all become friends. They feast for a year until his men remind Odysseus of his fatherland and he resolves to leave for home. Still, Circe tells him he must make one last voyage—to the end of the world and Hades in order to speak with the seer Tiresias.*

W E SOON DREW near to the island of Aeolia, where Aeolus, the son of Hippotas, dear to the immortal gods, lives on a floating island. Surrounding the island is an unbreakable wall of bronze—its steep rocky cliff rises straight up. Twelve children were born to Aeolus within his great hall—six daughters and six sons in their prime. And there in his house he offered his daughters to his sons to be their wives. And they are always feasting there alongside their dear father and diligent mother, with an abundant spread of food nearby."

10-19 Odysseus and his men remain feasting with Aeolus and his family for a full month, recounting everything that happened in Ilium and about the return of the Achaeans. When it is time for them to leave, Aeolus is very helpful, offering conveyance to speed them on their way, as well as an extraordinary ox-hide bagful of the winds.

20-53 "And he bound the paths of the blustering winds inside the bag since the son of Cronus had made him overseer of the winds, both to calm or to rouse the wind as he wished. Placing it in my hollow ship, he tied the bag with a bright cord of silver so that not even a little wind would escape. Nevertheless, he sent out Zephyrus, the West Wind, to blow and carry along my ships and men. But our homeward voyage was not destined to end well. No, by our thoughtless folly we perished.

"We sailed for nine days—travelling by day and by night. On the tenth day the fields of our homeland came into view so that we could see them plainly. [30] We could see men tending fires—that's how close they were.

"It was right then, when I was so exhausted, that sweet sleep suddenly fell on me. I alone had managed the ship's sail over the past days and nights, never giving it over to another man, in the hope that we might swiftly reach our fatherland.

"Meanwhile my men began to talk to one another, to proclaim that I was bringing home gold and silver gifts from Aeolus, the great-hearted son of Hippotas. And glancing at the one sitting next to him, one man would say, 'It's shameful to us how this man is honored and held dear by everyone everywhere, no matter the land or town he comes to. [40] He's already hauling home from Troy a boatload of beautiful treasure from all the booty we gathered there, while we're going home with nothing but empty hands, even though we went on the same journey. And now Aeolus has given him *this* in friendship and kindness! Come, then—let's take a quick look at how much gold and silver is in the bag.'

"That's what my comrades said, and so their evil plan prevailed among them. They untied the bag, and all the winds rushed out violently. Suddenly, a storm swept my weeping comrades toward the sea and far away from their fatherland.

"That's when I woke up. And I debated in my noble spirit whether I should throw myself from the ship and die in the sea or silently endure and remain among the living. I stayed and I endured."

54-72 A "cruel storm of wind" blows Odysseus and his men back to the island of Aeolia and Aeolus, master of winds, who is shocked to see him. When Odysseus asks him for help again, he refuses, knowing that some misfortune-bringing god has blocked his way home.

73-76 "'Leave this island immediately—you who, of all living things, are worthy of reproach! Be quick! It would not be right for me to aid in sending away a man hated by the blessed immortals. So leave!—since you've only landed here again because you're detested by the gods!'

"Speaking in this manner, he sent me sighing deeply from his house."

77-104 Odysseus and his men sail for six days and nights until they arrive at the "high and steep citadel of Lamus, to Telepylus, the city of the Laestrygonians." Most of Odysseus' ships anchor inside the Laestrygonian harbor. Odysseus alone moors his ship outside the harbor, fastening it with ropes to the rocks below the island's sheer cliffs. Then, having done some initial reconnaissance, Odysseus sends three men to scope out the island to find out what kind of men live there and in the city.

105-132 "Leaving the ship, they took a beaten road along which carts brought timber from the high mountains down to the city below. They met a young girl there drawing water in front of the city. She was the thickset daughter of the Laestrygonian Antiphates. She had come down to the beautiful flowing spring of Artacia from which the Laestrygonians carry water for the city. When my men stood alongside her, they spoke to her and asked [110] who the local king was and what people he ruled. Right then she showed them her father's high-roofed house. When they entered the glorious house, they found a woman who was as big as the top of a mountain and they felt nothing but disgust for her. At once she summoned her husband, glorious Antiphates, from the assembly place. And he plotted their destruction—a pathetic end for my men.

"Immediately he caught up one of my comrades and prepared his evening meal. As for the other two men, they jumped up and fled until they came flying to the ships. Antiphates then raised a cry throughout the city. Hearing it, the mighty Laestrygonians arrived from here and there, [120] countless in number. They didn't appear like men. No, they were like the Giants.

"Then from the rocky cliffs the Laestrygonians hurled boulders at us—stones as large as any man can lift or carry. And soon the dreadful din of dying men and ships breaking apart rose up from the ships. But the Laestrygonians were not finished. Spearing my comrades like men spear fish, they carried off the disgusting feast.

"While the Laestrygonians were killing those men in the deep harbor, I drew my sharp sword from my side and cut the ropes of my dark-prowed ship. A moment later I called to my comrades and urged them to grab their oars and row so that we might flee from misfortune. [130] Fearing destruction, they all dug into the water, tossing it behind with every sweep. They rejoiced as my ship flew out to sea and away from the overhanging cliffs. But all the other ships and men were destroyed there in the harbor."

133-209 They sail on—sad for their friends yet glad to leave—and finally come to the island of Aeaea, where Circe, the terrible goddess, lives. She is the daughter of Helios and Perse, and sister of Aeetes.

After two days and nights on the island, Odysseus spots smoke rising in the distance when he climbs to a high place to scope out the island on the third day. His plan is to have his men reconnoiter the smoke's source after feeding them. On the way back to the ship, a god sends a stag with lofty antlers before him that he easily drops with his spear. Dragging the beast back to his men, they feast on "abundant meat and sweet wine" for the rest of the day, Odysseus cheering them on by saying, "Friends, we will not go down grieving into the house of Hades before the day of fate arrives."

When dawn comes the next day, Odysseus explains that he has no idea where he and his men are—where the rising of the sun is or its setting. Rather, he only knows they are surrounded by endless sea. Still, there is smoke rising up on the island in the distance. Hearing this revelation, the men begin to weep with big tears pouring down their faces. "But," Odysseus relates, "the weeping did nothing for them." He divides his men into two groups—one led by Eurylochus and the other by him. They shake lots to see which group will go explore the smoke's source. The lots reveal that Eurylochus and his men will go. Lamenting their luck, twenty-two men march off with their leader.

210-250 "Within an opening in the forest they found the house of Circe, built of smooth stone in a remarkable place. All around were mountain wolves and lions, which Circe had charmed by giving them evil drugs. These creatures did not leap on my men but stood erect, wagging their long tails. As dogs fawn around their master when he comes from a feast because he always brings them treats they like, so around these men the strong-clawed wolves and lions fawned. Still, my men trembled at the sight of the dread monsters. [220] They stood before the gateway leading into the courtyard of the beautiful-haired goddess and heard Circe within singing with a beautiful voice, while working her divine loom, huge in size. She was weaving very fine cloth. It was graceful. Elegant. Marvelous— as are the works of gods.

"And among the men, Polites was the first to speak. He was a leader of men. Of all my comrades, he was nearest to me by marriage, and a diligent man, and careful. 'Friends, someone in the house is working a great loom and singing beautifully so that all the ground echoes. It is some goddess or a woman. Let us then quickly make some noise and call out.'

"So he spoke, and the others lifted up their voices and called out. [230] And suddenly, coming forward from within, Circe opened the shining gateway and summoned them inside. In ignorance, they followed her in. Only Eurylochus remained behind, supposing there might be a trap.

"When she had invited them into her house, she sat them down on couches and seats and mixed them a mixed drink made with cheese, pale honey, barley meal, and Pramnian wine. To this mixture she added her mournful drugs to make them wholly forget the land of their fathers. And when they had had their fill, Circe struck them with her wand and tossed them into her pigpens. And now the men were like wild swine—they had the form of a pig, its head and hair, and they grunted and squealed as a pig does. [240] Even so, their minds were the same as before.

"In this way they were confined in the pigpens wailing, and Circe threw them some acorns and other tree nuts such as pigs eat. But Eurylochus hurried back to the swift black ship to tell me about the bitter destiny of our comrades. He was so overcome with dismay that, even though he tried to speak, he could find no words to do so. Instead, his eyes filled with tears, and he could only sob and sigh, until in amazement we eventually forced the story out of him, [250] and he told us about the destruction of our other comrades."

251-273 Eurylochus relates the story of what happened—how he and his men came upon Circe's house, and how the goddess invited them in, and how he, suspecting a trap, remained behind waiting for them for a very long time to reappear. They never did. Hearing what happened, Odysseus readies his sword and bow to go to Circe's house to rescue his men. He commands Eurylochus to show him the way. The latter man, however, fearfully begs to be left behind with all the other men. Odysseus agrees, explaining he must nevertheless go help the others.

274-289 "Saying this, I left the ship and walked inland. When I was near the great house of the enchantress Circe, I met Hermes with his golden wand. He was disguised as a young man at the height of his youth and beauty, with a beard just now growing on his face. [280] He came up to me, took my hand, and said, 'Wretched man, where are you going alone and without knowing the way? Your men are trapped in Circe's pigpens. Are you hoping to free them? I can tell you that you will never get back to your ship nor will you return home. No, you'll stay there with the rest of them. But never mind—I will save and free you from this misfortune. Here, take this powerful herb with you. And when you go to Circe's house, it will defend you against every kind of wickedness."

290-312 Hermes tells Odysseus about the drug-laced mixture Circe will mix for him and how the herb will protect him. Then, he says, when Circe goes to strike you with her wand, quickly lay your sword against her neck as if to kill her. She'll fear you and beg to sleep with you. Agree to it—but make her swear by the blessed gods that she will not cast on you any more evil misery or unman you. Guiding him in this way, Hermes gives Odysseus the herb called moly—a black root and milk-white flower that is "hard for a mortal man to dig up" but easy for the gods—and flies off to Olympus. As for Odysseus, he moves toward the house with foreboding, calling out to Circe at the gates. Just as she had before, she comes out and invites him in.

313-347 "And I followed her with a troubled heart. Circe led me in and sat me on a silver-studded chair, beautiful, one cleverly fashioned. And below there was a footrest. Then she prepared a mixture for me to drink in a golden cup. She slipped a drug into it with wicked intentions in her spirit. But when she had given me the drink and I had finished it with no bad result to speak of—I was not bewitched—she nevertheless struck me with her wand and spoke these words to me: [320] 'Now, be off to the pigpens! And lie there asleep with the rest of your comrades!'

"That's what Circe said. But I drew a sharp blade from my side and rushed at her as though I meant to kill her. With a loud cry she ducked under the sword and took hold of my knees. And begging me with tears, she spoke to me with winged words:

"'Who are you among men? Where are you from? Where is your city? Who are your parents? I am amazed that you have downed this enchanted mixture without experiencing its strong effect. There's been no other man who has endured the drug once he has drunk the mixture and it has passed the barrier of his teeth. But the mind in your chest cannot be bewitched. [330] Surely you are much-wandering Odysseus. Argeiphontes of the golden wand always told me that you would come here on your way home from Troy in your swift black ship. Well then, come on, put away your sword in its scabbard. Let's climb into my bed so that mixing together there in love we may come to trust each other.'

"That's what Circe said. Nevertheless, in reply, I said to her, 'Circe, how can you now call on me to be kind to you? Gentle? You, the very one who has turned my comrades into swine in your great hall? And now you hold me here, and with treacherous thoughts you beckon me [340] into your inner chamber to go to bed with you so that once you've strip me naked you can unman me and turn me into a coward! Well, I am not willing to climb into bed with you — not unless you, goddess, agree to swear a mighty oath that you will not plot any more evil misfortune for me.'

"That's what I said. And at once she swore that she would not harm me just as I commanded her to do. When she finished swearing the oath, I climbed with her into bed, into the beautiful bed of Circe."

348-448 *While Odysseus and Circe mix in love, Circe's handmaidens, "children of the springs, groves, and the sacred rivers that flow into the sea," prepare refreshment and a bath for Odysseus. They later bathe and clothe him, offering him bread, meat, and wine. But he doesn't want any — not as long as his men waste away as pigs in Circe's pigpens.*

When Circe notices his glum mood, she reiterates the oath she has already made. She will not hurt him. It's not that, he says. It is his men. How can he enjoy himself while they remain penned up and unfree? Odysseus calls on the goddess to release them so that he may see his men with his own eyes. She does. Walking among the man-pigs, she smears another drug on each one, changing them from wild swine to men — but now they are younger, bigger, and handsomer. When they see Odysseus, they sob with relief, and even the goddess feels some measure of pity.

Circe approaches Odysseus and calls on him to retrieve his other men. He does. And when he first appears to them, they weep and joyfully receive him as calves receive their mothers that amble in from grazing. They want to know what happened to the other men. Odysseus tells them they will see their comrades, but first they must pull the ships onto the shore and store the gear away in nearby caves. Then, he says, they'll go see the other men who are eating and drinking an abundance of food and wine.

All the men agree to go — all but for Eurylochus. He asks them why they wish to go to Circe's house when she will turn them into lions, wolves, or swine. He goes on to blame Odysseus for the Cyclops disaster and the men they lost. "It was through this man's recklessness that they were destroyed!" Hearing this tirade, Odysseus ponders slaying Eurylochus even though he is his kinsman by marriage. He'll cut off his head with a sweep of his sword. Thanks to another man, though, he doesn't. Rather at this man's bidding, they make their way to Circe's house. Eurylochus even goes, fearing Odysseus' forceful rebuke.

449-475 "Meanwhile in her halls Circe [450] bathed the rest of my comrades kindly and anointed them richly with olive oil and threw on them fleecy cloaks and tunics. We found them all feasting with abundance in the halls. But when they saw and recognized one another face to face, they cried and mourned, and the house echoed with the sound of their crying.

"Then the divine goddess approached me and said, 'God-born son of Laertes, much-able Odysseus, stop this vigorous weeping. I know about all the pain and distress you have suffered on the fish-filled sea. I know as well all the damage hostile men have done to you on dry land. [460] Nevertheless come and eat food and drink wine until your spirits are once again revived in your chests just as they were when you first left rugged Ithaca, the land of your fathers. Now you are dried up, withered and spiritless, always remembering your torturous, never-ending roaming. Ah, you have suffered so very much that your spirits are never joyful.'

"That's what Circe said, and our courageous hearts consented. So, we stayed there day after day for a full year, feasting on an unspeakable quantity of meat and sweet wine.

"But when a year went by, and the seasons turned [470] as moon after moon waned and many days came to an end, then my faithful comrades called me out and said to me, 'God-possessed man, it is now time to remember the land of your fathers—if in fact it is decreed for you to be saved and to reach your high-roofed house and your homeland.'

"That's what they said. And my courageous heart consented."

476-561 *Later that night, after yet another day of feasting, Odysseus entreats Circe to send him and his men home. She agrees. But before making it home, she reveals that he must first journey to the house of Hades and dread Persephone in order to speak with the blind seer Tiresias, who will act as an oracle for Odysseus.*

Hearing the news, Odysseus collapses in tears, no longer wishing to remain among the living in the light of the sun. Yet then he regains his will and asks Circe about the voyage that no other man had ever made. Who will guide us?

The goddess explains that Boreas, the North Wind, will blow them to "the stream of Oceanus" where he will beach his black ship by the poplar and willow groves of Persephone. Then, moving on alone, Odysseus will come to a rock where the Pyriphlegethon and the Cocytus, which is a branch of the Styx, flow into the Acheron. There he must dig a pit and scatter barley grain over a milk, honey, wine, and water libation to the dead. And summoning the dead, Odysseus must promise them sacrifices upon their homecoming to Ithaca, including an all-black ram for Tiresias. After entreating the dead in this way, his men should sacrifice two sheep—a ram and black ewe—for their phantom-life souls. But, Circe goes on, he must not let them taste the blood until he has queried Tiresias about his return.

Finishing with her directions, the dawn comes at once, and Circe dresses in a white tunic tied with a golden belt. As for Odysseus, he wakes his men to tell them today is the day to sail.

Hearing Odysseus make the rounds and the noise of all the men rising to greet the day, the young man Elpenor wakes up and accidentally falls from the roof of Circe's house where he had sought cool air the night before when he was drunk. He plunges straight down, shattering the vertebrae along his neck, and his life-soul flies down to Hades. No one knows of his death.

Meanwhile, Odysseus is speaking to his men.

562-574 "'You think, perhaps, that you are going home to your dear fatherland. But it is not so. No, Circe has revealed another journey we must make—to the house of Hades and dread Persephone, where I will consult the phantom-life of Theban Tiresias.'

"That's what I said. And their dear hearts were broken within them. And so, sitting down right where they were, they wept and tore their hair. But no good came of their flowing tears."

"While we walked to the swift ship and the seashore, [570] sad all the way and shedding big tears, Circe passed us in order to leave a ram and black ewe at the ship. We didn't see her, though—for when a god does not want him to, what man can observe him moving here and there?"

BOOK 11

THE UNDERWORLD
SPEAKING WITH THE DEAD

IN BRIEF: *Odysseus and his men sail to the edge of the world to communicate with the dead in Hades. After pouring out a libation and sacrificing two sheep, Odysseus speaks with the seer Tiresias, who tells him what he must suffer before returning home, how he will slaughter the suitors, and about the final journey he must make. After speaking with him, he converses with many women, including his mother, and sees many more—among them, Epicaste, the mother-wife of Oedipus, and Leda, the wife of Tyndareus. After the Phaeacians ask to hear more, Odysseus reports his conversation with Achilles, his attempted reconciliation with Telamonian Ajax, and how he saw many others—Minos, Orion, Tityus, Tantalus, Sisyphus, and Heracles.*

NOW WHEN WE came down to the ship and to the sea, we first dragged the ship down into the divine sea. Then we set the mast and the sail in the black ship and took the sheep and put them aboard. Lastly, we ourselves embarked in sadness, shedding big tears."

"And Circe, dread goddess of human speech, sent for our aid a fair wind that filled the sail from behind our dark-prowed ship, one that was a useful comrade. So, when we had made fast all the tackling throughout the ship, [10] we sat down, and the wind and the steersman turned the ship straight ahead. All day long the sail was spread out as the ship sped over the sea until the sun set and all the ways grew dark.

"And now the ship came to deep-flowing Oceanus, the very limit of the Earth, where exist the land and city of the Cimmerian men, wrapped in mist and cloud. The bright sun never looks down on them with his rays—neither when he rides into the starry sky nor when he turns again toward the earth from the heavens. Instead, destructive night is stretched out over wretched mortals. [20] It was here that we came and beached our ship. And we led out the sheep and walked alongside the stream of Oceanus until we came to the spot that Circe had described.

"Perimedes and Eurylochus held the victims here, while I drew my sharp sword from my side and dug a pit measuring a cubit's length this way and that. Around the edges of the ditch, I poured a libation to all the dead—first with milk and honey, then with sweet wine, third with water, and finally, I sprinkled white barley-meal over the whole. And I earnestly beseeched the feeble corpse-heads of the dead, [30] vowing that when I came home to Ithaca, I would sacrifice in my halls a young cow, the best one that has not yet given birth, and I would fill the sacrificial fire with noble things, and to Tiresias alone I would sacrifice a ram, wholly black, the best of my flocks. So, when I had called upon the host of the dead with vows and prayers, I took the sheep and cut their throats, and dark, cloudy blood gushed out into the pit.

"Then the phantom-souls of the dead and gone gathered there from out of Erebus, the land of darkness. There were young brides and youths who never married, much-enduring old men, and delicate maidens with hearts yet new to sorrow. [40] There were many, too, who had been wounded with bronze-tipped spears, men slain by Ares, wearing their blood-stained armor. And with an awful cry, these phantom-souls came thronging in crowds around the pit from every side. And pale fear seized me!

"I nevertheless called out to my comrades and commanded them to flay and burn the sheep that lay there slaughtered by the ruthless bronze. I told them to pray to the gods as they did so, to mighty Hades and dread Persephone. As for me, I drew my sharp sword from my side and sat there. I would not let the feeble corpse-heads of the dead [50] go near the blood—not until I had learned what I needed to know from Tiresias."

51-91 *Nevertheless, when Odysseus sees the phantom-soul of his lost*

comrade Elpenor among the dead, he pities him and talks to him. Elpenor
explains how he died—the copious wine and the accidental fall from
Circe's roof and the snapped neck. Then he urges Odysseus to bury him
when he passes by the island of Aeaea on his way home. Burn me in my
armor, he says, and "pile up a mound for me on the shore of the gray sea,
a marker for an unhappy man, so that men yet to be will learn about me."
Elpenor finishes by asking him to stick his oar into the mound—the one he
used to row with next to the other men. Odysseus assures the unhappy
man that he will do as requested.

Next comes the phantom-soul of Odysseus' mother, Anticleia, the
daughter of Autolycus, whom he had left alive upon his departure from
Ithaca. Seeing her, he pities her. Even so, he holds her back from the blood
along with all the other dead.

Finally, Tiresias comes up from Erebus holding a golden scepter. He
recognizes Odysseus and speaks to him.

92-137 "'God-born son of Laertes, much-able Odysseus, what now
you unhappy man? Why have you left the light of the sun in order
to come here to see the dead in this place where there is no joy?
Whatever your reason, step away from the pit and pull back your
sharp sword so that I may drink of the blood and speak to you the
unfailing truth.'

"That's what Tiresias said. And so I drew back and thrust my
silver-studded sword into its sheath.

"When Tiresias had drunk the dark blood, then the blameless
seer spoke to me and said, [100] 'Glorious Odysseus, you seek out
an easy return home—honey-sweet. You want information. But let
me tell you, a god will make it hard for you. I do not think that you
will dodge the Earth-shaker since he bears a grudge against you in
his spirit. He's angry because you blinded his dear son.

"'Even so you may still reach home, though suffering misfortune,
if you will choose to restrain your own desires and curb those of your
comrades when you reach the island of Thrinacia with your well-
built ship, safe from the dark blue sea. There you will find the grazing
cattle and fat sheep of Helios the Sun, who sees and hears everything.
[110] If you leave these alone, unharmed, keeping in mind your

return home, then you may still reach Ithaca, though suffering hardship and misfortune. But if you hurt them, then I predict ruin—destruction—for your ship and death for your comrades. And even if you escape, your return will happen only after a long time has passed and after all your comrades have perished. And you will return in a ship that is not your own. And when home, you will find trouble in your house—proud men devouring your livelihood, wooing your godlike wife, and offering bridal gifts. Nevertheless, when you return you will pay those men back for their violent deeds.

"'But when you have slaughtered the suiters in your halls, [120] whether by some trick or openly with a sharp bronze sword, then go abroad, taking a shapely oar with you. Go until you come to men who know nothing of the sea and do not eat food mixed with salt. Indeed, they know nothing of ships with purple cheeks or of shapely oars that serve as wings for ships. And I will give you a sign that will be readily apparent to you, one that will not escape your notice. When you meet up with another traveler, and he says that you have a winnowing-fan on your shining shoulder, then plant your shapely oar in the earth [130] and make fine offerings to lord Poseidon—a ram and a bull and a boar that mates with sows. Then, go home and offer sacred hecatombs to the immortal gods, who possess the wide sky—offer them to each one in due order. And death will come to you away from the sea, a gentle death that will lay you low when you have grown old. And your people will exist in happy prosperity around you. With these words I speak unerring truth to you.'"

138-179 After hearing Tiresias' prophecy by the will of the gods, Odysseus asks him how his mother might come to recognize him. The seer explains that she must drink of the blood to see and speak to him. Saying this, Tiresias returns into the house of Hades, and Odysseus permits his mother some of the dark-colored blood. Now, recognizing her son she asks him how he came down to the land of the dead while still alive. Odysseus responds that the necessity to hear Tiresias brought him down to Hades. In response to other questions, he declares that he has not yet returned home after Troy. Then he asks her to tell him about his father and son, and whether he still

possesses the right to rule, and if they believe he is dead, and if his wife
Penelope has married again one of the best of the Achaeans.

180-224 "That's what I said. And my queenly mother answered me right away. 'In truth Penelope remains in your halls with a steadfast spirit and enduring heart, even though she is miserable, and day and night pass by for her in shedding tears. Even so, no other man holds the noble prerogatives and rights that were yours, but Telemachus commands the estate and joins in equal feasts as it is appropriate for one who judges others to do, for all men welcome him.

"'As for your father Laertes, he remains there in the fields and doesn't come into the city. He has no bed mattress, or a bed-robe, or colorful blankets for a bed. [190] Instead, covering himself with shabby clothes, he sleeps through the winter in the same house where the slaves sleep. There he sleeps stretched out on the dusty ground by the fire. But when summer comes and its flourishing end, then he sleeps along the slope of his vineyard plot in a pile of fallen leaves. There he lies in pain and distress as a great sorrow grows in his heart due to his longing for your return home. And meanwhile all the difficulties of old age have crept upon him.

"'This is how I died and met my own fate—just like the old man suffers now in sorrow and distress. Artemis, the keen-sighted archer goddess, didn't attack me in my halls and slay me with her gentle shafts, [200] nor did some disease suddenly come upon me as oftentimes happens when a hateful wasting away takes the spirit from the limbs. No, it was my longing for you and for your counsels, glorious Odysseus, and for your kindness, that robbed me of the honey-sweet spirit of life.'

"That's what she said, and I was torn in my heart by the wish to take in hand the phantom-life of my dead mother. Three times I dashed at her, my spirit urging me to take hold of her. But each time—three times!—she flew from the embrace of my arms like a shadow or a dream. And the pain I felt grew sharper in my heart.

"Finally, I spoke, addressing her with winged words: [210] 'My mother, why don't you remain here for me since I eagerly desire to hold you? Stay here so that even in Hades' house we might throw our arms around each other and take our fill of cold lamenting. Or is this just a phantom-image that wondrous Persephone has sent to me, to make me mourn and wail all the more?'

"That's what I said, and my queenly mother answered me at once: 'Ah me!—my child, ill-fated beyond all men! The daughter of Zeus, Persephone, is in no way fooling you, but this is usually what happens when mortals die. The sinews no longer hold the flesh and the bones together, [220] but the strong might of blazing fire over-powers and destroys these as soon as the spirit leaves the white bones, and the life-soul, like a dream, flies away, drifting here and there. But strive to move into the light as quickly as possible. And as you go, keep these things in mind so that you may tell them to your wife later on.'"

225-270 *After his mother vanishes into the darkness, Odysseus speaks to the other spirits of the dead, beginning with the wives and daughters of the best men, the ones who press forward to drink the dark blood. First, there is Tyro, who fell in love with the river Enipeus, even though she was the wife of Cretheus. In the end, she bore Pelias of Iolcus and Neleus of Pylos to Poseidon, who took on the form of the beloved river. And to her husband she bore Aeson, Pheres, and Amythaon. After Tyro comes Antiope. She slept with Zeus and gave birth to Amphion and Zethus. The latter founded Thebes and built its strong walls. Then Alcmene, the wife of Amphitryon and the mother of Heracles by Zeus, steps forward, as does Megara, the daughter of Creon, who married Heracles.*

271-280 "And I saw Oedipus' mother, beautiful Epicaste. In the ig-norance of her own mind, she did a monstrous thing. She married her own son—for he married her after killing his own father. Later, the gods proclaimed the whole story to the world. All the same, Oedipus remained king of Thebes, even though he suffered much pain thanks to the destruction the gods planned for him. As for Epi-caste, she went down to mighty Hades' house, having hanged her-self from a lofty beam for all her grief. Nevertheless, she left behind many woes for Oedipus. [280] And the Erinyes, the great avenging ones, haunted him because of his outraged mother."

281-297 Odysseus next sees the very beautiful Chloris, the daughter of Amphion. Neleus married her and made her the queen of Pylos. She gave birth to Nestor, Chromius, and Periclymenus, and to wondrous Pero, a beautiful girl. The seer Melampus won her once he had driven the cattle of Iphicles from Phylace.

298-304 "And I saw Leda, the wife of Tyndareus, who bore to Tyndareus two dauntless sons, [300] horse-taming Castor and the skilled boxer Polydeuces. The life-producing earth holds both men below, even though they are alive. There in the earth they possess honor from Zeus. On alternate days they live and die—one day alive, the next dead. Their allotment is like the honor the gods have."

305-327 Following Leda, Odysseus encounters Iphimedeia, the wife of Aloeus. She reveals that she slept with Poseidon and gave birth to the giants Otus and Ephialtes, the tallest and most beautiful men, after Orion. At nine years-old they were nine cubits wide by nine fathoms tall (about thirteen by fifty-four feet). These boys eagerly desired to create a stairway to the sky and heaven by stacking Mount Ossa on Mount Olympus, and Mount Pelion on Mount Ossa. They would have done so if they had reached their prime, but Apollo destroyed them before the hair began to grow on their chins.

Phaedra and Procris step up next, and beautiful Ariadne, Minos' girl, whom Theseus wished to bring from Crete to the heights of sacred Athens. Before he could enjoy her in love, however, Artemis killed her thanks to the testimony of Dionysus. And Maera and Clymene appear, and loathsome Eriphyle, who took gold in exchange for her husband.

328-334 "But I cannot recount or name all the many hero's wives and daughters that I saw. [330] If I tried, the immortal night would pass before I finished. No, now is the time to sleep. I'll either go sleep with the ship's crew on the swift ship or here. Regardless, my conveyance home is the gods' concern—and yours."

That's what Odysseus said. And the Phaeacians were all hushed in silence, fascinated by everything he had revealed in the shadowy hall.

335-472 Arete praises Odysseus for his mind and looks and suggests that the Phaeacian nobility should give him more gifts. The old man Echeneus agrees, but he says they must depend on Alcinous' word and deed for how to move forward. Alcinous supports his wife's proposal, adding that they must fully gather Odysseus' gifts before sending him on.

Odysseus eagerly agrees to stay for many days—even up to a year—as long as they'll give him glorious gifts and ultimately get him home. "For it would be far more profitable to return to my beloved homeland with hands full." Not only would he be wealthy, he says, but people would respect him more.

Alcinous tells Odysseus that the Phaeacians trust him. He doesn't seem like a liar, he explains, one who would make up stories. Indeed, he praises him for telling the tale so well—like a bard. Then he asks him if he saw any of his fallen comrades in Hades. Come, he says, we have all night to listen to your marvelous deeds.

Odysseus agrees to tell the Phaeacians of the many miseries his comrades experienced on the way home from Troy. And so, returning in word to the house of Hades, Odysseus explains that Agamemnon next appeared alongside all the men who were slain with him by Aegisthus.

Agamemnon, the son of Atreus, recognizes Odysseus after drinking the dark-colored blood, but he cannot embrace him since he's powerless to do so. Odysseus weeps and pities him before asking how the leader of the Achaeans died. Did Poseidon harm him on the sea? Or did enemy men harm him on dry land when he was stealing their sheep or fighting for their city and women?

Agamemnon responds that it was neither. Rather Aegisthus and Clytemnestra—Agamemnon's own wife and Aegisthus' lover—killed him and his men as a man would slaughter an ox or swine for a great feast. Agamemnon explains that Odysseus has surely never seen anything like it, so many men slaughtered in one hall, the floor flooded with blood. What a betrayal! Agamemnon thought his wife would welcome him home. Not at all! She didn't even close his eyes when he died and traveled down to Hades. He declares that his wife's dreadful act will be counted as a disgrace for all women to come, even for upright women who do well.

Odysseus laments the pain that has come to men through women—to Agamemnon's house through Clytemnestra and to the Achaeans through

Helen. Agamemnon advises Odysseus never to be gentle with his wife. And don't tell your wife everything, he says. Only some things but not others. Nevertheless, Agamemnon predicts that thoughtful Penelope will not harm Odysseus. No, unlike Agamemnon who was murdered before he could see his own boy, Odysseus will come home to his wife and to his son, who was an infant-child when they sailed for Troy, whereas he is now prosperous among men.

Agamemnon asks Odysseus if he has any news of his boy, where he is. Odysseus replies that he doesn't. So, they cry together and continue talking until Patroclus, Antilochus, and Telamonian Ajax walk up, along with Achilles, the son of Peleus, who speaks to Odysseus with winged words.

473-491 "'God-born son of Laertes, much-able Odysseus, you never stop! Tell me—what exploit will you plan that is greater than this? How did you dare to come down to Hades, where the senseless dead dwell, the phantom images of toil-worn mortal men?'

"That's what Achilles said. And in reply I said, 'Achilles, son of Peleus, the very best and bravest of the Achaeans, I came because I needed Tiresias, hoping that he would give me some plan [480] that would help me reach rugged Ithaca. The truth is I have not yet come near to the land of the Achaeans, nor have I set foot in my own land, but misfortune is always mine—unlike you, Achilles. There's never been a more blessed man than you, nor will there ever be one. When you were alive, we Argives honored you as we honor the gods, and now that you're here in this place you rule mightily among the dead. Therefore, don't feel bad that you are dead, Achilles.'

"That's what I said. And in response, Achilles said to me at once, 'Do not speak to me lightly about death, glorious Odysseus. If only I could, I would choose to live upon the earth, working as a day laborer for some other man, [490] some landless man who doesn't have much of what it takes to live. I'd rather be that man, Odysseus, than rule over all the rotting dead.'"

492-503 *After this rebuttal of Odysseus' assessment, Achilles asks about his own son, Neoptolemus, and about his father, Peleus—if he knows anything. Does his father still have honor among the Myrmidons, or do they dishonor him because of old age? Achilles wishes he could be strong again and alive just for long enough to harm those who dishonor him.*

504-516 "That's what Achilles said. In reply, I said, 'I have not yet heard anything about blameless Peleus. As for your dear son, Neoptolemus, I will tell you the whole truth, just as you ask me to. It was I—I myself, Achilles—who carried your son from Scyros in my well-balanced and hollow ship to join the army of the well-greaved Achaeans. [510] And when we debated plans around the city of Troy, he always spoke first, and his counsel never missed the mark. Godlike Nestor and I alone prevailed over him. And when we fought with bronze weapons on the plain of Troy, he never stayed in the crowd among the throng of men, but he ran out ahead of the many, yielding to no man in his strength. And he struck and killed many men in the battle-strife.'"

517-537 *Odysseus reports that Neoptolemus killed so many that he could not possibly name them all. That admitted, he does name one. He struck down Eurypylus, "the most beautiful man, next to godlike Memnon," along with many of his comrades. Then he tells of the sacking of Troy. When it was time for the best of the Argives to go into the wooden horse and to leave it in order to ambush the men of the city, Neoptolemus never shook or cried like the others, and his skin never changed color, but he was eager to do evil to the Trojans. And after sacking the city, he went home unharmed with his share of noble honor-prizes.*

538-540 "That's what I said, and the phantom-soul of the swift-footed son of Aeacus departed with long strides across the field of asphodel, [540] glad that I declared his son to be outstanding among men."

541-575 *Among the other sorrowful dead, Odysseus observes Telamonian Ajax standing back away from him—the hero still angry that Odysseus won the arms of Achilles. Thetis, Achilles' divine mother, had offered them as a prize to the Argive man judged the most dreadful warrior to the*

Trojans. Odysseus wishes he had never won. Because of his victory, the earth now covered Ajax. He blames the dispute on all the gods—especially Zeus. Nevertheless, Odysseus asks Ajax to overcome his pride and conquer his wrath in order to come forward and speak with him. But he refuses. Instead, Ajax turns and glides away to join the other dead.

Odysseus next sees Minos, the son of Zeus, who determines what is customary and right for the dead. He also spots Orion herding the animals he had hunted during his lifetime over the fields of asphodel.

576-604 "And I saw Tityus, the son of well-known Gaia, stretched out flat on the plain, his body covering over nine-hundred feet. And two vultures perched beside him, one on each side. They tore at his liver, plunging their beaks into his guts. Even so, he could not beat them off with his hands. [580] The reason? He had threatened Leto, the glorious wife of Zeus, with violence as she travelled to Pytho through beautiful Panopeus.

"I also saw Tantalus suffer pains horrible to endure. He stood in a pool of water that came right up to his chin. Even so, he was thirsty given that he couldn't take a drink. For whenever that old man stooped down, eagerly desiring to drink, the water would vanish, all swallowed up, and the dark earth would appear beneath his feet. Some god would dry it up. And more! Various trees, high and leafy, would dangle their fruit just above his head—pear, pomegranate, and apple trees, with their beautiful fruit, [590] and sweet fig and flourishing olive trees. But whenever that old man straightened up and reached his hand out to take one, the wind would hurl it up to the shadowy clouds.

"I also saw Sisyphus suffer pains horrible to endure while lifting a monstrous stone with both of his hands. Pressing on with hands and feet alike, he pushed the stone upward to the summit of a hill. Ah! But whenever he was about to roll it over the top, the stone's fantastic weight would turn it back. Then the cruel stone would once again come rolling down into the plain. Yet again he struggled intensely to push it up the hill—and sweat [600] flowed down from the limbs of his body, and a cloud of dust rose up around his head.

"And after Sisyphus I perceived the force of Heracles—his

phantom-image, not Heracles himself. As for Heracles himself, he dwells among the immortal gods, delighting in their feasts and living with his fair-ankled wife, Hebe, the child of great Zeus and gold-sandaled Hera."

605-616 *In Hades, Heracles carries his bow, with an arrow on its string, as if he is forever shooting. His belt and garb are a frightful mess of animals and horrors. Seeing Odysseus, he recognizes him and speaks to him with winged words.*

617-626 "'God-born son of Laertes, much-able Odysseus, you wretched man! Do you also endure an evil fate even as I once had to endure my lot beneath the light of the sun? [620] I was the child of Zeus, the son of Cronus—nevertheless I had to bear woe beyond measure. The reason? I was bound to a man who was very much my inferior—a man who pressed me with hard labors. He once even sent me here to bring back the dog—the hound of Hades. No, he could think of no other harsher task for me than this. I did it, too. I brought it up, dragging the dog all the way from Hades with Hermes as my guide and bright-eyed Athena.'"

627-635 *With that, Heracles' phantom-soul steps back into Hades' house. And though Odysseus desires to meet with other heroes—Theseus and Peirithous, for instance—the many dead begin to crowd around him so that Odysseus fears that Persephone may send up a monster with a gorgon-like head against him. Afraid of this, he turns to leave.*

636-640 "So then, I immediately went to the ship and ordered my comrades to embark . . . They stepped aboard quickly and sat down on the rowing benches. And the ship was carried down the Ocean's river by the swelling flow—[640] first with our rowing and later by a pleasant breeze."

BOOK 12

A Voyage with Many Dangers
The Sirens, Scylla and Charybdis,
and the Island of the Sun

IN BRIEF: *Odysseus and his men return from Hades to Circe's island to bury Elpenor. Circe warns Odysseus about the dangers of the voyage ahead and, as Tiresias did, she warns him to stay away from the island of the sun god Helios and his cattle. Departing the following morning, they first encounter the Sirens before passing between Scylla and Charybdis. They eventually approach the island of the Sun and stop for the night. It is a big mistake. There will be no homecoming for Odysseus' men after they slaughter and eat some of Helios' cattle. Finally, Odysseus survives an encounter with Charybdis and drifts to Calypso's island.*

A FTER OUR SHIP had left the flow of Oceanus' river and had come to the waves of the broad sea, we came to the island of Aeaea."

3-38 *Odysseus and his men return to Circe's island, Aeaea, "the dwelling of early Dawn." Early the following morning, and weeping, they burn Elpenor and his armor, as he wished, and pile a mound over his remains, topped with a block of stone and the young man's rowing oar. They feast with the goddess Circe, whose handmaidens offer the men an abundance of bread, meat, and wine. When it grows dark, the goddess takes Odysseus aside and asks him to relay the tale of his trip to Hades. He does. She then warns him about the dangers they will encounter during the voyage to come.*

39-58 "'You will first reach the Sirens, who [40] cast a spell on every man that comes to them. Whoever draws near to them in ignorance of this spell and hears the Sirens' clear singing, his wife and little children will never stand by his side, glad at his homecoming. Instead, the Sirens will enchant him with their sweet-sounding song. They are situated in a grassy meadow. Surrounding them is a huge pile of bones and rotting men, and on the bones the mushy skin is wasting away. Therefore, you should row past the Sirens and plug your comrades' ears with sweet beeswax that you have worked and pressed until it is soft so that none of them may hear. But if you yourself wish to hear them, [50] then let them tie you up in the swift ship by your hands and your feet, so that you are upright against the mast, with the rope winding around you and the mast itself. That way you'll be able to enjoy listening to the two Sirens. But if you implore your comrades and call on them to set you free, then let them tie you with even more rope. But now, when your comrades have rowed the ship past these deceivers, you will have a choice to make. At this point I will not fully reveal which of two paths will be your path. Rather, you should deliberate in your own spirit.'"

59-84 One path involves passing beneath the Overhanging Cliffs. These deadly rocks are called the Planctae by the blessed gods—the Clashing Rocks. And the towering wave of Amphitrite crashes against them. Not even birds fly by the Overhanging Cliffs without dying, and certainly not ships full of men. Jason's ship alone, the Argo, slipped by with the help of Hera.

The other path also involves cliffs. On one side is a cliff so high that it reaches into the sky, and so smooth that no man could ever climb it. Its top is surrounded by a dark cloud that never falls away. In the middle of the cliff is a cave "turned to the West, toward the darkness of Erebus." The cave is so high that a man could not shoot an arrow from a ship to its mouth.

85-110 "'Scylla dwells there in the cave, crying terribly. Her voice is about as loud as a newborn puppy. But be sure of this: she herself is an evil monster. No one would be glad to see her—not even if it were a god meeting her face to face. Scylla has twelve feet, all mismatched and misshapen. [90] And she has six very long necks. Atop each neck is an awful head that is terrible to look on. And within each head there are three rows of crowded teeth that are full of decay and black death.

"'Half of Scylla's monstrous body is plunged inside the hollow cave. As for the other half, she stretches her head out from the terrible pit and fishes there, eagerly looking around the side of the cliff for dolphins and seadogs and whatever other great fish or sea monsters she may happen to catch—the countless creatures that howling Amphitrite nourishes. No sailor in his ship may boast that he has slipped by her. But with each of her heads, she carries off [100] a man, snatching him from his dark-prowed ship.

"'As for the other cliff, Odysseus, you will see that it is lower. This cliff is nearby the other—so close that you could shoot an arrow from one to the other. On one of its lower rocks is a great and wild fig tree, blooming with leaves. Beneath this tree, wondrous Charybdis sucks down the deep, black water. Three times a day she releases the water, sending it up. But three times she sucks it down again—it's a terrible sight! May you not happen to be there when she noisily sucks down the water! In that case no one could deliver you from ruinous misfortune—not even Poseidon, the Earthshaker. Instead, draw near to Scylla's cliff, and quickly row your ship alongside it—since it is much better [110] to mourn six comrades out of the men in your ship than all of them at once.'"

111-126 Odysseus asks if there is any way to escape Charybdis or fight Scylla. Circe explains that Scylla is an immortal goddess, however troublesome and wild she is. The best he and his men can do is to flee rather than fight her. If he arms and battles her, he will risk losing even more men. Odysseus should pray to Scylla's mother Crataeis, who gave birth to this misery for mortals. She will hold off a second attack.

127-141 "'Next, you will reach the island of Thrinacia. The many cattle of Helios graze there, along with his fat sheep—seven cattle herds and just as many beautiful flocks of sheep, [130] with fifty sheep in each flock. These cattle and sheep bear no young, nor do they ever die. Goddesses are their shepherds, nymphs with beautiful long locks of hair. They are Phaethusa and Lampetia, whom divine Neaera bore to Helios Hyperion, the sun god who walks on high. Their queenly mother brought the two goddesses into the world and reared them, eventually sending them far away from home to dwell on the island of Thrinacia. There they guard their father's sheep and his cattle with curved horns. If you leave these animals alone, unharmed, keeping in mind your return home, then you may still reach Ithaca, though suffering hardship and misfortune. But if you hurt them, then I predict destruction [140] for your ship, and death for your comrades. And even if you escape, your return will happen only after a long time has passed and after all your comrades have perished.'"

142-183 Circe finishes speaking just as the morning comes. When Odysseus and his men embark on their ships and sail off, the goddess sends a friendly wind that blows them on their way. In the rear, the steersman guides the ship.

As they sail along, Odysseus reveals what will happen when they encounter the Sirens—how his men will plug their ears with beeswax while he listens to the deceivers' beautiful singing, bound by his men to the mast.

Thanks to the steady breeze sent by Circe, the well-built ship quickly reaches the island of the Sirens. Just as it comes into view, the wind stops, and the waves grow still. So, they lower the sail and row. Meanwhile, Odysseus prepares the wax with the help of the divine Sun's heat, and he plugs his comrades' ears. After, they tie him securely to the mast.

Soon the Sirens spot them nearing the island—they are as near as the distance is that one man can shout to another and make himself heard. The Sirens begin to sing.

184-200 "'Come here as you go, much-praised Odysseus, great glory of the Achaeans. Steer your ship landward so that you may hear our singing voices. Up to now, no man has rowed his black ship past this island until he has listened to the sweet singing voices streaming from our mouths. Instead, he takes pleasure in hearing us and goes away knowing more—for we know everything that happened throughout wide Troy. [190] We know all the pain that the Argives and Trojans suffered because of the desire and will of the gods. Truly, we know whatever happens upon the much-nourishing earth.'

"That's what the Sirens said, letting their beautiful voices flow. My heart longed to listen, and so I directed my comrades to untie me with the nod of my head and brows—but they fell to their oars and rowed on. And at once Perimedes and Eurylochus stood up and tied me with even more ropes and drew them even tighter.

"But when they had rowed past the island—far enough so that we could no longer hear their clear voices or their song—then my faithful comrades took out the [200] beeswax I had put in their ears, and they set me free from my bonds."

201-233 As soon as they leave the island behind, Odysseus and his men hear a loud thundering and see a great cloud of mist rising up in the distance. The men are terrified, and so Odysseus moves throughout the ship to encourage each one with gentle words and remind them of the evil they've experienced so far, particularly the horror of the Cyclops. But they escaped by means of his excellence, he claims, that of his counsel and his mind. He suggests that in the same way they remember that awful time now, they will eventually remember this. So row! he commands. He directs the steersmen to keep the ship away from the billowing mist and swollen waves, and to hold close to the cliff on the opposite side. Odysseus doesn't say anything about Scylla since—as he explains it to the Phaeacians—it was a problem they could not avoid. His comrades would only fear the monster and stop rowing. As for himself, Odysseus arms, forgetting Circe's advice not to fight Scylla. He takes up two spears and goes to the front of the ship to face the immortal monster.

234-259 "So it was that we sailed through the narrow strait weeping. On the one side there was Scylla, and on the other there was wondrous Charybdis, who sucked down the sea's salty water in a way that was shocking to see. Whenever she vomited it up, she would churn and bubble and roar loudly as water does in a caldron on a great fire, and overhead the spray would fall upon both cliffs. [240] But whenever she sucked down the sea's salty water, then everything within her stirred in chaos. And all around the rocks thundered terribly, while beneath the earth appeared black with sand. Pale fear seized my men as we looked at her and feared destruction!

"Even so, while we were looking the other way, Scylla snatched six of my comrades from the hollow ship—those who were the best in strength and might. Therefore, when I looked toward the swift ship and to my comrades, I observed their feet and hands already in the air as they were carried up. They screamed aloud, calling me [250] by name one last time in agony of heart. As when a fisherman stands on a jutting rock, casting his bait with a long pole in order to a lure in little fish, and when he catches them, he flings them writhing upon the shore, even so were the men gasping and squirming as they were carried up to the cliffs. Then at the entryway to the cave she devoured them—my men, shrieking and stretching out their hands to me in the terrible battle-strife, their struggle against death. Of all things my eyes had ever seen, that was the saddest sight I suffered while exploring the pathways of the sea."

260-278 *They sail on and come to the noble island of the Sun, the delight of men. As they approach it, Odysseus hears Helios' cattle lowing and his sheep bleating. The sound reminds him of Tiresias' and Circe's counsel to avoid the island. Therefore, he turns to his comrades in order to share with them their advice to row past the island despite all the evil they have suffered. Hearing this, his comrades are heartbroken. More than the rest, Eurylochus is angry and addresses Odysseus with hateful words.*

279-293 "'You're a cruel man, Odysseus! Hardhearted! Your strength surpasses other men and your limbs never [280] grow tired. You must be made of nothing more than iron since you won't let your own men—worn out as we are with toil and lacking sleep— go ashore, where we might prepare a satisfying evening meal upon this island surrounded by the sea. But no! Even as the night is swiftly approaching, you order us to leave the island to wander through the darkness and over the misty deep. But it is from the night that fierce winds blow, damaging ships. So tell me, how can a man escape utter destruction if a squall suddenly comes—a blast from Notos, the South Wind, or from storming Zephyrus, the West Wind? Of all winds, these very often [290] dash ships to pieces against the will of the ruling gods. No, let us yield to black night and prepare our supper, staying close by the swift ship. And in the morning, we'll climb into our ship and launch into the open sea.'"

294-339 *Every other man nods his agreement. At this, Odysseus believes some god is planning evil for them. Even so, he gives in to his men because he stands alone against them. His only stipulation is that they must swear not to slaughter any sheep or cattle they find. Rather, they must be satisfied with the food Circe gave them. They swear, and so they stop and eat. Later, they weep for their friends lost to Scylla, and they sleep.*

Overnight, Zeus causes a stormy wind to blow and covers the earth and sea with clouds. Consequently, when bright Dawn appears, Odysseus and his men drag their ship onto the shore and into a cave. With that, Odysseus reminds them of all the food and wine they have aboard their swift ship and warns them again to leave alone Helios' cattle and sheep—for the sun god sees and hears all things.

They agree, and everything goes well for a month. Even though Zeus doesn't send the right wind for them to sail away from the island, they have sufficient food and wine—for some time, anyway. Eventually, they grow hungry as their stores dwindle, and they're forced to fish "with bent hooks" and hunt. It is at this point that Odysseus treks up to a high place on the island to pray to the Olympian gods for help. In response, they cause him to fall asleep, while down below Eurylochus is giving evil counsel to the other men.

340-351 "'My comrades in arms, men bearing misfortune, listen to what I have to say. Every form of death is hateful to wretched mortals. But to die of hunger—to reach your destined end because of hunger—is the saddest way to go. So come on! Let's drive off the best of Helios' cattle and offer sacrifice to the immortals, who possess the wide sky. And if we ever reach Ithaca, our fatherland, we'll at once build a spacious temple for Helios Hyperion, and we'll put many pleasing and honorable gifts for the god inside the temple.

But if he's angry because of his long-horned cattle and wishes to destroy our ship, and the other gods agree to it, [350] then I would rather lose the spirit of my life all at once by drowning in the waves than to let it slowly be squeezed out bit by bit on this lonely island.'"

352-370 The men agree. Therefore, they take and slaughter the best of Helios' cattle. Since they have neither barley nor wine for the sacrifice or libation, they perform the ritual by using oak leaves and water. Finally, they burn the thighs and spit the meat.

Right at that moment Odysseus wakes up and ventures down to the ship. On the way he smells "the savory smell of fat"—and immediately he knows what his men have done. Groaning, he calls out to the gods.

371-388 "'Father Zeus and all you other blessed gods who live forever, surely it was for my ruin that you lulled me to persistent sleep, while my comrades who stayed behind planned a monstrous deed.'"

"And soon, the messenger Lampetia of the flowing robes came to Helios Hyperion and told him that we had slaughtered his cattle. At once he addressed the immortals with an angry heart: 'Father Zeus and all you other blessed gods who live forever, punish them now! Take vengeance on the comrades of Odysseus, the son of Laertes, the men who insolently slaughtered my cattle! For I [380] delight in them whenever I go up into the starry sky and whenever I turn back again from the sky to the earth. If they don't give me suitable compensation for the cattle, then I will plunge into Hades and shine among the dead.'

"In reply, cloud-gathering Zeus said to him, [385] 'Helios, go on shining your light upon the immortals and upon mortal men who live among wheat-bearing fields. As for these men, I will quickly strike their swift ship with my bright thunderbolt, blasting it to pieces in the middle of the wine-faced sea.'"

389-402 Odysseus explains to the Phaeacians that he later learned about this divine conversation from Calypso. As for the present moment of his story, he approaches his men and rebukes them one by one. Nevertheless,

*there's nothing anyone can do. The cattle are dead. Still, the gods send
frightful signs. Upon the fire, the meat bellows as though alive. Even so,
the men feast for six days. Then on the seventh Zeus stills the stormy
winds, and so Odysseus and his men sail off.*

403-419 "But when we had left the island behind us, and no other
land appeared so that now there was only the sky and the sea, then
the son of Cronus put a dark cloud above the hollow ship, and the
sea below grew dark.

"From then on the ship had very little time to make its run. At
once a screaming wind blew in from the west, Zephyrus, the West
Wind, raging with a furious storm. And the blasting wind broke the
stays that hold the mast in place [410] so that the mast fell back-
ward, and all its gear lay scattered in the ship's hold. And in the
back of the ship, the mast struck the steersman's head, dashing to
pieces all the bones in his skull. Like a diver he fell from the deck
and his proud spirit left his bones behind. Right then, Zeus flashed
lightning and cast a thunderbolt at the ship. And struck by the great
weapon of Zeus, the whole ship whirled around and filled up with
sulfurous smoke, and my comrades fell from the ship. Like sea
crows, they were carried along by the rolling waves around the
black ship—the god took away their return home.

420-449 *Odysseus rapidly constructs a makeshift raft when the ship
breaks apart. But now he's at the mercy of the stormy winds. And rather
than sending him homeward, they blow him back all night long to Scylla
and Charybdis.*

*In the morning he cannot steer clear of the whirlpool, but as Charybdis
sucks down the sea, he's pulled toward her. Instead of going down, though,
he leaps up to grab a branch of the lone fig tree growing on one of the lower
rocks and hangs there all day until the whirlpool spits up his raft again.
And falling to the water, he boards the raft and paddles away with his
hands, escaping destruction. With the gods' help, he eventually reaches
Ogygia, the island of Calypso, the goddess who treats him with affection
and cares for him.*

450-453 "But why should I tell you the tale? It was yesterday in this house that I told it to you and your noble wife. It seems distasteful to me to tell the same story again and again—especially if it has already been told well."

BOOK 13

ITHACA AT LAST

ODYSSEUS AND ATHENA

IN BRIEF: *Odysseus feasts one last time with the Phaeacians before they speed him home with many gifts while he sleeps. Poseidon punishes the Phaeacians. When Odysseus awakes in Ithaca, he doesn't recognize where he is until Athena, at first disguised as a young shepherd, shows him that he's home. Now he's full of joy! Still, until Athena reveals herself as she truly is and that he is truly home, Odysseus prevaricates with a story. Once Athena changes form, she reveals all the suffering he must endure and the work he has to do. They hide the many gifts in a cave, then Athena and Odysseus plan how the suitors will be punished. But first, the hero must endure much sorrow and pain. The goddess changes his appearance.*

THAT'S WHAT ODYSSEUS said, and all the Phaeacians fell silent, spellbound throughout the shadowy halls.

3-23 When Alcinous finally speaks, he calls on his fellow feasters to gather even more gifts for Odysseus—a tripod and a caldron from each man. He assures them that they will later "gather the cost" of the donations "from the common people" in order to repay themselves. When everyone agrees, the feast breaks up for the evening as each one goes home to sleep and gather the gifts. In the morning, Alcinous stows them aboard the ship that will speed Odysseus home. Then they all go to his house to prepare a feast.

24-30 And mighty Alcinous sacrificed a bull for them to Zeus of the dark clouds, the son of Cronus, who is lord of all. Then, when they had burned the thigh portions, they took pleasure in a glorious feast. And among them the sacred bard Demodocus, the one honored by the people, sang to the lyre. But again and again, Odysseus would turn himself toward the radiant sun, [30] willing it to plunge beneath the earth since he eagerly desired to return home.

31-39 *Like a man who waits for the sun to go down during a long day of hard work so that he can take his evening meal, Odysseus is glad when the sun finally sets. At once he asks for the libations that will end the feast so that he can board the ship and head for home. He blesses the Phaeacians, explaining why he has blessed them in the following manner.*

40-46 "For everything I love, all my spirit desires, has been accomplished—your help in getting home and the collection of dear gifts. May the sky-dwelling gods make them my happiness. And when I return home, may I find my blameless wife safe and sound in my house with all those who are dear to me. As for those of you staying here, may you happily delight your wedded wives and children, and may the gods give you every kind of excellence, and may misfortune be absent from among the people."

47-58 *Everyone praises Odysseus' speech, now eager to see him off. Alcinous calls on Pontonous to mix the wine and fill the cups. He does. And when they have finished pouring out libations to the gods, Odysseus stands to bless Arete with winged words.*

59-65 "May you fare well through all the years, dear queen, until old age comes to you [60] and you reach death, which is common to all human beings. As for me, I'm off. But may you delight in your children and king Alcinous in this house, as well as in your people."

   Godlike Odysseus spoke in this manner and stepped through the doorway. And mighty Alcinous sent a herald with him to lead him to the swift ship and to the seashore.

66-87 *As for Arete, she sends three slave women with Odysseus to carry clothes, a chest of goods, and bread and wine to the ship. Arriving, the young rowing men take everything aboard and prepare a bed for Odysseus. Once everything is ready, the ship flies over the water as fast as a soaring bird while Odysseus falls into a heavy, deathlike sleep.*

88-92 In this way the ship sped on swiftly, cutting through the waves of the sea. She carried a man that resembled the gods in counsel. [90] He was a man whose spirit had suffered much pain while living through the wars of men and sailing over the grievous waves of the sea. Even so, he slept now in peace, unaware of all he had suffered.

93-125 *Sailing on, the ship quickly reaches Ithaca by dawn and comes ashore in a ship-friendly harbor sacred to the sea god Phorcys. The Phaeacian men lift Odysseus, still asleep, out of the ship and set him down on the beach. Then they place all the gifts by an old olive tree off the path so that no one will take them before Odysseus wakes up. The tree is nearby a shadowy cave that is sacred to the river nymphs called the Naiads. Once everything is in order, the Phaeacians push off to return home again.*

126-138 Ah!—but the Earth-shaker Poseidon didn't forget how he had boastfully threatened godlike Odysseus with many perils. And so, he asked Zeus about his plans.

"Father Zeus, I will no longer be honored among the immortal gods when mortal men do not even honor me—[130] men such as the Phaeacians, who are my descendants. Just now I declared that Odysseus would suffer much misfortune before reaching his house. And since you first promised his homecoming with the nod of your head, I didn't wholly take it away from him. Yet these men have carried him home in a swift ship over the sea while he was sleeping. And now they have dropped him off in Ithaca and have given him an unbelievable number of gifts—bronze and gold things, and woven clothing. Altogether the gifts are far more than Odysseus would ever have carried off for himself from Troy, even if he had returned unharmed with his allotted share of the plunder."

139-186 *Zeus denies Poseidon's suspicion. It would be hard to dishonor the oldest and best of the gods, he claims. Still, if men dishonor him, then he should by all means do something about it. Relieved, the Earth-shaker declares he will. He wishes to strike down a Phaeacian ship and cover over their city with a giant mountain. Zeus agrees to it. And adding to the plan, he advises his brother to transform the returning ship into stone just as the townspeople spot it coming home.*

At this, Poseidon ventures off to punish the Phaeacians. They're amazed and perplexed when he turns the ship to stone, not knowing what is happening or why. When Alcinous finds out, he reveals that the strange event is the fulfilment of an ancient prophecy. He consequently advises them to sacrifice twelve of the best bulls to Poseidon and promise to no longer serve as escorts to men in need. In fear, they do. Meanwhile, as they huddle around the altar, Odysseus is waking up in Ithaca.

187-193 Godlike Odysseus woke up from sleep in his native land. Even so, he did not recognize the land since he had been gone for so long. Moreover, the goddess Pallas Athena, the daughter of Zeus, poured a mist around him [190] so that she might tell him everything, and in order to make him unknown to everyone—to his wife, the townspeople, and his friends—until the suitors had paid the full price of their transgressions.

194-235 *Everything looks strange to Odysseus, and he bemoans his luck, wondering what land he has come to and what the people are like. "Are they wild, insolent and unjust? Or do they love strangers and fear the gods?" And he wonders where to store all his wealth. He curses the Phaeacians for deceiving him and leaving him in a strange land. Then he goes to count everything to make sure nothing is missing, concluding all is present.*

Just then, Athena draws near him in the form of a young shepherd. Glad to see her, Odysseus turns to her in supplication, asking to know what land he is in, and whether it is an island or part of the mainland, and what sort of men live in the land.

236-249 The goddess, bright-eyed Athena, said to him, "You're silly, stranger, or you've come from a foreign land, if you're asking about this land. It's not a nameless land, not at all, but many know its name—[240] all those who dwell toward the dawn and the rising sun, and those who dwell in the other direction toward the murky darkness.

Anyway, this is a rugged island, not useful for driving horses. That said, it is not an exceedingly poor land even though the farmable ground is not spacious. Grain beyond measure grows in the land, as do grapes for making wine. Every tree is here. And there's always rain and copious dew. And the land is good for nourishing goats and cattle, as are the abundant springs for their watering. For all these reasons, stranger, the name of Ithaca has reached as far as the land of Troy, which is, they say, a long way from the land of Achaea."

250-286 Joy fills Odysseus when he hears the name of his homeland. Nevertheless, he conceals his true identity with a story. He's from Crete, he declares, and has come with all his wealth because he killed speedy Orsilochus, the son of Idomeneus. Orsilochus held a grudge against him for leading his own men before Troy rather than fighting under the leadership of his father. So he wished to confiscate all the booty he had collected there. To prevent this, he and another man ambushed Orsilochus at night while he was walking from his farm. Later on, he paid some Phoenician men to take him by ship to Pylos or Elis. But the wind didn't cooperate, and so, sailing far past their goal, they dropped him off in this spot and took off for Sidon in the land of the Phoenicians.

287-295 That's what Odysseus said. And the goddess, bright-eyed Athena, smiled and caressed him with her hand. Then she changed her form to that of a woman—one beautiful and tall, and skilled with splendid handiwork.

[290] And addressing him with winged words, she said, "There's no getting by you! Whoever wants to outdo you in guile must truly be cunning and full of wiles—even if it is a god facing you! You cruel man of many counsels, you cannot get enough of deception! It appears that even in your own land you cannot stop all the trickery and all the made-up stories that you adore from the bottom of your heart!"

296-306 Athena goes on to admit her own skill in the cunning arts. She declares that Odysseus is the best of men at devising plans and giving

speeches, whereas she is famous among the gods for giving counsel and de-
vising wiles. Still, she goes on, Odysseus did not recognize her who always
stood by his side among the Phaeacians. Now she assures him that she has
come to help him again, to concoct a plan and hide all the gifts, and to inform
him of all the trouble and sorrow he is destined to suffer in his house.

307-310 "Nevertheless, you must endure the trouble and pain—you
have no choice. And do not reveal to any man or any woman that
you have returned from roaming the earth. But in silence [310] suf-
fer all the pain and distress, and patiently bear the violent abuse of
men."

311-343 *Odysseus admits that it is hard even for a wise man to perceive*
the goddess since Athena is able to turn herself into anything. He knows
that she was with him during the war at Troy, but ever since then, aside
from her assistance in the land of the Phaeacians, he has not been aware of
her presence or help. Even so, he implores her by her father's name to tell
him the truth about where he is. Is he truly home? Or is she teasing him?
   Athena answers him by first mildly chastising him for his skepticism.
Most men would be eager to see their wives and children once home, she
says. Not Odysseus. He just wants to test his wife to make sure she's been
faithful—the very one who weeps for his absence during the day and sor-
rows at night. As for Athena, she has always believed he would return
home, though without his men. She didn't offer more help because she
didn't want to fight with Poseidon, who has been very angry with him for
blinding his son.

344-360 "But come, I will show you that this place is Ithaca so that
you may be confident. Before us is the harbor of Phorcys, the old man
of the sea. And here at the top of the harbor is the olive tree with the
long, pointy leaves. Nearby is the lovely dark cave that is sacred to
the nymphs who are called the Naiads. It is the wide vaulted cave in
which you [350] used to offer to the nymphs many hecatombs that
bring fulfillment. Over there is forest-clad Mount Neriton."
   The goddess spoke in this manner, and dispersing the mist, the
land appeared. It was then that much-enduring godlike Odysseus

was glad. He rejoiced in his own country and kissed the grain-bearing ground. And at once he prayed to the nymphs with his hands raised up to the sky. "Naiad Nymphs, daughters of Zeus, I said that I would never see you again, but now I greet you with kindly prayers. I will also give you gifts, as I used to give, if the daughter of Zeus, the plunder-bringing one, is willing that [360] I live, and if she strengthens my dear son."

361-428 *Athena bids Odysseus to be courageous. "Don't worry about these things," she says.*

She goes on to help him hide the Phaeacian gifts in the cave before planning with him "the destruction of the arrogant suitors." Odysseus is pleased that she has revealed how Penelope, his wife, has fooled the suitors for three years. He would have experienced the same misfortune as Agamemnon without this knowledge. But with the goddess by his side, he will be able to fight them, even if their number reaches three hundred.

Athena promises to be with him and suggests that some of the suitors will die with their blood and brains smeared all over the floor. Before that happens, however, she must change his appearance—his skin, limbs, and hair, and his clothing—so that everyone, even his wife and son, will think he's strange looking and repulsive instead of the handsome man that he usually is. Then Odysseus must go find and question the swineherd Eumaeus while she goes to summon Telemachus home from Sparta in spacious Lacedaemon.

Odysseus wonders why Athena let him leave Ithaca and suffer when she knew he was coming home. The goddess tells him not to worry too much—that she has been Telemachus' guide and that he has won noble glory while away. The big danger is the ship full of young men waiting to murder Telemachus before he returns home. Don't worry, though, she says. This will never happen. Instead, the suitors will die and be covered over by the earth.

429-440 Speaking in this manner, Athena touched Odysseus with her wand. [430] She shriveled the beautiful skin on his agile limbs, replacing it with the skin of an old man of many years. And she made him lose the yellow hair on his head. Then she darkened his two eyes, ones that were once beautiful with shining light. And she threw around him a tattered covering, an ugly tunic, filthy and torn and full of stale smoke. And about him she cast a swift deer's big hide, all stripped of its hair. And she gave him a staff, and a shameful leather pouch, all full of holes, hanging from him by a strap made of twisted rope.

So, when the two had deliberated in this manner and made their plans, they separated, and the goddess [440] went to divine Lacedaemon to retrieve the son of Odysseus.

BOOK 14

THE SWINEHERD EUMAEUS
LOYALTY AND HOSPITALITY

IN BRIEF: *The wandering, old stranger Odysseus visits the loyal swineherd Eumaeus, who behaves as an ideal host. When asked who he is and where he has come from, Odysseus lies, saying he is from Crete and fought next to Idomeneus at Troy. He cunningly relates how he has come to Ithaca after several misadventures—one in Egypt, another in Phoenicia. Eumaeus doubts the news the stranger offers about Odysseus' homecoming— that he will soon be home. He believes his master is dead. Not only that but many others have offered similar tales, he explains. They feast on boar's meat and sleep after Odysseus tells one last story to win a warm covering for the night. Eumaeus sleeps apart from the others with the boars.*

O DYSSEUS WALKED UP from the harbor, ascending a steep and rugged path through the woods and making his way up to the hills to the place where Athena had indicated he would find the noble swineherd, the slave who most took care of the wealth in property that godlike Odysseus had acquired.

5-36 Odysseus, old and ragged looking, finds the swineherd Eumaeus sitting in the porch of the stone dwelling he erected for himself. Built on the heights, it offers a spectacular view of the island. Surrounding the house are pig sties. The closest ones hold the sows for breeding, whereas the boars, the ones the suitors eat daily, are held further outside, guarded by four dogs. As Odysseus walks up to the dwelling, Eumaeus is making sandals for himself. The other men are off working. Three are pasturing the swine, and a fourth is delivering a boar to the suitors, who wish to satisfy their desire for meat. Before Odysseus can get to Eumaeus, the four dogs see him and rush at him, barking. In response, Odysseus sits down, dropping his

*staff. Yet it isn't enough. The dogs charge and would have attacked but for
the swineherd, who sees and calls them off with words and flying stones.
Speaking, Eumaeus says—*

37-47 "Old man, just like that, the dogs nearly ripped you to pieces!
And if they had, you would have blamed me, casting shame on me!
Oh well—the gods have given me other heartaches and groan-caus-
ing burdens. [40] While I sit here, I mourn and grieve for a godlike
master. And while I raise fat swine for other men to eat, he longs
for food, roaming through the land and city of men who speak an-
other language—if in fact he still lives and sees the light of the sun.
But follow me, old man, let us go to the shelter. When you have
satisfied your desire for food and wine, you can tell me where you
have come from and all the trouble you have endured."

48-52 *Eumaeus leads his guest to his dwelling and makes him comfortable,
sitting him down on a large and shaggy wild goatskin. Delighted with the
reception, Odysseus speaks to him.*

53-58 "Stranger, may Zeus and the other immortal gods grant you
whatever you ardently desire since you have readily welcomed me."
    In reply, the swineherd Eumaeus said, "Stranger, it is not right
for me to dishonor someone like you—not even if one more unfor-
tunate and of lesser account than you came to my shelter. I say this
because all strangers and beggars come from Zeus."

59-79 *Eumaeus admits that what he has to give is small because his master
is gone—he who was a kind man and would have given him property, Eu-
maeus says, "a house, an allotment of land, and a wife." Long ago he went
to fight the Trojans for the sake of Agamemnon's honor. He curses Helen
and her kind since so many men died for her. Finishing his invective, Eu-
maeus selects and prepares two boars for a feast. Giving Odysseus the
roasted meat and honey-sweet wine, he invites him to eat.*

80-96 "Eat now, stranger, whatever we slaves have to offer—the
meat of a younger lean pig. But the suiters—the heartless ones who

forget the watchful eye of the gods and their divine vengeance—eat the older fattened swine. The blessed gods do not love merciless deeds of men; rather, they honor justice and fitting behavior. And even though Zeus gives booty to implacable and hostile men who invade the land of other men, and even though they fill up their ships and go home, even these men experience the powerful fear of the watchful eye of the gods as thoughts of divine vengeance fill their minds. But these men here, the suitors, they must know something. They've heard the utterance of some god [90] about my master's mournful destruction. I believe this because they refuse to court the lady Penelope according to custom, and they refuse to go home to their own people and wealth. Instead, relaxing at their ease, they insolently devour everything he has, sparing nothing. Every Zeus-born day and night they slaughter one, two, and more victims, and they wantonly draw out wine and waste it—for my master's means of living were unspeakably vast."

97-121 *Eumaeus catalogs his master Odysseus' great quantity of wealth—the many herds of cattle, sheep, swine, and goats he has, both on the mainland and the island. But slowly they are dwindling. One goat and the best of the boars go to the suitors each day.*

Hearing the way they are wasting his wealth, Odysseus thinks about and plans evil for the suitors. Then, once he's satisfied with food and after the swineherd pours him another cup of wine, he asks Eumaeus to identify his master. It is possible he has news of him, he claims, since he's been roaming the world and only the gods know if he has seen him.

122-138 "Old man, no wanderer that came here and brought news of my master could win the confidence of his wife and his dear son. No, whenever roaming men need something, they tell lies and have no real desire to tell the truth. When a wanderer reaches the land of Ithaca, he goes to my mistress, the lady of the house, and speaks guilefully to her. Even so, she receives him well, welcoming him as a guest and treating him with affection. And she questions each wanderer while tears fall down from her eyes as she weeps—[130] since that is the way a woman behaves when her husband perishes in another land. And that's what you would do too, old man. You would quickly make up a story if someone would only give you a wool cloak and tunic to wear. But as for my master, dogs and swift birds have probably stripped the skin and flesh from his bones by now, and his life-soul has left them behind. That, or fish have eaten him in the sea, and his bones lie there in the infinite sand of the seashore, covered over by a deep pile of sand. In this way he perished somewhere out there. And for all those he held dear, nothing but sorrow remains—most of all for me."

139-160 Eumaeus emphasizes how much he still misses and cares for his master—more even than for his own parents—and how much his beloved master cared for him. In turn, Odysseus the wanderer, the ragged old stranger, offers to swear that Odysseus the master will come home. Doing so, he artfully asks for a reward, assuring the swineherd that he will not take it unless his master actually returns. Then, by Zeus and by the gifts of hospitality and Odysseus' hearth, he swears that everything will happen as he predicts.

161-164 "Odysseus will come to this land sometime this very year as the old moon falls dark and the new moon grows bright. He will return to his house and punish all those who dishonor his wife and his glorious son."

165-320 Eumaeus doesn't believe Odysseus' story even though its truth is what he desires most of all—he and Odysseus' whole family. Speaking of Odysseus' son, Eumaeus recalls Telemachus' noble beauty and explains how he went off to Pylos, eager to hear news of his father. And now the suitors hope to surprise and kill him on his way home, he reveals. His escape depends on the will of Zeus. Either way, they should talk about other matters. Eumaeus asks the stranger to truly declare what troubles he has known, as well as who he is and how he came to be in Ithaca.

In return, Odysseus the wanderer promises the exact truth, delivering the following fabrication. He boasts that he is from Crete, the child of a wealthy man, who was honored like a god for his land, riches, and happiness, as well as his glorious sons. He was part of a big family, he explains, though the son of a concubine. Nevertheless, his father, Castor, the son of Hylax, honored him as one of his true-born sons. When his father died, his sons divided his land and wealth by lot. Odysseus received very little in the process—a small plot of land and a small house. Still, by means of his excellence he won a wife from men wealthy in land.

He was no useless man, he says, nor one to flee from battle. Rather, he was good in war and useful during an ambush. He explains that he didn't care much for farming or the kind of work that increases a household's wealth. Nor was he interested in rearing children. Instead, he was fond of roaming ships and battles, with their flying arrows and spears—things that do not please most men. He supposes some god made these dear to him, "for different men delight in different things." Even before Troy, he led nine raiding missions against men in foreign lands, and he became very wealthy and respected by doing so. But then came the hateful expedition to Troy, during which he led the Cretans into battle with Idomeneus. Many men died there as they battled on year after year. Finally, after nine years of warfare, they conquered Priam's city in the tenth.

Odysseus was home in Crete for only a month, delighting in his children, wife, and wealth, before his restless spirit urged him to depart on yet another voyage—this time to Egypt. He bemoans all the misfortune that Zeus planned for him while there, declaring himself a wretched man because of it. Nevertheless, with the help of Boreas, the North Wind, he sailed off with nine ships full of men. They reached Egypt five days later, anchoring the ships in the Nile. And that's when the misfortune began. Although Odysseus had commanded his men to stay by the ships, they instead gave in to a desire for violence and began to raid the surrounding countryside, killing the men and taking the women and children. Soon the alarm was raised in the city, and the plain was filled with Egyptian footmen and flashing bronze chariots. In the end, his men were defeated. As for Odysseus, he quickly disarmed and threw himself at the king's knees as a suppliant. It was a risky move, but it worked. The king saved him because he feared Zeus Xenios, the stranger's god. Not only did it work for the moment, but he stayed with the Egyptians for seven years and grew wealthy thanks to all their gifts.

In the eighth year he went with a crafty Phoenician man to his house in Phoenicia where he lived for a year. Odysseus explains that the greedy *man's hope was to sell him into slavery. Pursuing this end, the Phoenician man took him along on a voyage to Libya. But on the way, Zeus' thunder and lightning sunk the ship somewhere off Crete, and all the men perished—all but for Odysseus. Zeus saved him, and he floated for nine days to Thesprotia, where the king's son rescued him and took him to his father's house. Pheidon welcomed him there as a guest. That's where, he claims, he heard news of Odysseus.*

321-330 "I heard news about Odysseus in Thesprotia. The king declared that he had affectionately received him as his guest on his way home to the land of his fathers. He showed me the possessions that Odysseus had gathered—the bronze and gold, and the well-wrought iron pieces. So great was the treasure stored for him in the king's halls that it would support his offspring for ten generations after him. Even so, Pheidon said that Odysseus had ventured off to Dodona in order to hear the will of Zeus from the god's towering oak. He wished to learn how to best return to the rich land of Ithaca [330] after being gone for so long—whether he should do so openly or concealed."

331-359 *Either way, Pheidon prepared a ship to convey Odysseus home whenever he came back from Dodona. As for the Cretan man, the old stranger telling the story to Eumaeus (but actually Odysseus himself), he claims that Pheidon sent him on a ship to Dulichium. On the way there, however, the Thesprotian men decided to sell him into slavery. They stole his fine clothes, dressed him in rags, and fettered him. But with the help of the gods, he escaped when they reached Ithaca. And that's how he came to be with the swineherd.*

360-364 In reply, the swineherd Eumaeus said to him, "Ah, wretched stranger, you've truly moved my spirit in telling me about how you have suffered and where you have wandered. But in this one thing I suppose you have not spoken appropriately. No, you won't convince me with this story about Odysseus."

365-417 *Eumaeus wonders aloud why the gods didn't slay Odysseus at*

Troy when his friends would have honored him with a glorious funeral. Instead, he likely died an inglorious death at sea. The truth, he says, is that many men have tried to deceive Penelope about Odysseus' return. One was an Aetolian man who came to Ithaca after killing a man in his homeland. When Eumaeus received him as a guest, the man deceived him with his own story. He claimed that Odysseus was on the island of Crete, staying with Idomeneus, and that he would soon return home with much wealth and his godlike comrades. But it never happened.

The point? Visitors do not have to win Eumaeus' hospitality with lies. Rather, the swineherd is kind to strangers because of the pity he feels and because he fears Zeus Xenios, the stranger's god.

Odysseus the wanderer nevertheless presses his story and tries to get Eumaeus to promise him clothing and conveyance to Dulichium if his master returns. If not, he suggests that the swineherd and his men can throw him from a tall cliff. Eumaeus reproaches him, reminding the old man that such an act—slaying a guest—would not win him the kind of reputation or success he wishes to have. Anyway, it is time for the men to return and have something to eat, he says. When they do, the swineherd asks them to select the best of the boars for their enjoyment.

418-434 Speaking in this manner, Eumaeus split wood with the ruthless bronze, and the others brought in a five-year-old boar that was very fat [420] and propped him up before the hearth. And since he was given a noble mind, the swineherd did not forget the immortals. Rather, he began by casting hair from the head of the white-tusked boar into the fire. Then he prayed to all the gods that much-thinking Odysseus might return home to his own house.

After that, Eumaeus struck the boar with a club of oak that he had kept when splitting the wood, and its life-soul left it behind. The other men cut its throat, burned off its bristles, and quickly cut the boar up. Then, before all else, the swineherd took raw flesh from the limbs and wrapped it in the rich fat. He threw these pieces into the fire once he had sprinkled them with ground barley. [430] The men cut up the rest and fixed the pieces on spits, roasting the meat with skill. And drawing it off the spits, they placed it in mounds on a carving board. Then the swineherd rose up to cut the meat since he knew in his mind what was right and fitting. And so, he carved all the meat, dividing it into seven portions.

435-439 *There is one portion for the nymphs and Hermes, one portion each for Eumaeus and the other men, and the best portion for his guest—a gift that gladdens Odysseus.*

440-445 "Eumaeus, may you be as dear to father Zeus as you are to me since you reward me with a good portion."

In reply, the swineherd Eumaeus said to him, "Eat, god-possessed stranger, and enjoy the food we have. The god gives on the one hand and withholds on the other depending on his spirit's wish, for the god is able to do all things."

446-522 *They pour libations and eat, served bread by Eumaeus' own slave Mesaulius, whom he bought from the Taphians. And finally, when they are satisfied with bread, meat, and wine, they go off to sleep.*

When they rise to go, a storm blows in with Zeus raining and Zephyrus, the West Wind, blowing. Odysseus grows cold. Consequently, he tells a story to Eumaeus to see if the swineherd will provide something warm for him to wear. He tells of the time he was waiting in ambush beneath the walls of Troy. He was there, he says, with Odysseus and Menelaus—and he alone foolishly didn't have a cloak. Sitting in the frost and chill, he was very cold and thus afraid he would freeze to death. When he explained his mistake to Odysseus, he figured out how to get another man to give up his cloak so he could survive. He finishes by wishing aloud that he were younger and in better form. Then, he says, someone would give him a cloak to wear out of respect and affection.

Eumaeus praises his guest's story and gives him clothing—what is due to a suppliant, he explains. He makes him a bed by the fire and offers him warm sheep and goatskins. Even so, he tells him that in the morning he will once again have to return to his ragged clothes—at least until Telemachus comes. The son of Odysseus will give him something to wear, he explains, and send him on.

523-533 Odysseus slept there in this manner, and the young men slept next to him. But it didn't please the swineherd to make his bed in that place. He didn't like sleeping away from the boars, so he prepared his things to go outside. Seeing this delighted Odysseus— that the swineherd earnestly looked after his master's property while he was in a distant land. First, Eumaeus flung a sharp sword over his stout shoulders. Then he covered himself with a wind-proof cloak. Lastly, [530] he picked up the fleece of a large, fully grown goat, took a sharp javelin to ward off dogs and men, and he stepped out to rest where the white-tusked boars slept within a hollow rock, in a place sheltered from Boreas, the North Wind.

Book 15

Stories and Returns
Telemachus Speeds Home, Eumaeus Gives His Story

In brief: Leaving Menelaus and Helen in Sparta and avoiding contact with Nestor in Pylos given his need to speed home, Telemachus returns to Ithaca from his long journey abroad gathering information and earning a reputation. The seer Theoclymenus joins him. Meanwhile, Odysseus tests Eumaeus' loyalty. The swineherd passes the test and tells of his past life—how, with the help of his nurse, he was taken by Phoenician men from the island Syria and his kingly father and sold to Laertes. When Telemachus reaches Ithaca, he goes to see Eumaeus.

NOW PALLAS ATHENA went to spacious Lacedaemon to remind the glorious son of great-hearted Odysseus of his return, and to speed along his homecoming.

She found Telemachus and the splendid son of Nestor lying in the porch of the palace of glorious Menelaus. The son of Nestor was still overcome by gentle sleep, but not Telemachus. Sweet sleep did not hold him. Instead, anxious thoughts for his father kept him up throughout the immortal night.

Bright-eyed Athena stood near him and said, [10] "Telemachus, it is no longer a fine thing to roam about so far from your home, abandoning your wealth in property and leaving behind arrogant men in your house. You must not let them divide and devour all your possessions, or your voyage will turn out to be a pointless one. Instead, go quickly to urge Menelaus, good at the battle cry, to send you on so that you may still find your blameless mother at home."

16-26 Athena explains that Penelope's father and brothers want her to marry Eurymachus, the suitor with the most gifts. If this wedding happens, the goddess is afraid that Penelope will take some of her son's property as part of the agreement in order to enrich her new household. It is what women do, Athena says. Therefore, Telemachus must return to prevent this.

27-42 "I will tell you something more, Telemachus—keep it in mind. The best of the suitors are waiting to ambush you in the strait between Ithaca and rugged Samos. [30] They long to kill you before you reach the land of your fathers. Yet I suppose this will never happen. Long before you die, the earth will hold in her depths some of the wooing men that gobble up the means of your living. Even so, keep your well-built ship far away from the islands and sail throughout the day and night. And one of the immortals who guards you and keeps you safe will send a fair wind from behind.

"When you have reached the nearest shore of Ithaca, then speed the ship and all your comrades on to the city. As for you, go first of all to the swineherd who watches over your swine, the one still united with you in kindly thoughts. [40] Sleep the night there. But send the swineherd into the city to carry the message to thoughtful Penelope that you have returned from Pylos and are safe."

43-109 *Just after Athena flies off to Olympus, Telemachus turns to his companion to tell him they must leave. Peisistratus, the son of Nestor, however, advises him to wait until morning when their host can give them a proper sendoff.*

When morning comes, Menelaus agrees to send them home with a full belly, giving a brief speech on the proper way to host a guest—a host should neither hold a guest when he longs to go nor send him off when he is not ready to leave; there's a proper balance between holding dear and detaining a guest and its opposite, for "what is suitable is better in all things." When Menelaus offers to escort Telemachus and Peisistratus on a tour "through Hellas and mid-Argos," Telemachus demurs, stressing his need to return home to Ithaca as soon as possible in order to protect his possessions.

With that, Menelaus orders his servants to prepare a meal and his neighbor Eteoneus, the son of Boethous, to stoke the fire and roast the meat.

Meanwhile, he goes with Helen and his son Megapenthes to choose gifts that will bring Telemachus glory, splendor, and profit—a two-handled cup, a silver mixing bowl, and an embroidered robe made by Helen that "shines like a star." When finished with their selection, they return to give their guest the gifts.

110-129 Yellow-haired Menelaus said to him, "Telemachus, may Zeus, the loud-thundering husband of Hera, bring you home as you so eagerly desire. And of the treasured goods that I keep stored in my house, I will give one that is the most beautiful and of greatest value—a well-wrought mixing bowl. The work of Hephaestus, it is all silver with its lips finished in gold. The hero Phaedimus, the king of the Sidonians, gave it to me when I sheltered in his house on my return home. Now, I wish to send it along with you."

[120] Speaking like this, the hero, the son of Atreus, set the two-handled cup in his hands. And strong Megapenthes carried the bright mixing bowl and set it before him. Then, holding the robe in her hands, beautiful-cheeked Helen stood by him. And calling him by name, she said, "I too give you this gift, dear child—something from my own hands by which you can remember me on your wedding day. Your wife can wear it. But until then, store it in your halls with your dear mother. As for you, may you with gladness return to your fatherland and to your well-built house."

130-171 *They all feast after the gift-giving and once the gifts are stored away in the chariot.*

When they are satisfied with food and drink, Telemachus and Peisistratus board the chariot to depart. But before they are able to drive away, Menelaus stops them in order to pour out one last libation. Doing so, he wishes them well and asks them to greet Nestor, who was "as kind as a father to me" when they were fighting in Troy. Telemachus promises to deliver the message and to report Menelaus' kindness to Odysseus—if indeed his father is home when he returns. Upon saying this, an eagle carrying a domesticated goose flies to their right, causing them all to rejoice. Menelaus ponders the sign at the bidding of Peisistratus, but it is Helen who suggests its meaning.

172-178 "Listen to me, and I will prophesy as the immortals give my spirit understanding—such as I believe will happen. Just as this mountain-born and raised eagle has snatched up this house-born and raised goose, so will much-wandering Odysseus, the man who has suffered so much misfortune, return and take vengeance. Or perhaps he's already home sowing the seeds of evil for all the suitors."

179-194 *Telemachus prays to Zeus that events may unfold as Helen has prophesied. And with this, the two speed off through the city and toward the plain, riding all day until night comes. They stay once again in Pherae, at the house of Diocles, the son of Ortilochus. In the morning, the chariot wheels its way to Pylos, where Telemachus speaks to Peisistratus.*

195-201 "Son of Nestor, will you promise me something and do what I ask? We boast that we are friends forever because of the friendship of our fathers. But more, we are the same in age and this road trip has united our hearts and minds. Do not take me past my ship, my friend, fostered by Zeus, but drop me off there. [200] Otherwise the old man, hoping to show me affection, will detain me in his house against my will. But I need to return home quickly."

202-270 *Peisistratus considers how to fittingly accomplish the request for Telemachus. Finally, he turns the horses toward the ship, loads the gifts, and urges Telemachus and his men to embark quickly and leave. Otherwise, Nestor will come and angrily insist that Telemachus stay. Hearing this advice, Telemachus prepares to leave as the son of Nestor rides off to Pylos. The men ready the ship while Telemachus prays and offers sacrifices to Athena by its stern for a safe voyage.*

Seeing him there, the seer Theoclymenus approaches the ship and introduces himself to Telemachus. He is the descendant of Melampus, the man who won for his own brother the daughter of Neleus by driving cattle from Phylace to Pylos. Afterwards, Melampus went to live in Argos and rule over some of the people there. He married and his family line was great and long, including his grandson Cleitus, whom Dawn carried off to live with the immortals, and Theoclymenus' own father, Polypheides, whom

Apollo made a seer. Once Theoclymenus finishes, he asks Telemachus to tell him about his own lineage, city, and parents. Inform me truly, he bids. Telemachus is short with his reply. I'm from Ithaca, he reports, and my father is Odysseus—"if he ever lived," a man who has probably already perished. He explains that he is in this land seeking news of his father.

271-281 Then godlike Theoclymenus answered him, "Like you, I am far from my homeland. I killed a man who is part of my tribe, a man who has many brothers and other relatives there in horse-nourishing Argos—and mightily do they rule over the Achaeans. I'm running from there to avoid the black doom of death since I suppose it is now my destiny to roam among men. Therefore, let me board your ship since in my flight I have approached you as a suppliant. I think they are now chasing me, but may they not slay me!"

And mindful Telemachus answered him, [280] "Since you wish to come aboard, then I will not push you off the well-balanced ship. Rather, come along with us. And there in our home you will be welcomed as a guest with whatever we have."

282-291 *With this invitation, Theoclymenus boards the ship with Telemachus, and they sail away with the help of Athena, who sends a fair wind to speed them across the sea.*

292-302 So they sailed past Krounoi and Chalcis, with its beautiful streams. And as the sun was setting and all the ways were growing dark, the ship drew near Pheae, sped on by the wind of Zeus, and sailed past divine Elis, where the Epeians rule. From there he steered for the Pointed Islands, [300] anxiously wondering whether he would escape death or be seized by it.

As for the others, Odysseus and the noble swineherd were eating the evening meal in the shelter alongside the other men.

303-325 *When everyone is satisfied, Odysseus tests the swineherd to see if he will let him stay or encourage him to leave. He tells Eumaeus and the other men that he plans to go to the city to beg so that he doesn't become a bother to them or use up all their resources. His only request is for advice and a guide to the city. Perhaps he will go to the house of Odysseus and Penelope, he says, and offer his services to the suitors there since, thanks to Hermes, he's very skilled at all the necessary tasks: splitting wood, keeping a fire, pouring wine, and roasting and carving meat. Hearing Odysseus' suggestion, Eumaeus is upset.*

326-336 "Ah me, stranger! Why has such a thought come into your mind? You must truly yearn for your own destruction if you wish to fall among the crowd of suitors whose arrogance and violent acts reach the iron sky. [330] Not only that, but you are not like their serving men. No, they are young. And you are well-dressed in cloaks and tunics, with shiny, oiled hair and handsome faces. That's the type of serving man that stands by their polished tables weighed down with bread, meat, and wine. Even so, remain here since no one is bothered by your presence—neither I nor any of my comrades."

337-362 *Pleased with the swineherd's response, Odysseus blesses him, praying that he may be "dear to father Zeus," explaining what Eumaeus has done for him—that he's saved him from more roaming and hunger. Then he asks the swineherd to tell him about his master's mother and father. Are they still living, or have they gone down to the house of Hades?*

In response, Eumaeus reports that his master's father, Laertes, is still alive, even though he prays to Zeus for death on two counts. One, he is mourning his son's ongoing absence. Two, he misses his wife, who died of sorrow when Odysseus failed to return. Eumaeus goes on to talk about his master's mother.

363-372 "She brought me up with long-robed Ctimene, her noble daughter, whom she bore as her youngest child. I was raised with her and given nearly as much honor as that given to Ctimene. Nevertheless, when we both reached the prime of youth, that period of life most desired, they sent her to Same to wed, taking countless bridal gifts in exchange for the marriage. As for me, my lady dressed me in beautiful clothes, a cloak and a tunic. And giving me sandals for my feet, [370] she sent me out into the fields—though she continued to hold me dear in her heart. But now, even though I miss her love, the blessed gods prosper all the work I do."

373-402 Eumaeus finishes by relating, once again, the house's troubles thanks to the suitors, who are "arrogant men," and how the servants have been cut off from Penelope.

Odysseus asks Eumaeus to tell him how he first came to Ithaca. Tell me truly, he bids. Was his city sacked? Or was he snatched up while shepherding or tending the cattle—taken by roving men and sold to his master? Hearing these questions, Eumaeus invites Odysseus to sit back, enjoy the wine, and listen to his tale since they have all night to exchange stories. As for the other men, he dismisses them to sleep elsewhere, if they wish, or they may stay with Eumaeus and Odysseus while they tell and enjoy stories about their prior sufferings—"for after a man has wandered and suffered much, he takes pleasure in his hardships."

403-436 "There's an island called Syria—perhaps you've heard of it? It sits above Ortygia, where the sun turns. Even though the island is not densely populated, it is nevertheless a good land—good for cattle and sheep, full of vines for wine, and rich in grain. Hunger and famine never enter the land, nor does any other hateful plague fall on wretched mortals. But when the tribes of men grow old throughout the city, [410] Apollo of the silver bow arrives with Artemis, slaying them with their gentle shafts.

"There are two cities in the island, and all the land is divided between them. My father ruled over both—my father, Ctesius, the son of Ormenus, who was a man like the immortals. It was to this island that the Phoenicians came. These men are greedy scoundrels, famed for their ships. Anyway, they came in their black ship carrying a whole load of trinkets.

"Now in my father's house there lived a Phoenician woman, who was tall and beautiful and skilled in splendid handiwork. Even so, this woman was deceived by these conniving Phoenicians. [420] First of all, when she was washing clothes by their hollow ship, one of them flirted with her and lay with her in love—an act that is enough to beguile the mind of a woman, even if she is a hard worker. Then he asked her who she was and where she came from. Right then she pointed at my father's high-roofed house and said, 'I boast that I am from Sidon, rich in bronze. I am the daughter of Arybas, a man of abundant wealth. But Taphian pirates seized me as I was returning from the fields. They carried me across the sea and brought me here to the house of this man. He paid a good price for me.'

[430] "Then the man who had secretly joined with her in love said to her, 'Now, why don't you return with us to your home, so that you may once again see your father and mother's high-roofed house, and see them too? I ask because they are still alive, and they have the reputation for riches.'

"In reply, the woman said to him, 'I would do this—if only you sailors would promise me with an oath that you will take me home unharmed.'"

437-463 Once the men swear the oath, the woman makes plans with them for the best time to depart. They'll go when the Phoenicians have sold all their merchandise, she says, having filled their ship with new goods. To pay for her own passage, she will bring along gold and the young boy she takes care of for the king. They can sell him for a good price, she promises. When they are ready to sail, they should send a messenger who will give her a sign that it is time to go.

This is precisely what happens. When the ship is full, a man comes to the king's house. And pretending to offer a fine necklace to the women there, he signals to the Phoenician woman with the nod of his head. It is time to go.

464-492 "The man then walked to the hollow ship, while she seized me by the hand and led me from the house.

"Now in the front portion of the house the woman found the cups and tables of men who had been feasting, those who work with my father. They had gone out of the house to the assembly where the people talk and make judgments. Seeing this, the woman quickly concealed three costly goblets in the fold of her robe, [470] and she carried them away while I followed along in thoughtless folly. The sun was setting, and everything was growing dark as we quickly went and reached the glorious harbor where the speedy ship was anchored—that of the Phoenician men.

"Entering the ship and bringing us onboard as well, the men set sail along the watery ways. And Zeus sent them a fair wind. We sailed for six days—travelling by day and by night. But when Zeus, the son of Cronus, brought us to the seventh day, then the archer Artemis hit the woman with one of her many arrows, and she fell with a thud into the hold of the ship, just as a sea bird plunges into the sea when fishing. [480] And so they threw her from the ship, so that she became food for seals and fishes, while I was left behind, heartbroken.

"Now the wind drove the ship and the water carried them to Ithaca, where Laertes purchased me with his own wealth. And that's how I saw this land with my own eyes."

God-born Odysseus once again replied to him, "Eumaeus, you've truly moved the spirit in my chest in telling me these things—about how you have suffered and endured all these sorrows in your spirit. Yet surely in your case Zeus has given something good alongside all the evil since after all your suffering you have come to the house [490] of a kind man, who thoughtfully offers you food and drink so that you live a good life. As for me, I come here a wanderer, roaming through the many cities of mortal men."

493-511 *While Eumaeus and Odysseus tell their stories, Telemachus and his comrades come ashore in Ithaca and have their morning meal. Once they're satisfied with eating and drinking, Telemachus orders the men to row the ship to the city where, he says, he will meet them after he goes out to visit his herdsman in the fields. Hearing these directions, Theoclymenus asks Telemachus where he should go—should he go to his and his mother's house or another man's?*

512-517 Then mindful Telemachus said to him, "If things were other than they are now, I would urge you on to our house since there you would not long for friendship or hospitality. Yet as things stand, you would be worse off since I will be away, and my mother will not see you given that she does not often appear before the suitors in the house. Instead, she weaves at her loom far away from them in the upper room of the house."

518-554 *Rather than go to his house, Telemachus advises Theoclymenus to go to Eurymachus' house, one of his mother's suitors. Just as Telemachus is finishing with these directions, a bird of omen flies by on his right, carrying a wild pigeon. Theoclymenus interprets the sign from Apollo in favor of Telemachus, suggesting that his house will always rule Ithaca. Pleased, Telemachus wishes it would be as the seer has spoken and tells him that he would receive many gifts from him if it were so—so many that men would call him blessed. Then, turning to his comrade Peiraeus, he asks him to host the stranger and show him honor until he comes for him. Peiraeus agrees, promising him hospitality. With that, the men row off and Telemachus ventures with his spear in hand to find the swineherd Eumaeus.*

555-557 And quickly walking on, his feet carried him forward until he reached the outer yard where the many swine were kept. And among them slept the noble swineherd—the one with kind thoughts for his masters.

BOOK 16

FATHER AND SON
ODYSSEUS REVEALS HIMSELF TO TELEMACHUS

IN BRIEF: *Telemachus comes to Eumaeus' shelter. He asks the swineherd about the stranger. Telemachus is upset he cannot host him in his own house thanks to the suitors. The stranger Odysseus expresses anger at the suitors. Telemachus sends Eumaeus to report his homecoming to Penelope. Athena appears to Odysseus and strengthens him. In turn, he reveals himself to his son, and they plan how they will deal with the many suitors. Meanwhile, the suitors plot against Telemachus in the place of assembly. When they come back to the house, Penelope rebukes them for their insolent behavior. Eumaeus returns to his shelter.*

ODYSSEUS AND THE noble swineherd kindled a fire in the shelter at dawn and were preparing their morning meal. They had already sent out the herdsmen with the droves of swine. As Telemachus drew near the shelter, the usually loud-barking dogs wagged their tails around him without barking.

5-98 Telemachus suddenly appears in the doorway. The swineherd is astonished. He jumps up to greet him as a loving father would greet his only son after years of absence — one who has escaped death. He embraces him, kissing his head, eyes, and both hands, weeping all the while, and telling him that he thought he would never see him again after he went to Pylos.

Telemachus explains that he came to ask Eumaeus about his mother's status with the suitors. The swineherd reports that Penelope stays in the house weeping. When Telemachus steps inside the hut, the old man Odysseus rises to give his son his seat, but the latter refuses, telling the "stranger" that he would find a seat elsewhere. At this the swineherd prepares a seat of sticks covered with fleece and serves roasted meat, bread,

and honey-sweet wine. Finally, when they're all satisfied, having "set
aside the desire for drink and food," Telemachus queries Eumaeus about
the stranger. The swineherd declares what he knows—that he came from
Crete and has wandered and suffered much in conjunction with the lot
given him by some god. Eumaeus hands him over to Telemachus, reporting
that he has declared himself his suppliant.

Hearing this, Telemachus expresses dismay at his inability to properly
host a guest-friend in his house given his own youth and his mother's wa-
vering indecision. He resolves to clothe and arm the old man and send him
on his way with sandals on his feet to wherever he wishes to go. Or he can
stay with Eumaeus, and Telemachus will provide the clothing and food so
that the stranger will not exhaust their resources. Whatever he does, he
cannot go join the suitors, who are reckless and arrogant. Telemachus pre-
dicts that the suitors would taunt the old man, and this would cause the
young hero terrible distress. He can't fight them alone, he observes, since
they are stronger. Such a feat would be hard even for a strong man against
so many!

Much-enduring godlike Odysseus turns to his son and expresses the an-
ger flooding his heart in response to the reckless suitors. He asks him if he
has willingly allowed the suitors to overcome and master him. Or do the
surrounding people hate you? he queries. Or are your brothers to blame, "in
whose fighting a man trusts, even when a great strife arises"?

99-111 "I wish that I were young—as young as I am in spirit! [100]
Or the son of blameless Odysseus! Or even Odysseus himself come
home from his roaming! Then there would be some measure of
hope. I'd invite any other man to lop off my head if I did not become
a misfortune to all those suitors when I entered the great hall of
Odysseus, the son of Laertes.

"But if they were to conquer me all alone thanks to their num-
bers, then that's what I would want. I'd rather be slain in my own
halls than forever to see these shameful deeds. Strangers abused!
The women servants disgracefully dragged from room to room in
the beautiful house! [110] Wine flowing continuously and men de-
vouring my bread as if the supply would never end! There's no
point to it!"

112-154 Telemachus responds by ensuring the old man that it is neither the people nor his brothers who are to blame. He has no brothers, he reveals. Rather, Zeus has caused his lineage to be one of single sons—Telemachus from Odysseus, Odysseus from Laertes, and Laertes from Arceisius. He explains that Odysseus left him alone once he was born, and that now the suitors from Ithaca and the surrounding islands court his mother, consuming and wasting his household wealth with all their feasting. Soon they'll destroy him! Still, things will happen as the gods will.

Turning to the swineherd, Telemachus orders him to go tell thoughtful Penelope that he has returned safely from Pylos. He also bids him not to let anyone else know of his return since many wish him harm. As for the young hero, he will stay in Eumaeus' hut. The swineherd asks if he should give the same message to unhappy Laertes, who hasn't directed the workers in the field or eaten since his grandson went to Pylos; rather, he wastes away in sorrow. The answer is no—even though the thought of it is distressing. Telemachus explains that mortals don't always get what they want—otherwise he would choose his father's return. Instead, he orders Eumaeus to have his mother's handmaid give word to the old man. With this, Eumaeus ties his sandals upon his feet and departs.

155-215 Noticing that the swineherd Eumaeus was gone from the dwelling, Athena drew near in the likeness of a tall and beautiful woman, one skilled in splendid handiwork. She stood by the door of the shelter, appearing to Odysseus. [160] Telemachus did not see her there by the door, nor was he aware of her—for in no way do the gods appear in bodily form to all men. But Odysseus saw her as did the dogs, though they didn't bark. Rather, whimpering, they crawled off to the other side of the dwelling.

Athena motioned with her eyebrows. Noticing the sign, godlike Odysseus left the house, went past the courtyard's great wall, and stood before her. And Athena said to him, "God-born son of Laertes, much-able Odysseus, go ahead now and tell your story to your son. Do not conceal it. Then, when you have planned death and doom for the suitors, [170] you may go to the glorious city. And I myself will not be away from you for too long—no, I eagerly desire to fight."

Saying this, Athena touched him with her golden wand. She first draped a well-washed cloak and a tunic around his chest. Then she increased his height and made him appear younger. Once more his skin grew dark, his jaws stretched square, and his beard darkened upon his chin. When she had done these things, she departed. But Odysseus went into the shelter.

And when his dear son Telemachus saw him, he was amazed. Fearing that he was a god, he turned his eyes away. [180] And addressing him with winged words, he said, "You seem different to me, stranger, than you did before—a new man, fresh. Your clothes, your skin—they're no longer the same. You're clearly some god, one of those who possess the wide sky above. Be gracious, then, so that we may freely offer you acceptable sacrifices and well-made gifts of gold. Spare us!"

Then much-enduring godlike Odysseus answered him, "I tell you, I'm not a god! Why, then, do you say I'm like one of the immortals? Rather, I am your father! It is for me that you have suffered much pain and distress, groaning all the while, enduring the strong violence of men."

[190] Speaking in this manner, Odysseus kissed his son. And he let a tear fall from his cheeks to the earth below, whereas before he had always held them back.

Telemachus did not yet believe that he was his father, and so he once again answered him and said, "You are not my father, Odysseus, but some god is bewitching me to make me weep and groan even more. No mortal man could contrive this by his own mind unless a god himself came to that man and easily made him young or old by his own wish. Just a moment ago you were an old man clothed with shame, [200] but now you are like the gods, who possess the wide sky above."

In reply, Odysseus of many counsels said to him, "Telemachus, it is not fitting for you to be overly amazed that your dear father is in the house or to be astonished. I tell you that no other Odysseus will ever come here. But here I am! Such as I am, I'm here! After suffering much and enduring much, I have returned in the twentieth year to my homeland! I tell you that this is the work of Athena, the driver of spoil. By her own wish she makes me as I am. She has the power to make me resemble a beggar at one moment and [210] a young man with fine clothes hanging from his body at another. But for the gods, who possess the wide sky above, it is easy both to glorify a mortal man and to shame him."

Speaking in this manner, Odysseus sat down. But Telemachus, throwing his arms around his noble father, wept and shed tears. And the longing to weep stirred in both of them.

216-232 *The father and son embrace and cry, wailing aloud like sea-eagles for a very long time, until eventually Telemachus asks Odysseus how he came to Ithaca. His father reports that the Phaeacians returned him home with much wealth that is now stored away in the caves.*

233-280 "I have come here now at the bidding of Athena so that we may discuss the slaughter of our enemies. But come—count for me the suitors. Give me a list of them so that I may know who they are and how many men there are. Then, pondering the matter in my noble spirit, I will decide whether we will be able to fight against them alone without others, or whether we will have to look for others to help us."

[240] In turn mindful Telemachus answered him, "Father, I tell you that I have always heard of your great glory—that you were a strong warrior and a thoughtful advisor. But what you say is too great! I'm stunned with amazement! Two men can't fight against so many strong men. There are not just ten suitors alone, nor twice that number, but many more. But quickly you will learn their number. There are fifty-two distinguished young men from Dulichium. Six serving men attend them. And from Same there are twenty-four men. [250] There are twenty young Achaean men from Zacynthus, and from Ithaca itself there are twelve men, all of them the best. The herald Medon is with them, as well as a godlike bard and two attendants skilled in carving meats and waiting tables. If we face all these men within the house, your mission to make them pay for all their violence will turn out to be bitter and grim. So, if you are able to think of one, consider the man who will help us with a ready heart."

Then much-enduring godlike Odysseus answered him, "In that case, then, I will tell you. Listen to me [260] and decide whether Athena and father Zeus will be help enough for us, or whether I should consider some other helper."

In turn mindful Telemachus answered him, "Noble indeed are the two helpers you mention, enthroned high in the clouds. They rule over everything—over men and the immortal gods."

Then much-enduring godlike Odysseus answered him, "I tell you that these two will not stay out of the mighty battle for long when we fight the suitors in my halls. [270] But for now, go home when dawn appears and join the company of the arrogant suitors. Later on, the swineherd will lead me to the city in the likeness of a miserable old beggar. And if they dishonor me while in the house, then let the dear heart in your chest endure it while I suffer misfortune. Even if they drag me by the feet through the house and out the door or throw missiles at me—even then just look on and bear with it. Sure, you may urge them to stop their thoughtless behavior, encouraging them to do so with gracious words. But they won't [280] listen to you, for their day of doom is at hand."

281-332 *Odysseus further orders Telemachus to stow all the war gear in the storeroom when he gives him the signal—a nod with his head. When the suitors ask what he's doing, he should explain that he wishes to protect the gear from all the smoke and prevent the suitors from using it in anger when drunk. That said, Telemachus should leave behind two spears, two swords, and two shields for them to use. Lastly, Odysseus commands Telemachus to keep his father's presence a secret, even from Laertes, the swineherd Eumaeus, and his mother Penelope, so that he and his son can test everyone's loyalty—the women and the serving men. Telemachus agrees with the plan but advises against testing the men scattered about the island, farming the land. They should do it after taking revenge, he suggests.*

While they discuss the best strategy for moving forward, the ship Telemachus had used during his voyage sails into Ithaca's harbor. Coming ashore, the men carry his collected gifts to Clytius' house and send a herald to inform Penelope that Telemachus has returned. The herald meets the swineherd Eumaeus on the way to the house.

333-342 So the two met, the herald and the noble swineherd, on the same errand, carrying their report to the mistress of the house. And when they reached the halls of the godlike king, the herald stood among the handmaids and said, "Even now, queen, your dear son has come back from Pylos."

But the swineherd drew near to Penelope and told her all that her dear son had ordered him to say. [340] And when he had declared all that had been commanded him, he stepped away to go be with the swine, leaving the hall and the courtyard.

But the suitors felt annoyed and downcast in spirit.

343-370 *Leaving the house and going some distance away, the suitors sit down to confer with one another. Eurymachus accuses Telemachus of arrogant behavior in going off to Pylos. He says they should send men to warn the others out at sea that they should return. Amphinomus breaks in, however, and pointing to the harbor, he explains that there is no need to send men since the others in the ship have already returned. The suitors go down to help their comrades drag the black ship ashore. After, they walk to the place of assembly to talk, not letting anyone else, young or old, join them in their discussion. Antinous, the son of Eupeithes, begins by suggesting that the gods have saved Telemachus. There's no other explanation, he asserts. Their men would have apprehended and slaughtered him if not for the help of some god. Still, Antinous has not given up.*

371-386 "But here and now let us plan a miserable destruction for Telemachus, not letting him escape. I say this because I imagine that while he lives our endeavor will not prosper since he is himself shrewd in his thoughts and plans, and the people no longer favor us. But let's act before he gathers the Achaeans to the place of assembly—for if he does, I don't think he will let us go. No, he'll be full of wrath. And rising up among them he will declare how we plotted sudden death for him but did not catch him. [380] The people will not praise us when they hear of our evil deeds. Instead, they may harm us, driving us from our own land until we come to the land of strangers. Let us act first, then, and seize him in the fields far away from the city—or at least on the way home. As for

whatever Telemachus has for living, all his property and posses-
sions, let's hold on to it, dividing it among ourselves fairly—though
we should give the house to his mother to possess, and to him who
marries her."

*387-399 Antinous finishes with an ultimatum. If they don't like his plan,
they should leave Telemachus' house and woo his mother from their own
halls.*

*Amphinomus, the son of Nisus, who above all the other suitors pleases
Penelope, speaks next.*

400-405 "Friends, I surely would not wish to kill Telemachus—it is
a terrible thing to slay the offspring of a king. Let us first inquire
into the will of the gods. If the oracles of great Zeus recommend it,
then I myself will slay him and order all you other men to do so.
But if the gods turn us away from the act, then I order you stop."

*406-475 The suitors like what Amphinomus has to say. And so, they leave
the place of assembly and return to the house. There, Penelope meets them
in anger in order to rebuke them for their threat to Telemachus. Speaking
to Antinous first, she demeans his ability as a leading man before remind-
ing him of the care that men owe to suppliants, the same care her husband
gave to Antinous' father when he came to Odysseus as a suppliant many
years before. It is this hospitable house that Antinous now wastes, and
Odysseus' wife he hopes to woo, and his son he hopes to slay! Not to men-
tion all the distress he has caused her. She calls on him and the rest of the
suitors to stop.*

*Eurymachus steps in to assure Penelope that Telemachus will not suf-
fer harm as long as he, Eurymachus, lives. If someone tries to kill her son,
then that man will himself know death. Telemachus is dear to him, he fin-
ishes, because Odysseus was kind to Eurymachus when he was a small
boy.*

*Homer observes, "That's what he said to encourage Penelope, while all
along he was plotting his destruction."*

*Hearing Eurymachus' words, Penelope returns to her room and weeps
for Odysseus before falling asleep.*

Later on, when Eumaeus returns to his shelter, Athena changes Odysseus back into an old man once again so that the swineherd will not know and possibly reveal the truth of his return home. Telemachus asks Eumaeus for any news. Have the ambushers sent out by the suitors returned to the house? The swineherd explains that he didn't roam the city asking for news, but he did see a ship return to the harbor when he was journeying back. He saw it from atop Hermes' hill. Still, he's not certain it was them.

476-481 That's what Eumaeus said, and glancing at his father with his eyes, strong and mighty Telemachus smiled—but he avoided the swineherd's gaze.

And when they had finished their work and had prepared the meal, they feasted. Each man had a full share of the spread—no one's hunger went unsatisfied. [480] But when they had set aside the desire for drink and food, they thought of bed and took the gift of sleep.

BOOK 17

THE STRANGER AND THE SUITORS
ODYSSEUS RETURNS TO HIS HOUSE

IN BRIEF: *Telemachus returns to the city where he meets up with his mother, Penelope, and the seer Theoclymenus, who foretells Odysseus' return and plan for revenge. Odysseus and Eumaeus journey to town and the house. On the way, the goatherd Melanthius verbally abuses them. After seeing the dog Argos, Odysseus enters the house and begs for food. When Telemachus gives him some, he prays for his happiness, that he may get what he desires. Begging some more, Odysseus is battered by the suitor Antinous. Penelope curses the suitors and sends Eumaeus to fetch the stranger. Odysseus suggests they talk later in the evening.*

WHEN THE EARLY-BORN rosy-fingered Dawn appeared, Telemachus, the dear son of godlike Odysseus, tied his fair sandals beneath his feet and took his mighty spear that fit well in his hand. And setting off for town, he spoke to his swineherd, saying, "Father, I'm off to the city so that my mother may see me, for I suppose she will not stop her hateful weeping and tearful lamentation until she sees me in the flesh. That said, I charge you [10] to lead this wretched stranger to the city so that he may beg for his food there. And whoever wishes will give him some bread and a cup of wine."

12-152 Odysseus agrees that it would be best to go to the city, suggesting that he is too old to stay on and work in the fields.

When Telemachus returns to the house, he's greeted by all the women. Eurycleia, his childhood nurse, and the serving women see him first. Then, appearing "like Artemis or golden Aphrodite," his mother Penelope sees him and expresses great relief at his return. But Telemachus is all business. He commands her to go pray to the gods for revenge and to bathe and prepare for a guest since, he explains, he's off to fetch the seer Theoclymenus in the assembly place.

As Telemachus goes through the city, the people are amazed to see him. When he arrives at the assembly place, the suitors approach him, feigning respect but planning evil in their hearts. Rather than speaking with them, however, Telemachus joins Mentor, Antiphus, and Halitherses, long-time friends of his father's house. While they are questioning him about everything, Theoclymenus walks up with his host Peiraeus. The latter man calls on Telemachus to send someone to retrieve all the gifts Menelaus gave. Telemachus says it will be better to wait until after he has slaughtered the suitors—if, that is, he is able to do so.

Taking Theoclymenus home with him, Telemachus provides him with a bath, clothes, water for his hands, and food and wine.

While they eat, Penelope sits apart from them spinning yarn. When they are satisfied, she reveals her disappointment in Telemachus, that he has not related the results of his journey to her before all the suitors came for the day—particularly any news regarding his father.

Her son explains that he will tell her at once—all of it and the truth. He went to Pylos, he says, to the house of Nestor, who hosted him and treated him kindly as a father would. Nestor had no news of Odysseus, whether he was alive or dead. He eventually sent him on to Menelaus' house where he saw Helen, the cause of the great war at Troy. There his host told him much—of his own sojourn, and how the old man of the sea had revealed that Odysseus was alive, though he was stuck on Calypso's island without a ship or men to get him home. Still, if he could, he would return and slaughter the suitors with a "shameful death," as a lion would slaughter a female deer and her new-born fawns that have happened to take refuge in his den. If only he could meet the suitors with the strength he displayed while wrestling Philomeleides in Lesbos, then they would know a quick death! Menelaus finished by reporting his own rapid trip home from Egypt thanks to winds sent by the gods.

The story stirs Penelope to the core. Yet before she is able to reply, the seer Theoclymenus updates Menelaus' account.

153-165 "Listen to my words. I will prophesy to you so that you may be sure, and I will hide nothing. I call on you Zeus, first of the gods, to be my witness, and on this table belonging to friendship, and the hearth of blameless Odysseus to which I have come. I tell you that Odysseus is already in the land of his fathers. Whether he's stationed in one place or he's moving about, he's investigating these evil deeds you speak of, and he's planning evil for all the suitors. [160] Such was the bird sign that I pointed out and declared to Telemachus when I sat on the benched ship."

Then thoughtful Penelope said to him, "Ah, stranger, if only this word would come true, then you would quickly know my friendship and receive many gifts from me—so much so that a man would call you blessed if he met up with you."

166-214 *Meanwhile, the suitors are outside taking their pleasure in throwing the discus and hurling spears. Finally, when it is time to feast, the herald Medon calls them inside where they go to prepare the meal.*

As for Odysseus and Eumaeus, they hike along the rough path that leads into the city. Looking like the miserable old beggar that he is, Odysseus walks on with the aid of a walking stick. When they reach the beautiful well built by Ithacus, Neritus, and Polyctor, the one from which the town's people draw their water and by which they make offerings to the nymphs on their altar, they encounter two herdsmen moving along with the goatherd Melanthius, the son of Dolius. They're taking the best of the goats to the suitors for their feast.

215-253 When Melanthius saw them, he called out and spoke to them, abusing them with terrible and shameful words. The words stirred Odysseus' heart. "Look at this now! As always, one contemptible man is leading another! The god matches like with like! Where are you leading this greedy man, you miserable swineherd? [220] Where are you taking this annoying beggar who will spoil the pleasure of our feasting? He's the kind of man that stands in many doorways, begging for scraps of food but not for swords or cauldrons. If you would let me have him to keep my farm, then by drinking whey he might grow strong and sweep out the pens and carry grass to the young goats. But since he has only learned evil deeds, he will not want to busy himself with work. Instead, he plans to go begging throughout the land so that by begging he will be able to feed his insatiate belly.

"But I will speak out to you, and this word will be fulfilled. [230] If he comes to the house of godlike Odysseus, many footstools will fly at him, thrown by the men, and they will break his ribs as he hobbles through the house."

That's what Melanthius said, and as he passed by, he thoughtlessly kicked Odysseus on his hip. Even so, the goatherd did not drive him from the path, but he stayed firm, unmoved. And Odysseus considered whether he should rush him and club him to death with his walking stick or lift him up by the middle and smash his head against the ground. But he checked himself and endured.

The swineherd looked the man in the face and rebuked him. And lifting up his hands he prayed aloud, [240] "Nymphs of the fountain, daughters of Zeus, if ever Odysseus burned thigh pieces of lambs or young goats wrapped in rich fat upon your altar, then accomplish for me my longing. Grant that Odysseus himself, the man in the flesh, may return home, led along by some god.

"If this happened, Melanthius, he would then scatter to the wind all the vain glories that you now trail behind you in your arrogance, always roaming about the city, while worthless herdsmen destroy the flock."

Then the goatherd Melanthius said to him, "I'm amazed at how the dog goes on, his mind full of destructive thoughts! Someday I will take him on a well-benched black ship [250] far from Ithaca so that he may fetch wealth for me—much of what it takes to live. If only Apollo, the god with the silver bow, would today strike down Telemachus in his house, or he would be struck dead by the suitors, just as surely as Odysseus, far away from us, has lost his day of return."

254-262 Finishing his threatening remarks, the goatherd Melanthius ventures on to the city and house and takes his place by Eurymachus, the suitor he likes best, and he begins to eat. Odysseus and the swineherd follow from behind, pausing before the great house when they finally draw near and hear the playing of the bard Phemius from within.

263-271 Taking the swineherd by the hand, Odysseus said, "Eumaeus, surely this is Odysseus' beautiful house. Even if it were seen as one among many, it would be easy to spot. Each building joins the other, the court is carefully finished with a cornice-topped wall, and the doors are well made. No man may scorn it. I notice too that many men are feasting inside the house, [270] for the smell of roasted meat rises up from it, and the lyre sings within—the lyre given by the gods to be the companion of the feast."

272-281 *Confirming Odysseus' observations, Eumaeus strategizes about who should enter the house first. If the stranger stays behind, he says, he should not wait for long, or someone might throw stones at him to drive him away. Odysseus approves.*

282-289 "Go ahead and go in, and I'll stay behind, for in no way am I unused to blows and missiles. I have a spirit that knows how to endure since I've suffered much misfortune upon the waves and in war—so let this come as well. But there is no hiding a hungry belly. It is an accursed, destructive thing, which introduces many evils to all men. It is because of hunger that well-benched ships are made ready to sail the barren sea and carry misery and sorrow to hostile men."

290-335 *Nearby, an old dog called Argos lifts his head and wags his tail when he hears his long-gone master speaking—Odysseus, who left for Troy before the dog was grown. Since then, he has become old after many years of hunting. When Odysseus asks Eumaeus whose dog he is and why he rests atop a dunghill, Eumaeus laments his demise. He used to be a fast dog, and strong, he says. And quite a hunter. But over time, no one cared for him.*

Finishing his explanation, the swineherd enters the house and sits by Telemachus. The herald gives him a portion of food—meat and bread. As for Argos the dog, he dies right then, just after seeing his master return home after twenty years.

336-355 Soon after the swineherd, Odysseus entered the house in the likeness of a wretched old beggar, leaning on a staff. The clothing on his back was sad to see. He sat down on the ash wood threshold just within the doorway [340] and leaned against a cypress wood doorpost that a carpenter had skillfully planed long ago, levelling it to the line.

Telemachus called the swineherd to him. And taking a whole loaf from the beautiful basket, and all the meat his hands could hold, he said, "Take all this and give it to the stranger. And urge him on to beg from all the suitors. Shame is no good for a man in need." That's what Telemachus said, and the swineherd walked off as soon he heard the order.

Standing nearby Odysseus, Eumaeus spoke to him with winged words, [350] "Stranger, Telemachus gives you these and urges you to beg from all the suitors. Shame, he says, is no good for a begging man."

In reply, Odysseus of many counsels said, "Lord Zeus, may Telemachus be happy among men, and may everything happen as he desires in his heart."

356-413 Odysseus takes the food and eats apart from the suitors while they feast in the hall and listen to the music of the lyre.

Sometime later, after the suitors have become quite noisy, Athena urges Odysseus to go and beg for scraps among them in order to see who behaves in a suitable manner and who does not. Many give to him out of pity, asking aloud who he is and where he came from. The goatherd Melanthius reveals that the swineherd brought him to the house. Hearing this, Antinous rebukes him, telling the swineherd that they already have enough wandering beggars to spoil their fun. Plus, he should be mindful of his master's store of food. Eumaeus denies that he would ever go out looking for beggars to invite to Odysseus' house. Then he rebukes Antinous for being so harsh to all the servants. Telemachus advises Eumaeus to let it go. It's just the way Antinous is, he says. Then he turns on Antinous and expresses surprise at his counsel to turn out a stranger. Rather, he should give food to him. He finishes with the observation that Antinous prefers eating to giving. Antinous denies being stingy. And finishing his speech, he seizes a footstool from beneath the table while everyone else fills Odysseus' pouch with bread and meat.

414-424 Odysseus stood by Antinous, and said, "Give me something, friend. You don't seem like the worst of the Achaeans here but the best since you appear like a king. Therefore, you should give me an even better portion of food than the rest. If you do, I will glorify you throughout the endless earth. For I too once dwelled in a house among men attached to me. [420] I was a happy man in a wealthy house. And often I gave to wanderers—whoever they were and with whatever need they came to my house. And I had countless slaves and everything and more for living well, those things for which men are called wealthy. But Zeus, the son of Cronus, destroyed all of it. I imagine it was what he wanted."

425-444 *Fabricating a story, Odysseus relates how Zeus sent him to Egypt with a roving band of plundering pirates. After meeting with some initial success in slaying the local men in their fields and carrying off their wives and children, he says that he and the pirates met with disaster when the rest of the population came out to fight in a full force of foot and horsemen. Many were killed, Odysseus reports, others were taken as slaves, and he himself was handed over to Dmetor, the son of Iasus, the ruler in Cyprus.*

445-465 Antinous answered him and said, "What god has brought this pain here to spoil our feasting? Stand over there in the middle and stay away from my table—unless you want to see an even crueler Egypt and Cyprus! What a bold and shameless beggar you are, [450] going to every man—and in turn they give recklessly. Ah, there's no reluctance to give, or holding back, when giving from another man's goods and when each man has plenty!"

Stepping back, Odysseus of many counsels said to him, "How strange! It seems that your wits don't match your royal form! You wouldn't even give a suppliant a grain of salt from your own store of goods since now, sitting at another man's table, you won't let a scrap of food leave his house. Yet here there's plenty!"

That's what Odysseus said. And Antinous grew angrier in his heart, and with a glance of anger from beneath his brows, he spoke to him with winged words, [460] "I don't think you'll be going around the house anymore saying fine things now that you've addressed me with words of reproach!"

Saying this, he seized the footstool and threw it. The missile struck Odysseus on his right shoulder, just where it joins the back, but Odysseus stood firm as a rock. It didn't make him fall. He just stood there, silently shaking his head and pondering evil deep in his heart.

466-538 *Odysseus sits down in the doorway, and, praying for his death, he reproaches Antinous for hurting him on account of his hungry belly. Antinous tells him to eat quietly, or the men will drag him away and strip off his skin. The men, however, are not pleased with Antinous' treatment of the wanderer, who may be a god, since gods "roam our cities in the guise of strangers from afar." Witnessing Antinous' abuse, Telemachus is indignant, contemplating evil for the suitors deep within.*

Penelope, sitting with her servants, also criticizes them and prays for Antinous' death—the suitor who is like "black death," she says. Calling on Eumaeus, she asks him to go and fetch the stranger so that she can talk with him and see if he has any news of Odysseus to offer. Eumaeus tells her about the three days and nights the stranger spent with him in his shelter—how he could sing as though one taught by the gods, and how he told him about all the bad things that had happened to him, and how he claimed to be from Crete and Odysseus' ancestral friend, and, lastly, how Odysseus is nearby in the land of the Thesprotians, preparing to return home with a pile of treasure. Reiterating her command, Penelope once again bids Eumaeus to go and fetch the stranger so that she might hear his story face to face. Meanwhile, she laments Odysseus' absence and the suitors' behavior in wasting the household's wealth.

539-550 "But if Odysseus would only come home and return to the land of his fathers, [540] then he and his son would quickly make these men pay for their violent deeds."

That's what Penelope said. And right then Telemachus sneezed loudly, and the whole room echoed in a way that was terrible to hear.

But Penelope laughed, and at once she spoke to Eumaeus with winged words, "Go and call the stranger over to me. Didn't you hear it?—how my son sneezed at all my words? I told you that death would come to all the suitors! Not one will escape the fate of death! And I'll tell you another thing that you should keep in your heart. If I learn that the stranger reports all things truly, [550] I will clothe him in a cloak and a tunic—in beautiful clothes."

551-575 When Eumaeus goes to retrieve the stranger and relates to him Penelope's sorrow and promise of clothes in exchange for truthful news, Odysseus tells him that he would be happy to speak with her, but he fears the men in the hall and their response. He suggests waiting until the sun sets. Then he can sit by the fire and give a full report to the mistress of the house. Eumaeus returns to Penelope without the stranger.

576-590 "You're not leading him, Eumaeus. What is the wanderer thinking? Is he unnecessarily afraid of someone? Or is he otherwise ashamed to beg throughout the house? But a shamefaced beggar is an unfortunate beggar."

In reply, the swineherd Eumaeus said to her, [580] "He speaks rightly, even as any other man would think, in seeking to shun the arrogance of overbearing men. But he asks you to wait until the sun sets. Anyway, it is better for you to speak to the stranger alone, and to hear his report."

Then thoughtful Penelope said to him, "The stranger is no fool. He understands how things might be, for doubtlessly there are no mortal men who devise reckless deeds as these arrogant men do."

That's how Penelope spoke to him, and the noble swineherd went [590] into the throng of the suitors when he had told her everything.

591-601 Quietly, Eumaeus tells Telemachus that he's off to watch over the swine. He counsels the young hero to guard himself since the suitors are plotting evil. "May Zeus destroy them before they harm us!" Telemachus agrees, ordering the swineherd to bring more swine in the morning. As for the suitors, they will be his and the gods' concern.

602-606 That's what Telemachus said, and the swineherd sat down again on the polished stool. But when he had satisfied his desire for food and drink, he stepped away to go be with the swine, leaving the hall and the courtyard that was full of feasting men. The latter were making merry with dance and song, for evening was now following day.

BOOK 18

NAVIGATING A DANGEROUS HOUSE
ODYSSEUS BOXES IRUS AND DEALS WITH THE SUITORS

IN BRIEF: *The beggar Irus arrives and is rude to Odysseus. With the encouragement of the suitors, Odysseus boxes with him, knocking him out, thereby winning a prize and their blessings—at least for the moment. Odysseus warns Amphinomus that the fortunes of men rapidly change. He was once wealthy, he claims, but after behaving recklessly, he lost everything. The suitors should be careful. Penelope shows herself to the suitors. They are awed by her. After she chastises them for pursuing her contrary to custom, they bring her gifts. Later, the housemaid Melantho shamefully upbraids Odysseus. In turn, he threatens her with what Telemachus will do to her. The suitor Eurymachus makes fun of Odysseus. After his defensive response, the suitor throws a stool at him, but Odysseus ducks. There is such a racket that Telemachus orders them all to leave. Amphinomus backs him up, advising them not to abuse the stranger anymore. After one more drink, they depart.*

THERE CAME INTO the hall a man who begged from everyone throughout the whole town of Ithaca. He was known for his greedy belly, eating and drinking without end.

4-13 *Although his real name is Arnaeus, the suitors call him Irus. He's a big, hulking man, but weak. And coming into the hall, he tries to drive Odysseus from the doorway. Get up, he says, or I'll drag you away! They might have to fight if Odysseus doesn't move, he hints.*

14-24 But with an angry glance from beneath his brows, Odysseus of many counsels said to Irus, "God-possessed man, I harm you neither in word nor in deed, nor am I jealous if some man gives you much. This doorway will hold us both. Therefore, you don't have to begrudge the goods of other men. You seem to be a wanderer like me. As for the happiness of wealth, it is up to the gods to give it or not. [20] As for you, don't overdo it by challenging me with your fists, or you may anger me. And if that happens, old man that I am, I might shower your chest and lips with blood. Ah, but then I would have more peace tomorrow—since I don't imagine you would return again to the hall of Odysseus, the son of Laertes."

25-89 *Irus balks at Odysseus' threat and challenges him to a fight. When Antinous learns about the proposed fight, he's delighted and offers to the winner sausages "full of fat and blood" and an ongoing seat at the feasting table. Odysseus protests. Why should an old man fight a young man? he asks. Still, his hungry belly urges him on, he says. He only asks for the guarantee that no man will step in to help Irus. They all agree and accordingly swear an oath, with Telemachus as host confirming their good faith.*

Odysseus prepares for the fight so that his shoulders, arms, and thighs are bare of clothes. When Athena draws near and fills out his limbs, all the suitors are astonished. And Irus, seeing Odysseus' body, visibly shakes with fright. Observing this, Antinous schools him for being afraid of an old man. If you lose, he says, I'll ship you off to king Echetus, who will maim you by cutting off your nose and ears before giving your innards to a dog to eat. Irus shakes even more. The suitors lead Irus and Odysseus to the middle of the great hall, and both men raise their fists to fight.

90-99 Then much-enduring godlike Odysseus pondered whether he should punch him so that his life would leave him when he fell, or whether he should strike him lightly in order to stretch him out flat on the earth. Thinking in this manner it seemed better to hit him just a little so that the Achaeans wouldn't discover him.

So, then they raised their hands, and Irus punched Odysseus' right shoulder. But Odysseus struck him on the neck just beneath the ear and crushed the bones within. And at once, red blood gushed from his mouth. He fell down to the dusty ground, moaning and crying like a wounded animal. And gnashing his teeth, he kicked the ground with his feet.

100-111 *The suitors nearly die with laughter at the knockdown while Odysseus grabs Irus by the foot and drags him outside, propping him up against a wall as a scarecrow for dogs and stray pigs. He orders him to stop lording it over other strangers and beggars—not while he himself is so pathetic, anyway. Turning around, Odysseus returns to his seat in the doorway. And laughing with delight, the suitors address him.*

112-123 "Stranger, may Zeus and the other immortal gods grant you what you most desire and what is dear to your spirit since you have stopped this insatiate man's begging in the land."

115-121 *Odysseus is pleased to hear the prayer. Antinous gives him the sausages, and Amphinomus gives him bread and a golden cup of wine, and further blesses him.*

122-123 "Rejoice, father-stranger! May happiness eventually be yours, though now you are carrying the heavy weight of wretchedness."

124-129 *Odysseus acknowledges Amphinomus for his rich and noble father, Nisus of Dulichium, and for his apparent wisdom. Then he tells him to pay attention to what he has to say.*

130-150 "Of all things that breathe and move along the earth, there is nothing weaker than a human being—I tell you, the earth nurtures no frailer thing. For as long as the gods give him excellence, and as long as his knees stand strong, he believes he will never suffer misfortune in the days to come. But when the blessed gods send him misery, he must bear it with an enduring spirit even though it is against his will. For the mind and mood of men on earth is led along by the father of men and gods even as he leads each day. I was also once destined to be happy in wealth among men, but giving way to force and strength, I behaved recklessly many times, [140] relying on my father and my brothers and cousins to back me. The point: let no man ever be lawless. Instead, let him be silent when the gods give gifts—whatever they give.

"I see the suitors behaving recklessly, consuming the household wealth and dishonoring the wife of a man who, I tell you, will not be gone for long from his friends and homeland. No, he is very near. May some god, therefore, lead you to your homes. And may you not meet him face to face when he returns home to his dear homeland. For not without bloodshed, I think, [150] will the suitors and this man part from one another when he steps into this hall."

151-205 *Finishing, Odysseus pours out a libation to the gods and drinks some of the wine. Amphinomus returns to the hall with the golden cup and a heavy heart, foreboding ill to come.*

Sitting in the chamber above, Penelope decides to go and show herself to the suitors even though she hates them. Turning to the housemaid Eurynome, she explains her plan and tells her she also wants to give a message to her son—that Telemachus should avoid the suitors since they say good things but plan evil. In response, Eurynome advises Penelope to bathe first and anoint herself with olive oil. Penelope balks! The gods took her beauty away on the day her husband went off to Troy, she says. She orders Eurynome to go and get the handmaids Autonoe and Hippodameia so that they can walk by her side when she enters the hall. It would be shameful, she notes, to go alone. Eurynome obeys.

Meanwhile, "Athena has another idea." She causes Penelope to fall asleep. And while she's sleeping, the goddess makes her beautiful.

When Penelope wakes up, she wishes that Artemis would send her death so that her sorrows would vanish. Even so, she gets up and ventures down to the hall with the two handmaids.

208-213 Now when Penelope, divine among women, reached the suitors, she stationed herself by the doorpost of the well-built hall, [210] holding a shining veil in front of her face. Her faithful handmaids stood by her side, one on each side. The knees of the suitors were loosened at once—their spirits enchanted by desire. And they all prayed to lay by her side in bed.

214-319 *Turning to Telemachus, Penelope rebukes her son for the way he has allowed the stranger to be treated. You used to be wiser! she says.*

Telemachus defends himself, saying that it's hard to plan when the suitors are present. Furthermore, the stranger beat Irus. Ah, he prays, if only all the suitors "limbs were loosened" as Irus' are—the man who sits outside with his head slumped over like a man drunk with wine.

Suddenly, Eurymachus yells out that if other Achaeans could see Penelope, then she would have far more suitors because of her great beauty and balanced mind.

In reply, Penelope claims that the immortal gods destroyed whatever excellence she possessed when the Argives and her husband went to Troy. She wishes Odysseus were present to help her. Then she recalls his words to her before he departed. He said that, thanks to the fighting skill of the Trojans, he may not return from the expedition. Still, she should take care of his mother and father. And when their son becomes a bearded man, she should leave and marry another man. That's what he said. But now, Penelope laments, Zeus has destroyed my happiness since I will have to get married. She goes on to explain that the suitors are pursuing her in a way opposed to custom. Usually, suitors bring food and gifts to the woman's house; they, by contrast, are eating everything she has!

Hearing these words, Odysseus is glad. As for the suitors, Antinous speaks up to declare that they will send heralds to fetch gifts for them, but they themselves will stay until she marries one of them.

The heralds bring back many gifts for Penelope—a robe with golden brooches from Antinous; a golden chain with inset amber from Eurymachus; earrings from Eurydamus; and a necklace from Peisander, as well as other gifts from the other suitors.

Penelope returns to the upper chamber with all the gifts carried by her handmaids. Below the suitors dance and make merry, waiting for the turn of day into evening. When the sun sets, they set up three braziers for light, and the housemaids light the fire. Turning to the women, Odysseus tells them to go join Penelope in her room. He will stay and tend the fire for the rest of the evening, even if they wish to stay until dawn. They will not tire him in this way, he says, for he's used to enduring much.

320-345 That's what Odysseus said. Hearing him, the women laughed and glanced at one another. And beautiful-cheeked Melantho shamefully berated him—Melantho, Dolius' daughter, whom Penelope had reared and cherished as her own child, giving her the toys she desired. Nevertheless, Melantho did not feel sorry for Penelope. Instead, she liked Eurymachus and mixed in love with him. Melantho now upbraided Odysseus with disgraceful words.

"Wretched stranger, something must be wrong with your mind since you're unwilling to go to the blacksmith's shop to sleep, or to a public house. Instead, you go on and on here, [330] undaunted among the other men without any fear in your heart. Surely wine holds your mind captive—unless your mind is always like this, causing you to speak without a point. Are you so excited that you have beaten that wandering man Irus? Beware! A better man than Irus may rise up to beat your head with heavy hands and send you from the house covered with blood."

But with an angry glance from beneath his brows, Odysseus of many counsels answered her, "You bitch! I'm going right now to tell Telemachus what sort of things you're saying so that he'll cut you up, limb from limb, right here on the spot!"

[340] Speaking in this manner, he scattered the women with his words. They fled through the hall, and the limbs of each were loosened beneath her with terror, for they thought that he spoke the truth. But Odysseus stood by the burning brazier, keeping the fire, observing all the men. Yet as he stood there, he pondered other things with his heart—things that would not remain unfulfilled.

346-386 *Athena stirs up the suitors so that Odysseus becomes even more irritated. Eurymachus, the son of Polybus, makes fun of him for his bald head, saying that the gods have sent him along to them for the extra light that his head reflects from all the torches. He goes on to say that he would hire him to work but Odysseus prefers to beg. Odysseus responds by saying that if they competed in a work contest, cutting hay or driving oxen, then Eurymachus would see how hard Odysseus could work. He would see the same if there was a war and Odysseus marched into battle holding a shield and two spears and wearing a bronze helmet on his head. He would fight out front with the best of the fighters. He finishes with an insult: Eurymachus is a harsh man! He thinks he's great and powerful, but if*

Odysseus happened to return, the door wouldn't be big enough for his and the other suitors' flight!

387-398 That's what Odysseus said, and Eurymachus grew more and more wrathful at heart. And with an angry glance from beneath his brows, he spoke to Odysseus with winged words, "You wretched man! You'll know misfortune soon enough thanks to me and your own going on and on! [390] You're so daring among the other men, without any fear in your heart! Surely wine holds your mind captive—unless your mind is always like this, causing you to speak without a point. Are you really so excited that you have beaten that wandering man Irus?"

Saying this, Eurymachus grabbed a footstool. But fearing him, Odysseus ducked by the knees of Amphinomus of Dulichium, and so Eurymachus struck the wine-pourer on the right hand, so that the wine-jug fell to the ground with a clang, and the pourer himself fell moaning in the dust.

399-422 *Witnessing this accident, the other suitors regret Odysseus' presence, which has caused so much turbulence. Telemachus speaks up and tells them all to go home—now that they've had their fill of food and drink, he says. The suitors are astonished at Telemachus' boldness. Amphinomus calls on them all to stop abusing the stranger. They should pour out one last libation and go home to rest. As for the stranger, they should leave him alone in the hall where Telemachus will care for him. Everyone agrees to Amphinomus' plan.*

423-428 And so the hero Mulius, a herald from Dulichium and the attendant of Amphinomus, mixed a bowl of wine for the suitors. He served everyone in turn. And making libations to the blessed gods, they drank the honey-sweet wine. Then, when they had made libations and had drunk as they desired, they departed, each man to his own house, desiring rest.

BOOK 19

THE STRANGER SPEAKS WITH PENELOPE
ODYSSEUS PLANS FOR THE SUITORS' DEATH

IN BRIEF: *At the direction of Odysseus, Telemachus stores the weapons away from the suitors. Penelope enters the hall from her chamber. The handmaid Melantho abuses Odysseus. After reprimanding her handmaid, Penelope interviews the stranger, who praises her for her well-known glory. She explains her misfortune—how now, after having deceived them for so long, she must marry one of the suitors. When asked about himself, Odysseus claims he is Aethon from Crete. He says he once hosted Odysseus and gives proof. Not only that, he declares, but Odysseus is on his way home. Penelope is skeptical. The old nurse Eurycleia washes Odysseus and recognizes him by the scar above his knee. He swears her to silence. Penelope tells the stranger about the dream she had of the eagle that killed her geese. Odysseus confirms its truth—the suitors will die. No, says Penelope, he won't come home. Instead, she will hold a great contest to determine the suitor she will marry. They go to sleep.*

G ODLIKE ODYSSEUS WAS left behind in the hall, plotting the slaughter of the suitors with Athena's help.

3-99 After the suitors leave for the night, Odysseus turns to Telemachus and directs him to put the weapons away in the storeroom, with the excuse— when the suitors ask—that they are becoming dirty with smoke and that he's afraid they'll use them to turn on one another when drunk. Obeying, Telemachus has Eurycleia shut and lock the doors to the hall and order all the women to their rooms while he and his father carry the weapons and armor to the storeroom—helmets, shields, and spears. Athena stands by with a golden lamp, shining a beautiful light. When Telemachus notices and comments on the divine presence, Odysseus hushes him. "Yes," he reveals, "it is the gods who hold Olympus." Then the father dismisses his son to go rest while he talks to his mother. Telemachus goes off to bed.

Penelope emerges from her chamber, "like Artemis or golden Aphrodite," and sits down on a fleece-covered chair placed by the fire—a chair fashioned by Icmalius with ivory and silver spiral work and an attached footrest.

The servants clean up the mess left by the suitors and stack new wood in the braziers. Seeing Odysseus, Melantho upbraids him once again, telling him to leave or be hit with a torch.

Angry, Odysseus asks Melantho why she's treating him in such a begrudging manner. Is it that he's a dirty beggar? Well, he's driven on by necessity, he says. He goes on to explain that he was once rich and happy among his own people and slaves in his own household, and yet he gave to roaming men. But Zeus took all he had away as was his will. In a similar way, Melantho should hope she doesn't lose her shining beauty and so her privileged spot among her mistress' handmaids. And she should fear her master's homecoming, or, if he never returns, Telemachus' punishment for her insolence.

Hearing the conversation, Penelope turns to Melantho and scolds her. You bold and shameless bitch! she cries out. You'll pay for this! You knew I wanted to question the stranger about my husband. Turning to Eurynome, Penelope asks for a chair and fleece for the stranger to sit on so that he may tell his story.

100-105 That's what Penelope said, and Eurynome quickly brought a well-planed chair and set it down, casting the fleece on it. Then much-enduring godlike Odysseus sat down on the chair.

And thoughtful Penelope spoke first, and said, "Stranger, I will ask you this question first: Who are you and where do you come from? And tell me about your city and your parents."

106-128 *Odysseus avoids answering her questions. Rather, he lauds Penelope for her well-known glory. It is like that of a just king, he observes, whose good rule is the cause of his people's prosperity. He begs her not to ask him about his family and homeland for fear it will cause him more pain since he is "a man of sorrows." He doesn't want to weep in a strange house or have the servants making fun of him for drinking too much.*

Hearing the stranger's praise, Penelope denies any special glory. It all vanished on the day Odysseus and the Argives sailed off for Troy. If only Odysseus would come home, then things would be better! she says.

129-163 "But now I am grieving—some god has sent me so much misfortune. [130] For all the best men who rule over the islands — Dulichium and Same and wood-covered Zacynthus—and those who dwell in far-seen Ithaca itself, all these woo me, even though I am unwilling, and they consume the wealth of my house. Consequently, I don't pay attention to strangers or suppliants—or even to the heralds, who serve everyone. Instead, my dear heart melts in longing for Odysseus.

"These men—they urge me to marry. And meanwhile, I weave deception. First some god inspired my heart to set up a great loom in my room and begin weaving an enormous cloth [140] made of very fine and very long thread. And at once I said to them, 'My young suitors, godlike Odysseus is indeed dead. Still, do not press me to marry again immediately. Wait until I have finished this burial shroud for the hero Laertes so that he'll have one when the destructive fate of death takes him down. If I don't make him one, the Achaean women will shame me. They'll express astonishment that a man of so many possessions and wealth went down to death without a burial shroud.'

"That's what I said, and their manly spirits were persuaded. And from that day forward I would weave on the great loom during the day, [150] and by torchlight I would unravel what I had done at night. In this manner I persuaded the Achaeans for three years and was never discovered. But when the fourth year came along, and the seasons turned as moon after moon waned and many days came to an end, then with the help of my servants—the disrespectful bitches!—they came to me and took me by the hand and scolded me.

"So, I finished the shroud against my will, by the force of necessity. And now I am unable to put off the marriage, nor am I able to discover some other cunning ruse. Not only that, but my parents encourage me to marry, and my son is vexed by the men devouring the household's wealth. [160] He observes it all since he's already a man and cares very much for the household that Zeus glorifies.

"But even so, tell me about your family lineage and where you come from—for you are not from an oak tree or a rock, as an ancient tale might have it."

164-202 Odysseus agrees to tell Penelope about his background, even though, he explains, it will cause him great sorrow. He says that he's from Crete, the land of many cities and languages, and that his name is Aethon. He's the son of Deucalion and grandson of Minos. His brother is Idomeneus, "the older and better man," who went to Troy. He claims that he (Aethon) saw Penelope's husband when Odysseus himself was on his way to Troy. A wind blew him off course to Crete, and so he came looking for Idomeneus, his friend. But Idomeneus was already gone, and so Aethon hosted Odysseus and his men for twelve days until the wind permitted their departure on the thirteenth day.

203-219 As Odysseus spoke, he made the many falsehoods of his tale seem like the truth. And as Penelope listened, tears flowed and her face melted as the snow melts on the high-ranging mountains— the snow that Euros, the East Wind, melts after Zephyrus, the West Wind, has dumped it. And as it melts, the rivers flow full. In this manner her beautiful cheeks melted as she lamented and wept for her husband—the very man at her side.

Odysseus [210] felt pity in his heart for his weeping wife. Even so, his eyes remained motionless—as though they were horn or iron—between his eyelids. With guile he hid his tears.

But when Penelope had had her fill of tearful weeping, she once again answered him and said, "Now, stranger, I believe I will question you to see whether you, as you say, truly hosted my husband and his godlike comrades there in your halls. Tell me what sort of clothes he wore upon his body. And describe the kind of man he was, and the comrades who followed him."

220-248 The stranger—Aethon (Odysseus)—agrees to try to remember. But it's been twenty years, so it will be challenging, he says. Nevertheless, he goes on to describe what he was wearing—Odysseus' purple, double folded cloak; a golden brooch depicting a dog clutching a young deer; and a shining, soft tunic. Of course, he could have received these clothes from a comrade or a host. Aethon himself gave him gifts when Odysseus departed. Then he describes Odysseus' herald—a dark-skinned, curly-haired man called Eurybates, a man Odysseus honored above his other comrades because he and Odysseus were like-minded.

249-250 That's what Odysseus said. And doing so, he aroused in Penelope the longing to weep [250] as she recognized the certain signs that Odysseus pointed out.

251-267 *After crying, Penelope declares that the stranger will be honored in her house due to his truthful story. She knows because she herself gave Odysseus the clothes and the brooch. But, she pessimistically finishes, he will never return.*

Aethon (Odysseus) tells her to cry no more, though he doesn't blame her since any woman would cry at the loss of her husband.

268-273 "Even so, stop weeping and listen to my words, for I will speak unerringly and hide nothing [270] of what I recently heard about Odysseus' return home. He's nearby and alive in the rich land of the Thesprotians, and he's bringing with him many valuable treasures, asking for good things as he goes through the land."

274-466 *Aethon (Odysseus) goes on with the story, explaining how Zeus and Helios, the Sun, destroyed Odysseus' men after they ate the cattle of the Sun. This is what Pheidon, the Thesprotian king, told him. Odysseus didn't die with his men, however, but he escaped to the land of the Phaeacians, who honored him, gave him gifts, and sent him on. Aethon saw the great treasure that Odysseus had gathered—wealth enough for many generations. As for the man Odysseus, he's gone to the oracle of Zeus at Dodona, the sacred oak. Aethon finishes with an oath sworn by Zeus and Odysseus' hearth that Odysseus is safe and will soon return home.*

Penelope declares that if his word is true then the stranger will know her friendship, and she'll give him many gifts, and men will call him blessed.

Nevertheless, she doubts it will happen. Even so, she calls on the women to wash the stranger's feet and prepare his bed. She further orders them to bathe and anoint him in the morning so that he may eat with Telemachus and the others in the hall. And curse the man who distresses the stranger, she says, for people blame a harsh man and praise a gentle one.

Odysseus tells Penelope that he doesn't need a fine bed—he's used to sleeping roughly, he says. Nor does he want his feet washed by any of the women, unless there's an older woman who has known many sorrows. Penelope says there is such a one, Eurycleia, who took care of Odysseus from the moment he was born.

Eurycleia agrees to wash his feet. But first she mourns for Odysseus. Finally, pulling the stranger toward herself, she tells him that he is very much like Odysseus in body, voice, and feet. Odysseus tells her that many have said the same. Pouring warm and cold water into a basin, she prepares to bathe his feet and lower legs. It is then—right when Eurycleia takes up his foot—that Odysseus suddenly worries that she'll detect and remember a scar from long ago. If she does, his true identity will be discovered.

She does. Washing him, she immediately recognizes the scar that Odysseus received long ago while on a trip to Parnassus to see his grandfather Autolycus—Anticleia's father—and Autolycus' sons. A wild boar inflicted it with its white tusk. It was Autolycus who had given Odysseus his name when he was born—Autolycus, who "surpassed all men in thievery and oaths," thanks to his devotion to the god Hermes. Eurycleia had set the newborn boy in the man's lap and asked that he name him. And so Autolycus had called him "Odysseus" and invited him to Parnassus when he was grown. Odysseus travelled to his grandfather's homeland when he was older and was welcomed with kisses by his grandmother, Amphithea, and all of his uncles, who prepared a feast for him. And so, they feasted all day long until at night they slept. The following morning, the sons of Autolycus took Odysseus hunting. The hounds followed the scent of a wild boar to its resting place in a dark thicket. Trapped there, the fierce boar rushed out right when Odysseus stabbed at it with his spear. The boar cut right above Odysseus' knee with its sharp tusk just as Odysseus dealt it a death blow with his spear. When Odysseus later returned home to Ithaca with many glorious gifts, his father and mother asked him how he had gotten the scar, and so he told them.

467-475 "This was the scar the old woman felt with the flat of her hands—she knew it by the touch. And so, she dropped the foot, and his leg fell into the basin. The bronze vessel rang aloud, [470] tumbled over, and all the water spilled out upon the ground. At once, joy and grief seized her heart, and her eyes were filled with tears, and the fullness of her voice was checked.

Touching Odysseus' chin, she said, "You really are Odysseus, dear child, and before now I didn't recognize you—not until I had felt my lord all over."

476-534 *Eurycleia attempts to catch Penelope's eye to let her know the truth, but Athena prevents it. Quickly, Odysseus grabs his old nurse by the throat and commands her to keep silent. If she doesn't, he says, then he will slay her with the other serving women after he takes revenge on the suitors. Hearing his threat, Eurycleia is shocked! She promises to be quiet and to tell him who has been faithful among the servants, and who has not, when he conquers the suitors. And she finishes washing his feet.*

When Eurycleia is finished, Penelope begins talking to Odysseus once again. She tells him how hard her life has become, and how she weeps at night as does Pandareus' daughter, the nightingale, for her own child Itylus, the son of Zethus, whom she accidently killed with a sword. Penelope anxiously wonders whether she should stay and honor her husband's household and bed or marry one of the gift-bearing suitors. When Telemachus was young, she reveals, he wanted her to remain in the house. Now that he's a man, he would like her to depart so that the Achaean suitors would also leave. This is why she cries at night.

535-550 "But come, hear and interpret this dream of mine. About the house I have twenty geese who come out of the water and eat grains of wheat. I am warmed with joy when I watch them. Ah, but down from the mountain there came a great eagle with a hooked beak! It broke all their necks—killing them. And so, they lay scattered [540] about the halls while the eagle was carried high into the bright sky. Seeing this, I began to weep and wail—still in the dream. And so, the fair-haired Achaean women gathered around me as I lamented sadly that the eagle had killed my geese.

"Then the eagle came down again and landed on a jutting roof-beam. And with the voice of a mortal man, it checked my tears and said, 'Be courageous, daughter of far-famed Icarius. This is no dream, but it is reality in truth that will be fulfilled. The geese are the suitors. And I—I who was before the eagle—have now come again as your husband, [550] who will inflict a shameless doom on all the suitors.'"

551-570 Odysseus confirms the eagle's words. All the suitors will die. As for Penelope, she doubts it. She explains some dreams come through a gate of horn and some through one of ivory. The latter are false whereas the former bring truth and fulfillment. Her dream, she expounds, came through the ivory door and will thus not happen. Anyway, here's what she has decided to do.

571-587 "Even now—this morning—is the fatal dawn that will cut me off from Odysseus' house. For now I will propose a contest. It will be with those axes, twelve in all, that Odysseus used to set up in a line in his halls. He would stand at a distance and shoot an arrow through all of them. I will now propose this contest to the suitors. I will go with whomever most easily strings Odysseus' bow with his hands and shoots an arrow through all twelve axes. I will go with him and forsake this house, [580] the one of my wedded life, a beautiful house full of wealth and livelihood, which, I imagine, I will always remember in my dreams."

In reply, Odysseus of many counsels said to her, "Honored wife of Odysseus, the son of Laertes, do not any longer delay this contest in your hall. For Odysseus of many counsels will be here among the suitors. And handling the polished bow, he will string it and shoot an arrow through the iron."

588-601 Penelope wishes the stranger could entertain her for longer. But, she says, since the gods have appointed a proper time and fate for each thing, she must go sleep upon her bed of sorrows—for, she declares, she has been sorrowing ever since Odysseus left for unhappy, evil-causing Ilium. As for the stranger, he should also sleep in the hall.

602-604 And when she had gone to the upper chamber with her handmaids, she grieved over Odysseus, her dear husband, until bright-eyed Athena cast sweet sleep upon her eyelids.

BOOK 20

ODYSSEUS ENDURES
THE SUITORS' DESTRUCTION WILL COME

IN BRIEF: *Odysseus endures the insolent women in his halls. Athena en-
courages him when he worries about how he will fight so many men. With
her, she promises, he can accomplish the deed. Still, Odysseus asks for a
sign. In response, Zeus sends an omen—thunder and the words of a
woman—portending destruction for the suitors. The herdsman Philoetius
meets the stranger Odysseus, wishing him well and explaining his own
plight with the suitors. When the stranger predicts Odysseus' return and
the slaying of the suitors, Philoetius prays for fulfillment. And, he assures
him, he'll help in the fight! Within the hall, the suitors are amazed at Te-
lemachus and his bold words. Athena drives them on in their foolishness.
The seer Theoclymenus sees blood on the walls and dead men descending
to Hades. Soon the suitors will pay.*

GODLIKE ODYSSEUS LAY down to sleep in the portico of the
house *upon oxhide overlaid with many fleeces. Eurynome covered
him with a cloak.* He lay sleepless there, contemplating misfortune
for the suitors in his spirit. And the women came out from the
hall—those who mixed in love with the suitors. They were laughing
and making merry with one another.

Odysseus' spirit stirred within his dear chest, [10] and he con-
sidered in his heart and spirit whether he should rush upon them
and kill each one or let them mix in love with the arrogant suitors
one last time. His heart howled and barked within him at their evil
deeds. And as a bitch stands over her tender whelps howling and
barking at a man she does not know, and she is eager to fight, so his
heart howled and barked within him with indignation at their evil
deeds. Even so, he struck his chest and admonished his heart,

saying, "Endure, my heart! You once endured an even worse thing than this when the irresistible Cyclops devoured your [20] mighty comrades. But you endured until your cunning wisdom led you out from the cave where you imagined you would die."

That's what Odysseus said, addressing the dear heart in his chest. And in complete obedience his heart continued to endure even though he himself tossed from side to side.

25-43 Athena appears in the form of a woman next to Odysseus and asks him why he's not sleeping. After all, he's in his own house with his wife and child. Odysseus admits that he's been worrying about how he alone will slay all the suitors. And if he's successful, then where will he flee?

44-62 The goddess, bright-eyed Athena, said to him, "Unhappy, obstinate one! Many a man puts his trust in a friend who is even weaker than I am, one that is mortal and not as wise as I am. But I am a god!—and I will guard you to the very end, through all your toils. Now I say to you plainly, even if fifty groups of speech-endowed men [50] stand around us, eagerly desiring to kill us in battle, even then you would seize and drive off their cattle and fat sheep.

"But now let sleep take you in hand—there's trouble and distress in keeping a wakeful watch all night long. And know that even now you're already emerging from your misfortunes."

That's what Athena said, and she poured sleep upon his eyelids. As for the heavenly goddess, she returned to Olympus.

Now, while sleep seized him, limb-relaxing sleep releasing the cares of his spirit, his sage wife woke up. And sitting on her soft bed, she began to cry. But when her spirit was satisfied with weeping, [60] the godlike woman prayed to Artemis, saying, "Artemis, queen goddess, daughter of Zeus, I pray that you would now shoot your arrow into my breast, taking my life away this very instant!"

63-96 Penelope further prays for death, even as the daughters of Pandareus were blotted out by the gods, she prays. At least then she can go down to Hades without making another man glad. Ah, but the gods send her evil

dreams, she says, untruthful dreams—as with the dream she earlier had of
a young Odysseus laying by her side before he went off to Troy.

The dawn comes as Penelope is praying. Odysseus hears her and
muses. Gathering his bed, he lifts his hands and prays to Zeus.

97-121 "Father Zeus, if you gods willingly brought me over dry
earth and the watery sea to my own land, even though you have
afflicted me with distress, [100] then let someone who is now awake
inside the house utter some good word of omen for me, and may
another sign from Zeus be given from outside the house."

That's what Odysseus said in prayer, and Zeus the counselor
heard him. At once, the god thundered from radiant Olympus, out
of the clouds above, and godlike Odysseus was glad.

Then a woman grinding at the mill uttered a word of omen. She
was within the house and nearby—where the shepherd of the peo-
ple's mills were located. Twelve women usually worked at the mills,
preparing barley meal and grinding the wheat, the nourishment of
men. Now, however, the other women were sleeping, having already
ground their wheat. [110] This one woman alone had not finished her
work since she was very weak. But stopping the mill, she uttered a
word, a sign for her master. "Father Zeus, you who rule over gods
and men, you have thundered very loudly from the starry sky—yet
there's no cloud anywhere in the sky! Surely this is a portent you are
showing to some man. I ask you, then, to fulfill for me—for wretched
me—this word I speak. May the suitors this day hold their glad feast
in Odysseus' halls for the very last time—those men who have loos-
ened my limbs with heart-grieving, troublesome toil, while I ground
for them their barley. May this be their final meal!"

[120] That's what she said, and godlike Odysseus was glad to
hear the omen and Zeus' thunder. And he declared he would make
the wrongdoers pay.

122-184 *Telemachus awakes from sleep soon after, dresses with a tunic,*
sword, and sandals, and taking his spear, he ventures out to the hall where
the serving women are kindling the fire. Seeing Eurycleia, he asks her if she
has made provisions for the stranger. His mother, he says, neglects such men,

even though she is wise. Eurycleia asks Telemachus not to blame his mother. She explains that they took care of him the night before. Satisfied with the report, Telemachus marches off with his two dogs to the assembly place.

Eurycleia turns to the serving women and commands them to prepare the hall for the day—wipe down the tables, clean the cups and mixing bowls, cover the chairs with purple, and go to the well for water. The suitors are coming, she declares. The many women obey. When they return from the well, there are men splitting wood for the fire. And soon, the swineherd Eumaeus comes along, driving three fat hogs. Spotting Odysseus, he asks him if the Achaeans have been kinder to him. Or do they still hurl their insults? Odysseus curses the suitors for their lack of shame, praying for revenge.

While they are talking, the goatherd Melanthius shows up with two shepherds, driving the best of the goats ahead of him for the suitors. He's once again rude to Odysseus, asking him if he, the stranger, plans to stay on at the house in such an unfitting manner. Odysseus doesn't answer. Instead, he silently contemplates evil for the goatherd.

185-186 A third man joined them. He was Philoetius, a leader of men, driving a barren cow and fat goats for the suitors.

187-196 *Approaching Eumaeus, Philoetius asks him who the stranger is—his land and people. He calls the stranger "ill-fated" since he looks like a lord who has been reduced to wandering by the gods.*

197-203 Drawing near to Odysseus, Philoetius stretched out his right hand in greeting, and spoke to him with winged words, "Rejoice, father-stranger! May happiness eventually be yours, though now you are carrying the heavy weight of wretchedness! Father Zeus, no other god is more destructive than you are! You have no pity on men, even though it is you yourself who have brought them into being. Instead, you plunge them into misfortune and wretched pains."

204-212 *Philoetius explains that he was distressed to see the stranger, for he reminds him of Odysseus, who must likewise be clothed in tatters and roaming, or dead in Hades. But if he is dead, then I am unhappy, he declares—I to whom he entrusted his cattle long ago.*

213-217 Ah, but now strangers call on me to drive these cattle and fat goats for themselves to eat. They disregard the son of the house, and they don't fear the wrath of the gods. Instead, even now they eagerly desire to split up our absent master's possessions. As for me, the spirit in my dear chest whirls with thoughtful consideration.

218-229 *Philoetius explains that he has long considered leaving his master's estate for another, except that he still thinks that maybe—just maybe—he will return and scatter the suitors. Acknowledging the herdsman's evident wisdom and goodness, Odysseus swears an oath.*

230-246 "Be my witness now, Zeus, god above all gods, and this table of hospitality, and the hearth of blameless Odysseus to which I have come. Truly, while you are here, Odysseus will come home. And you will see with your own eyes, if you are willing, the slaying of the suitors who rule here."

And the herdsman of the cattle said to him, "May the son of Cronus fulfill your words! Then you would know the strength I have and how my hands act with might!"

Using similar words, Eumaeus prayed to all the gods that wise Odysseus might come home.

[240] That's how these men spoke to one another. Yet meanwhile, the suitors were plotting the fate of death for Telemachus. Nevertheless, a bird came flying at them on their left—a soaring eagle, clutching a trembling dove. Observing this, Amphinomus spoke among them in the assembly place, saying, "Friends, our plot won't go well—the plan to murder Telemachus. Let us instead turn to feasting."

247-267 *The suitors gladly walk to the house and prepare for the feast, roasting the meat and mixing the wine. When they recline to eat, Philoetius serves the bread and Melanthius the wine.*

And now, Telemachus cunningly seats Odysseus inside the hall, giving him meat and pouring wine into a golden cup. He assures the stranger that he will defend him against the suitors' jeering and rough handling. It's his house, he claims, the one secured for him by his father. And turning

to the suitors, he orders them not to harass the stranger so that no strife
will arise.

268-274 That's what Telemachus said, and the suitors all bit their
lips in astonishment that Telemachus had spoken so boldly.

[270] Antinous, the son of Eupeithes, said to them, "As hard as it
is to bear, Achaeans, let us accept the command of Telemachus, even
though he threatens us with his berating rant. I say this because Zeus
himself, the son of Cronus, hindered our plan. Otherwise, we would
have long ago silenced him in these halls—shrill speaker though he
is!"

275-332 *Telemachus ignores his speech, and the suitors turn to feasting. At
the prodding of Athena, the wealthy suitor Ctesippus jests and throws an ox
hoof at Odysseus, calling it an honor-gift in addition to the large portion of
meat Telemachus has rightly given him. Seeing it fly, Odysseus ducks, and
the missile zips past him and hits the wall. Angry, Telemachus scolds Ctes-
ippus. Lucky you! he declares. If that had hit him, I would have killed you
with my spear! And this feast would have turned into a funeral!*

*And turning to the rest of the suitors, Telemachus commands them to
stop any outrageous behavior. He explains that once he was young and
didn't know any better. But now he knows the difference between noble and
ignoble behavior. He only puts up with all the feasting because of their great
number. What can he do? Still, he insists there must be no more deliberate
harm. He would rather die at the tip of their bronze swords than witness
such shameful behavior—strangers and servants abused!*

*Hearing his speech, everyone falls silent until Agelaus, the son of
Damastor, advises everyone to heed Telemachus' words and leave the
stranger and servants alone. And directing his speech to Telemachus and
Penelope, he expresses his understanding that they have put off the marriage
as long as they expected Odysseus would show up.*

333-344 "But now it is clear that he will not return home. But come,
Telemachus, go and sit by your mother and tell her that she must
marry whomever the best man is, the man who offers the most gifts,
so that you may keep and enjoy everything your father left for you,

eating and drinking, while your mother manages the house of another man."

In turn mindful Telemachus answered him, "No, Agelaus, I swear by Zeus and by the sufferings of my father, [340], who has perished far from Ithaca or is roaming somewhere, that it is not I myself who delay my mother's marriage. Rather, I call on her to marry whatever man she wishes to marry. Moreover, I give gifts past counting! Nevertheless, I feel shame to drive her from the house with a speech compelling her to go. May god not do such a thing!"

345-366 At this point, Athena causes the suitors to behave crazily. They laugh wildly with wandering thoughts—and yet they cry and feel horrible. Observing them, the seer Theoclymenus speaks out, describing the situation, including the blood dripping from the meat and down the walls. Not only that, but he sees a great number of phantom-forms waiting to go down to the dark gloom of the world below. Laughing with the others, Eurymachus commands the youngest among them to carry him out of the hall and outside. Theoclymenus, however, suggests he can leave with his own feet.

367-370 "With them I'll go through the door, for I perceive evil nearing you, misfortune that not one of you suitors may escape or avoid—[370] you men who behave with reckless arrogance in the house of godlike Odysseus."

371-383 Theoclymenus goes to his host Peiraeus, who gladly takes him in. As for the suitors, they begin to tease Telemachus for the kind of guests that come to his house—the wanderer and the prophet! How unfortunate he is in his guests! they say. Telemachus should pack them off to Sicily to sell as slaves.

384-394 That's what the suitors said. But Telemachus ignored their words. Rather, in silence he watched his father, patiently waiting for the moment when he would lay his hands on the shameless suitors.

Now the daughter of Icarius, thoughtful Penelope, had taken her very beautiful chair and set it down opposite the door. From there she listened to the words of each man in the hall, [390] where they had prepared their meal amid great laughter—a delicious meal, one that would satisfy their desires with all the beasts they had slaughtered. But how could any meal be more unpleasant, more unfavorable, than the one that a goddess and a strong man would soon set before them? Still, they were the first to contrive shameful deeds!

BOOK 21

THE CONTEST OF THE GREAT BOW
ODYSSEUS PARTICIPATES

IN BRIEF: *Penelope retrieves and presents the great bow of Odysseus to the suitors for a contest. Whoever strings the bow and shoots an arrow through twelve axes will win her hand in marriage. The suitors try without success. Meanwhile, Odysseus reveals himself to Eumaeus and Philoetius, who assure him of their loyalty and willingness to fight. Contrary to the suitors' wishes, he takes up and attempts to string the bow.*

A ND NOW THE goddess, bright-eyed Athena, slipped into the mind of thoughtful Penelope, the daughter of Icarius, the thought to offer the suitors in the halls of Odysseus the bow and gray iron—this to be a contest and the beginning of the slaughter. And so, Penelope climbed the long stairway of her house, took the curved key—bronze with an ivory handle—and went with her handmaids to a far-off storeroom, where her lord's treasures were stored. There lay [10] bronze, gold, and well-wrought iron. There was also his curved bow, bending backwards, and the quiver for his arrows, with many groan-causing arrows still in it. These were gifts that Odysseus' friend Iphitus, the son of Eurytus, a man like the immortals, had given him when he met him in Lacedaemon.

15-67 Odysseus met Iphitus when he was in Messene, on the mainland, retrieving lost sheep, while Iphitus was at the same time looking for horses. Heracles later killed Iphitus. But before then, Odysseus gave him a sword and spear, and Iphitus gave the bow to Odysseus—one that he never took into war.

Penelope opens the well-crafted door and steps through the oak threshold into the storeroom. Before her are chests holding fragrant clothing.

Reaching up, she retrieves the bow from its peg and holds it, weeping as she takes it from its radiant case. Then, having enough of weeping, Penelope walks to the hall with the bow and arrows in hand, her handmaids carrying the rest. And coming to the hall and the suitors, she speaks to them from behind a veil she has draped before her face.

68-79 "Listen to me, you proud suitors. You have plagued this house by eating and drinking without end, [70] even though its master has been gone for a very long time. You have no excuse to offer aside from your wish to marry me, to take me as your wife.

"But come, suitors, since your prize has appeared to you. I offer you the great bow of godlike Odysseus. And I will go with the man who is able to string the bow most easily with his hands and shoot an arrow through all twelve axes. Yes, with him I will go, and I will abandon this home where I have lived my married life, one so beautiful and filled with wealth and whatever else it takes to live. I imagine that I will forever remember it in my dreams."

80-89 *Turning to Eumaeus, Penelope has him deliver the bow and axes to the suitors. He weeps as he does so, along with the herdsman Philoetius, causing the suitor Antinous to scold them for crying in front of the mistress of the house, and thus troubling her. He goes on talking.*

90-100 "And leave the bow here to be a mad contest for the suitors. I suppose that this polished bow will neither be bent nor strung with ease since there is no man among all the suitors who is so powerful as Odysseus was. I myself saw him once and remember him, though I was then only a child."

That's what Antinous said. Even so, the spirit in his chest hoped to string the bow and shoot an arrow through the iron. Yet he would be the first man to taste an arrow sprung from the hands of blameless Odysseus, the very man whom he dishonored [100] as he sat in Odysseus' halls.

101-139 *Antinous encourages his comrades to come and take their turn. Before they do, however, Telemachus stands and speaks out. Here, he says, is your prize—a lady unlike any throughout the Achaean land. He bids them forward to try their strength on the bow. But first, let me try it, he says. He wants to see what kind of a man he is. Telemachus sets up the axes by planting them in the dirt of the packed floor, and he tries—once, twice—to bend and string the bow. On the third try, he's very close, but Odysseus nods to him to back off. He does, lamenting his feigned weakness. He places the bow on the ground and sits down.*

140-142 Then Antinous, the son of Eupeithes, spoke among them, "Rise up in order, all you comrades, from left to right, beginning from where the cupbearer pours the wine."

143-192 *The diviner Leiodes, the son of Oenops, who abhors the suitors and their behavior, stands first to try. Pulling hard, he cannot bend or string the bow. After his attempt, he prophesies failure for the suitors, suggesting that "this bow will take the life and breath of many of the best men." He advises they look for other women to marry after they fail at the bow.*

Antinous is offended by his remarks—as if the bow will take the breath and life of many just because he, Leiodes, cannot bend it! No, your mother simply didn't give birth to one who could accomplish such a deed!

Turning to the goatherd Melanthius, Antinous sends him to build a fire and collect a great cake of fat so that the "young men" can warm the bow and lubricate it. Nevertheless, when they try this, they still cannot bend the bow. Homer judges they "lack the strength." Even so, Antinous and Eury-machus, the leaders of the suitors and the best in manly excellence, were still making an attempt.

Meanwhile, the swineherd Eumaeus and the cowherd Philoetius leave the house. The stranger Odysseus trails them to the gate and beyond in order to speak to them.

193-216 "Cowherd—and you too, swineherd. Should I tell you something, or should I keep it to myself? No, my spirit calls on me to speak. How ready would you be to defend Odysseus if he suddenly came from some land—if some god brought him home? Would you support Odysseus or the suitors? Speak now as your heart and spirit call on you to speak."

And the cattle herdsman answered him, [200] "Father Zeus, may you fulfill this longing wish! May Odysseus return and some god guide him! Then you will know what sort of power mine is and how my hands obey."

Eumaeus prayed in a similar manner to all the gods—that wise Odysseus might return to his own home.

Consequently, when Odysseus knew with certainty the mind of each man, he answered them once again, saying, "It is me! I am Odysseus here in my house! After much suffering and many toils, I have come in the twentieth year to my homeland. [210] And of all my servants, I know that you two alone long for my homecoming. I've heard none of the rest praying that I might come home again. To you, then, I will tell the truth about what will be. If a god subdues the lordly suitors by my hand, then I will bring each of you a wife, and I will give you possessions and build you a house near to my own. And from that time on, I will consider you to be the comrades of Telemachus and his brothers."

217-244 To prove his claim, Odysseus shows Eumaeus and Philoetius the scar caused by the boar. They instantly know the truth! And so, they cry and hug and kiss Odysseus, and Odysseus does the same until he suggests they must stop, or someone will see them and tell the suitors. He orders them to go into the hall one by one—after he goes in, he says. When inside, Eumaeus will give the bow to Odysseus and tell the women to lock the doors and leave. And if the women hear any strife-caused noise, they should simply go on with their weaving. Otherwise, Philoetius will close and bar the gates of the court.

When Odysseus finishes giving directions, he goes inside, and they follow him some moments later.

245-255 Eurymachus was now holding the bow in his hands, trying to heat it up in the bright fire. Even so, he was not able to string it, and so he groaned in his noble heart. Frustrated, he spoke to the others, "I can't believe it! Truly, I'm distressed for myself and for all of you. [250] I don't so much bewail the lost marriage—though I am annoyed at that. After all, there are many other Achaean women, some in sea-girt Ithaca itself, and some in other cities. Rather, I bewail the possibility that in strength we fall so far short of godlike Odysseus because we cannot string his bow. If this is the case, then it will be a disgrace that men to come will hear about!"

256-273 Antinous agrees that no one of the suitors will string the bow—at least not on this day, he says, for it is Apollo's feast day. He suggests that today is more appropriate for eating and drinking—and that tomorrow will be better for the contest. And so, the suitors put aside the bow for now, and the wine pourers pour so each man can drink to his heart's content.

274-288 But with a mind set on deception, Odysseus of many counsels spoke to them, "Listen to me, you suitors of the glorious queen, let me tell you what the spirit within my chest calls on me to say. Most of all, I entreat Eurymachus and godlike Antinous since you appropriately suggested that you presently stop with the bow and leave the matter with the gods. [280] In the morning the god will grant strength to whomever he wishes. But come and give me the polished bow so that in your presence I may prove the strength of my hands. I wonder whether I still have the strength I used to have in my agile limbs or whether my wanderings and lack of proper care have destroyed it."

That's what Odysseus said, and the suitors all grew excessively indignant, fearing that he would bend and string the polished bow. Antinous scolded him, saying, "Wretched stranger! You have no sense! Not even a little!"

289-319 Antinous suggests that Odysseus should be glad to sit and feast with them—never mind string the bow! He must be drunk—even as Eurytion the centaur was drunk when he stirred up the men in the household of Peirithous against him so that they cut off his ears and nose. It is why humans have long feuded with the centaurs. Antinous concludes with a threat: if Odysseus strings the bow, no one will be happy with him or kind. Rather, they'll send him off to king Echetus, a man who revels in hurting other men. So drink in silence, he commands, and don't compete with young men!

Hearing this, Penelope rebukes Antinous. What, she asks, do you suppose he will take me as his wife if he is successful? It won't happen, she says.

320-336 In response, Eurymachus, the son of Polybus, said to her, "Daughter of Icarius, thoughtful Penelope, it is not that we imagine the man will lead you away to his home. That's unlikely! But we do dread the talk of men and women that would shame us. What if some other cowardly man among the Achaeans were to say, 'Men far inferior are wooing the wife of a noble man. They are not able to string his polished bow. But another man, a wandering beggar, showed up, and he was able to string the bow with ease and shoot an arrow through the iron.'"

[330] Thoughtful Penelope once again spoke to him, saying, "Eurymachus, there can be no glory report in the land for men who dishonor the best of men and consume the goods of his house. Why, then, do you count this as disgraceful? Look—the stranger is very tall and well-built, and he calls himself the son of a good father. But come and give him the polished bow so that we can see."

337-347 *Penelope promises the stranger good clothing, a spear, a sword, and sandals for his feet if he succeeds. More, she promises to send him wherever he wishes to go. And speaking up, Telemachus asserts his right to do as he wishes with the bow.*

348-355 "No man here will thwart my will, even if I wished to give this bow to the stranger as a gift for him to take away. [350] But you, mother, go to your chamber and busy yourself with your own tasks, the loom and the distaff, and call on your handmaids to ply their own tasks. As for the bow, the men will worry about it, but I most of all since I have the authority in the house."

Seized with amazement, Penelope went back to her chamber, storing the wise saying of her son in her heart.

356-377 *Going upstairs, Penelope cries for her dear husband until Athena causes her to fall soundly asleep. Meanwhile, the swineherd Eumaeus is*

carrying the bow to Odysseus amid a storm of suitor frenzy and indigna-
tion. Where are you taking that, you fool? They threaten him with death.
Frightened in this way, Eumaeus sets the bow down. But from the other
side of the hall, Telemachus calls on him to carry on. He even threatens
him if he doesn't—at which the suitors laugh.

378-389 And so the swineherd carried the bow through the hall.
And coming up to wise Odysseus, he put it into his hands.

[380] Then, calling aside Eurycleia the nurse, he said to her, "Te-
lemachus commands you, wise Eurycleia, to bar the close-fitting
doors of the hall. And if any of the women hear groaning or noisy
strife within the walls, do not let them rush out. But they are to re-
main where they are in silence at their work."

When he spoke in this manner, Eurycleia offered no winged
words in response; rather, she closed and barred the doors leading
into the very comfortable halls.

In silence, Philoetius passed out of the house and closed and
barred the gates of the well-enclosed court.

390-403 *After securing the gates, Philoetius returns to his seat and*
watches Odysseus, who is holding and inspecting the bow to see if it has
become rotten through the years. One of the suitors teases him for being a
bow expert or a trader in bows. Another wishes good luck to him in pro-
portion to his ability to string the bow.

404-434 That's what the suitors said. But Odysseus of many coun-
sels strung the great bow just after he lifted it and scanned it on
every side. Even as one well-skilled in lyre playing and singing eas-
ily stretches a string around its peg, securing at each end the twisted
sheep-gut, so did Odysseus string the great bow without effort.
[410] And he held it in his right hand and tried the string, which
sang sweetly beneath his touch, singing like a swallow.

Seeing this, great consternation fell upon the suitors, and all
their faces changed color. And Zeus thundered loudly, manifesting
his signal to begin. Hearing this, much-enduring godlike Odysseus
was glad at heart that the son of scheming Cronus had sent him a

portent. And so, he took up the swift arrow, which lay by him on the table, drawn, whereas the other arrows were still in the hollow quiver—even those that the Achaeans were destined to taste. Odysseus took this arrow and set it upon the bridge of the bow. Then he drew the bowstring and the notched arrow. [420] And from the chair where he sat, he let fly the shaft with sure aim. He didn't miss one axe's ring from first to last, but the bronze-tipped arrow cleanly sped through all.

And turning to Telemachus, he said, "Telemachus—the stranger that sits in your halls brings no shame on you, nor in any way did I miss the mark or labor for long in stringing the bow. My strength is unbroken—not as the suitors have mockingly despised. But now it is time for the evening meal to be prepared for the Achaeans while there is still light. And thereafter we will make sport [430] with song and with the lyre since these things attend a feast."

He spoke, making a sign with his eyebrows, and Telemachus, the dear son of divine Odysseus, fastened his sharp sword around his waist, took his spear up in his right hand, and stood by the chair at his father's side, armed with gleaming bronze.

BOOK 22

SLAUGHTER IN THE HALL
THE SUITORS PAY

IN BRIEF: *Odysseus and his men—Telemachus, Eumaeus, and Philoe-*
tius—kill the suitors, showing mercy only to a few. After the slaughter,
and after Eurycleia identifies the women who betrayed Odysseus, the
twelve guilty serving women clean the hall. They punish these same
women with a shameful death, as well as the goatherd Melanthius. Once
the work of revenge and cleansing is complete, the other women, including
Penelope, come into the hall and see Odysseus for the first time.

N OW ODYSSEUS OF many counsels stripped off his rags and
sprang to the great threshold with the bow and quiver full of
arrows. He poured out the swift shafts by his feet and addressed
the suitors, saying, "At last this awful contest is over! And now I
turn to another target in order to hit what no man has hit be-
fore—may Apollo grant me the glory-boast!"

So he spoke. And he aimed the sharp arrow at Antinous, who
was just raising his beautiful cup to his lips. [10] The cup was gold
and double-handled. Even now he guided it with his hands so that
he might drink the wine. Death was far from his mind and
thoughts—for who could imagine that in the company of feasters
one of the crowd, however strong, could deliver to him evil death
and black fate? But Odysseus aimed an arrow and struck Antinous
in the throat. The sharp point passed through his tender neck and
out the back. The man slumped over to the side, and the cup fell
from his hand as he was struck. At once there came a thick stream
of blood through his nostrils. Roughly, [20] he pushed the table
from him with a kick of his foot, scattering all the food on the floor.
And the bread and roasted meat were ruined.

22-33 Seeing this and believing the shot was an accident, the suitors reprimand Odysseus, telling him how he will pay for what he did. Soon, they say, vultures will be devouring his flesh! And quickly they reach for a spear and a shield. But they're gone!

34-54 Then with an angry glance from beneath his brows, Odysseus of many counsels answered them, "You dogs! You thought that I would never come home again from the land of the Trojans, and so you squandered my household goods, and you forced yourself on my servants to sleep with them! And while I was still alive, you unlawfully wooed my wife, having no fear of the gods, who possess the wide sky above [40], nor do you fear the indignation of men that will come in due time. But now the ropes of destruction have been tied around all of you!"

That's what Odysseus said, and pale fear seized them all. Each man glanced around to see how he could escape utter destruction.

In response, Eurymachus alone said to him, "If indeed you are Odysseus of Ithaca come home again, then you've spoken justly regarding all that the Achaeans have done—the reckless, arrogant behavior here in the great hall and out in the field. But now Antinous, the man who was to blame for it all, has fallen and is dead. He was the one who began this business—[50] not so much because he desired or needed to marry, but with another purpose in mind, one which the son of Cronus did not accomplish for him. He wished to be king in the land of settled Ithaca, and so he desired to lay in ambush for your son to slay him. Even so, now he has been struck down, as was his due. Now he is dead. Still, spare your own people."

55-59 Eurymachus promises recompense for all the waste—the drink and food. They will repay Odysseus in oxen, bronze, and gold.

60-94 Then with an angry glance from beneath his brows, Odysseus of many counsels said to him, "Eurymachus, I won't stop my hands from slaughtering the suitors until they've paid the full price of their many transgressions—not even if they gave me everything their fathers left them, or all they now have, or whatever wealth they can get their hands on. Your choice now is to fight or flee—if anyone wishes to escape the fates of death. But some men, I imagine, will not evade utter destruction."

That's what Odysseus said, and their knees and dear hearts were loosened. Eurymachus spoke again for a second time, saying, [70] "Friends! You see that this man will not check his invincible hands. Now that he has the polished bow and the quiver full of arrows, he will shoot from the planed threshold until he kills us all. Come now, let us take thought of battle. Draw your swords and hold the tables up against his deadly arrows. Let's move against him together. It's possible we can thrust him from the threshold and the doorway. Then we can reach the city and quickly raise the alarm, and this man will have soon shot his last."

Saying this, Eurymachus drew his sharp, two-edged sword [80] made of bronze, and he sprang at Odysseus with a terrible cry. But at the same moment, godlike Odysseus released an arrow that flew and struck him on his chest right by the nipple. The swift arrow stopped in his liver, fixed there. And Eurymachus dropped the sword, letting it fall from his hand to the ground. He squirmed over the table, bent over and fell down, spilling his food and two-handled cup on the floor. His spirit in agony, he struck the earth with his forehead, and kicking with both feet he shook his chair until it toppled over as the mists of death poured over his eyes.

Amphinomus then darted at glorious Odysseus, [90] rushing straight at him with his sharp sword drawn in the hope that Odysseus might give way before him from the door. But Telemachus was too quick for him. He cast and struck him from behind with a bronze-tipped spear. He hit him between the shoulders and drove the spear through his chest. Amphinomus fell with a thud and struck the earth with his forehead.

95-159 Fearing someone might strike him, Telemachus returns to his father without retrieving the spear. Reaching him, he offers to go and fetch armor and spears from the storeroom. Odysseus nods, ordering him to be quick so that the other men won't have enough time to drive him from the doorway. Telemachus runs off and grabs four shields, eight spears, and four bronze helmets with horsehair plumes. Quickly, then, he, Eumaeus, and Philoetius arm while Odysseus fires a stream of arrows at the suitors, killing a man with each shot. They fall side by side. When there are no more arrows, Odysseus sets the bow down. He arms and picks up two bronze-tipped spears.

Meanwhile, the suitor Agelaus wonders if they can get a man out through a side door to raise the alarm. The goatherd Melanthius says it is unlikely if not impossible. He then offers to get arms from the storeroom. And so, making his way through a narrow passageway, Melanthius goes to the storeroom and selects twelve shields, spears, and helmets, and returns to the suitors.

Seeing the suitors arm themselves, Odysseus grows weak with fear thinking about the great task ahead of him. He turns to Telemachus and blames the treachery on one of the women. Surely one of them, he says, supplied the suitors with the arms. Telemachus immediately admits his own fault. It was me, he says. I left the door ajar when I fetched the arms. He turns and orders Eumaeus to go and close the door and to see if, as he suspects, Melanthius, the son of Dolius, is responsible for what has happened.

160-177 They spoke to one another in this manner. But the goatherd Melanthius went again to the storeroom to bring even more beautiful armor. The noble swineherd saw him, and at once he said to Odysseus, who was standing nearby, "God-born son of Laertes, much-able Odysseus, there is that destructive man again, the one we suspected, going to the storeroom. Speak the truth, then. Should I kill him if I prove to be the better man, or should I bring him here to you so that he can pay for the many crimes that he has plotted in your house?"

[170] In reply, Odysseus of many counsels said to him, "Telemachus and I will hold the noble suitors here in the hall, however eager they are to fight. As for the two of you, take Melanthius and bend his feet and arms behind him. Drag him into the storeroom and tie wooden planks behind his back. Then lash a twisted rope around him and hoist him up along the post until he reaches high to the roof beams. That way he will stay alive for a long time and suffer pains hard to bear."

178-186 *That's what they do. As soon as Melanthius, carrying a helmet and Laertius' old shield, moves to exit the storeroom, they seize him.*

187-193 Eumaeus and Philoetius dragged him by the hair and flung him down to the ground. Melanthius was terrified. They bound his feet and hands with painful bonds, [190] binding them firmly behind his back, just as the son of Laertes had ordered, much-enduring godlike Odysseus. And they lashed a twisted rope around him and hoisted him up along the post until he reached high to the roof beams.

194-204 *Eumaeus mocks Melanthius. And leaving him there to suffer, they return to Odysseus and Telemachus. Now it is the four of them against the many in the great hall.*

205-207 But Athena, the daughter of Zeus, drew near them. She was like Mentor in form and voice. Odysseus saw her and was glad.

208-247 *Odysseus calls on Mentor for help, even though he knows it is truly Athena. From the other side of the hall, the suitor Agelaus, the son of Damastor, threatens Mentor. If you help Odysseus, we will kill you once we have killed the four of them. And your children will lose their inheritance since we will take all your property. Athena grows angry and chastises Odysseus. Where is your might? she asks. Now that you are home, you cower, whereas when you were battling for Helen in Troy, you fought mightily. Still, she promises help. Stand by my side and watch what I do, she commands. Rather than helping, however, she changes form to a swallow and flies up to a roof beam. She wishes to test his strength—his and his son's.*

Agelaus—who is now in the lead with Eurynomus, Amphimedon, Demoptolemus, Polybus, and Peisander, the son of Polyctor (Homer declares that these stand out as "the best in excellence" of the remaining suitors)—calls out to the suitors.

248-291 "Friends—at last this man will check his invincible hands. Mentor has left them after uttering empty boasts. [250] There they are, left alone by the front door. Therefore, let's not all throw our long spears at once, but you six throw yours first in the hope that Zeus will deliver Odysseus up to be struck, and that we will win glory. Once he falls, we don't have to worry about the rest."

That's what Agelaus said, and they all eagerly hurled their spears as he urged them to do. But Athena made their effort useless. One man struck the door post of the well-built hall. Another hit the close-fitting door. Yet another man's ashen spear, heavy with bronze, struck the wall.

[260] And when the men were safe, having avoided the suitor's spears, much-enduring godlike Odysseus was the first to speak among them. "Friends—now I give the word. We too will cast our spears into the crowd of suitors, those men who intend to kill us in addition to all their former wrongs!"

That's what Odysseus said. And they all carefully aimed and cast their sharp spears. Odysseus struck Demoptolemus. Telemachus hit Euryades. The swineherd speared Elatus. And the cattle herder killed Peisander. So, at the same moment, all these men bit the dust of the broad floor with their teeth, [270] while the suitors drew back to the innermost part of the great hall.

Nevertheless, the others rushed forward and yanked the spears from the dead bodies. Again, the suitors hurled their spears, but Athena made their effort useless, despite their numbers. One man struck the door post of the well-built hall. Another hit the close-fitting door. Yet another man's ashen spear, heavy with bronze, struck the wall. Still, Amphimedon struck Telemachus on the hand by the wrist—a grazing blow—and the bronze tore the surface of the skin. And with his long spear, Ctesippus [280] scratched Eumaeus' shoulder just above his shield, but the spear flew over and fell to the ground.

Once again Odysseus, the wise and cunning man, along with his men, hurled their sharp spears into the crowd of suitors. And once again, Odysseus, the sacker of cities, struck Eurydamas. Telemachus hit Amphimedon. The swineherd speared Polybus. And after these fell, the cattle herder struck Ctesippus on the chest. He boasted over him, saying, "Son of Polytherses, fond as you are of jeering at others, never again will you give in to folly and speak big words. But leave the matter to the gods since they are far mightier than you. [290] This gift should balance out the hoof you earlier gave to Odysseus when he went begging throughout the house."

292-296 And now, fighting hand to hand, Odysseus wounds Agelaus, the son of Damastor, with his spear, and Telemachus wounds Leiocritus, the son of Evenor, with a spear to his belly.

297-309 Athena then held up her aegis, the destroyer of mortals, high up by the roof, and the suitors' minds were panic-stricken. They fled through the hall like a herd of cattle [300] that the darting gadfly falls on and drives along in springtime when the days grow long. And even as vultures with crooked talons and curved beaks descend from the mountains and dart at smaller birds that skim the plain, flying low beneath the clouds—and the vultures swoop on them and kill them as the tiny birds have no defense or way of escape, and men rejoice at the chase—even so did the four men attack the suitors in the hall, striking them right and left. Wretched groaning rose from them as their heads were struck and beaten. And the ground swam with blood.

310-319 The diviner Leiodes rushes forward to take hold of Odysseus' knees and beg for mercy, claiming that he took no part in the suitor's wrongdoing, and that he actually tried to stop them.

320-329 Then with an angry glance from beneath his brows, Odysseus of many counsels said to him, "If you declare yourself the diviner for these men, then you must have often prayed for the delay of my joyous return, and that my dear wife would go with you and bear children for you. Therefore, you will not escape grievous death."

Saying this, Odysseus seized in his strong hand a sword that was nearby—one that Agelaus had dropped to the ground when he was killed—and with this sword he struck him, cutting through the middle of Leiodes' neck. The man was still speaking when his head fell to the ground and rolled in the dust.

330-370 *Similar to Leiodes, Phemius, the son of Terpes, also rushes for-*
ward to receive mercy from Odysseus—this rather than darting to the
safety of Zeus' altar in the courtyard, as he first thought to do. Setting his
lyre down, Phemius takes Odysseus' knees and makes a case for the value
he brings to the master of the house as a singer. Not only that, he says, but
the suitors forced him to sing in the house.

Hearing this, Telemachus calls out that Phemius is without guilt. The
herald Medon is too, he asserts, and so we must save him, he advises, unless
he's already been struck and killed. As for Medon, he is hiding beneath a
chair, wrapped in oxhide, hoping to avoid death. When he hears Telemachus'
speech, he rushes forward to his knees and asks him to stop his father from
slaying him in his wrath.

371-389 Odysseus of many counsels smiled and said to him, "Take
courage—Telemachus has delivered and saved you so that you may
know in your spirit and tell others how much better it is to do good
than evil. Both of you—you and the singer of many songs—leave the
hall and sit outside away from the bloody slaughter until I have fin-
ished everything I need to do in the house."

That's what Odysseus said, and the two walked from the hall and
sat down by Zeus' great altar. And sitting there, [380] they glanced
from side to side, still expecting death.

Inside the hall, Odysseus also glanced around, looking through
the house to see if anyone was still alive, hiding there, hoping to
evade black death. But he found no one. Every man had fallen in
the blood and dust. They were like fish that fishermen have caught
in their nets and have pulled up from the gray sea, up to the beach.
And there they lay, heaped on the sand, longing for the waves of
the sea. But the bright sun takes their lives away. Even so, the suit-
ors now lay heaped upon one another.

390-401 *Odysseus now orders Telemachus to go fetch Eurycleia and the*
other women. He does and Eurycleia enters the great hall.

402-418 Eurycleia found Odysseus there among the bodies of the
slain, soiled with all the blood and filth. Like a lion that comes from

feeding on a field-dwelling ox—his great chest, face and sides are stained with blood, and he is terrible to look on—even so was Odysseus soiled, his feet and his hands above. When Eurycleia saw the bodies and the great quantity of blood, she prepared herself to utter loud cries of joy, seeing what a mighty deed had been done. But Odysseus stopped her. He checked her in her eagerness, [410] speaking to her with winged words, "Rejoice in your own spirit, old woman, but hold yourself back and do not cry aloud. It is an unholy thing to boast over slain men. The fate of the gods and their own cruel deeds have conquered these men. They honored no one on earth, whoever came among them, whether a noble or a base man. Therefore, they brought on themselves a shameful death because of their foolish recklessness.

"But come now, name for me the women in the halls. Tell me which ones dishonor me and which ones are without guilt."

419-445 Eurycleia tells him. Out of fifty women, twelve have behaved shamefully, neither honoring Penelope nor her. When Eurycleia offers to go wake Penelope and tell her the news, Odysseus orders her to wait. First, he says, tell the disobedient women to come to the hall. She goes to fetch them. Turning to Telemachus, Eumaeus, and Philoetius, Odysseus explains what they should do—how they should kill the serving women in the courtyard after the women have cleared out the corpses and cleaned the hall "so that they will forget the love of the suitors."

446-479 That's what Odysseus said, and the women came clinging to one another in a throng, wailing terribly and shedding big tears.

First, they carried the bodies of the slain out from the hall and set them down beneath the portico of the high-walled courtyard, [450] propping them up one against another. Odysseus gave the orders and sped on the work. So it was that the serving women carried off the corpses under the force of necessity. And when they were finished, they cleaned the beautiful chairs and tables with water and porous sponges. Telemachus, the cowherd, and the swineherd scraped the floor of the well-built house with hoes, and the serving women carried the scrapings and threw them outside.

When they had ordered everything in the hall, they led the women from the well-built hall to a place between the conical-roofed vaulted chamber and the courtyard's excellent wall. [460] They shut them up there in a narrow space where they could not possibly escape.

Mindful Telemachus was the first to speak to the others, saying, "Let it be by no clean death, free from shame, that I take the lives of these women—the ones who have poured out reproaches on my own head and on my mother, sleeping by the side of the suitors."

That's what Telemachus said, and he tied the cable of a dark-prowed ship to a great pillar and flung it around the vaulted chamber's conical roof. He stretched it high so that none of the women would be able to reach the ground with her feet. And as when wide-winged thrushes or doves fly into a net that has been set up for them in a thicket, [470] seeking their resting place but finding instead a hateful bed—even so the serving women held their heads in a row, and a noose was slipped around the neck of each one so that they would all die in the most pathetic manner. There feet twitched a little, but not for long.

Then Melanthius was led out through the doorway into the court. They cut off his nose and his ears with the ruthless bronze. And they yanked out his intestines and chopped off his genitals and gave them raw to the dogs. And raging with anger, they hacked of his hands and feet.

Afterward, when they had completed this grisly task, they washed their hands and feet and went into Odysseus' house. All their work was done.

480-491 *Inside, Odysseus calls on Eurycleia to bring him sulfur and fire so that he may clean the hall. He also asks her to fetch the other women, including Penelope. She agrees to do so after offering him new clothes. Odysseus orders her to wait on the clothes—the cleaning must come first.*

492-501 That's what Odysseus said, and his dear nurse Eurycleia did not disobey. She brought the sulfur and the fire, and Odysseus thoroughly cleaned the hall, the house, and the courtyard.

After, the old woman passed through Odysseus' beautiful house in order to carry the message to the other women and encourage them to come. They came out from their hall holding torches in their hands. And they gathered around Odysseus, embracing him with affection, kissing his head and shoulders, [500] and taking his hands in their own in loving welcome.

As for Odysseus, a sweet longing to weep and wail aloud seized him. In his heart he knew them all.

BOOK 23

ODYSSEUS AND PENELOPE
SIGNS AND RECOGNITION

IN BRIEF: *Eurycleia reports Odysseus' homecoming to Penelope, who is still doubtful. Penelope goes to see for herself, and though she is standoffish at first, she finally comes to believe the stranger is her husband when Odysseus reveals the sign of the olive tree bedpost. And so, they are finally happily reunited. Lying in bed in love, they tell each other what has happened over the past twenty years. In the morning, Odysseus arms with Telemachus, Eumaeus, and Philoetius. They leave the city for the fields.*

REJOICING AND LAUGHING aloud, the old woman went up to the upper chamber to tell her mistress that her dear husband was in the house. Her knees moved quickly—too quick for her tottering feet. But finally, she stood above Penelope's head, and she spoke to her, saying, "Wake up, Penelope, dear child! Wake up so that you may see with your own eyes what you've desired to see for so many days. Odysseus is here! He's come home at last, and he's killed the arrogant suitors—the very men who have troubled this household, devouring his property and overpowering his son!"

Then thoughtful Penelope said to her, "Dear nurse, the gods have made you crazy—the ones who can make a very thoughtful person thoughtless, and one who rarely thinks things through sound in mind and with discretion. It is the gods who have misled you. Until now your thoughts were always fitting."

15-84 Penelope asks Eurycleia why she's mocking her. And why did she wake her up when she was sleeping so soundly? Any other serving woman would be sorry if she had roused her with such a message! The nurse assures her she's not mocking her. The stranger himself is Odysseus! she

says. And Telemachus knew it all along, but in prudence he kept it to him-
self until his father got revenge. Penelope turns glad. Weeping for joy she
asks if it is true. Has her husband returned? And how did he—one man
alone—slay the suitors? Eurycleia explains that she didn't see the act but
only the result. Odysseus was like a lion stained with the blood of his
prey—a sight that would've warmed your heart! And now the bodies are
stacked by the courtyard gate, and he and the other serving women are
cleaning the hall. He's here! she exclaims. He's come back to you and your
son, and he's won revenge from the suitors!

Penelope warns Eurycleia not to laugh and boast about the suitors. Not
yet. Although she longs for Odysseus' return, she declares, surely the
truth is that one of the immortal gods killed all the suitors out of anger for
all their arrogant deeds, their lack of respect for anyone. Therefore, she
concludes, they suffered because of their own reckless folly. As for Odys-
seus, he'll never return home.

Eurycleia is shocked by Penelope's disbelief. "Your heart is always
doubting," she observes. She goes on to reveal the sign she herself saw
when she was bathing Odysseus, the scar given by the boar. She nearly
told Penelope, but Odysseus forced her to be silent. Anyway, she finishes,
come and see. And if I'm lying, you may slay me.

Penelope agrees to go—to see her son, at least, and the slain suitors,
and the man who killed them.

85-122 Saying this, Penelope went down from the upper chamber.
She debated back and forth in her heart whether she should stand
apart from her dear husband and question him from a distance, or
draw near to him, taking his hand and kissing his head. When she
entered the hall, crossing over the stone threshold, she sat down
across from Odysseus. She sat in the light of the fire, [90] by the
other wall.

As for Odysseus, he was sitting by a tall pillar, looking down
and waiting to see whether his noble wife would say anything to
him when she saw him. But she didn't. She just sat there for a long
time in silence, her heart full of amazement. At one moment she
would gaze upon his face with a long look. But she didn't know
him thanks to the wretched clothing he wore.

Telemachus upbraided her. And speaking to her, he said, "Mother, cruel mother, you have a hard spirit. Why do you hold back from my father? Why do you not sit next to him and question him? [100] No other woman would harden her spirit as you do, nor would she stand apart from her husband, one who after much unfortunate suffering and grievous toil has come to his homeland after twenty years. Even so, your heart is ever harder than stone."

Then thoughtful Penelope said to him, "My child, the spirit in my chest is dazed with wonder. I am unable to speak to him or ask him a question or look him in the face. Even so, if he is truly Odysseus, and if he has really come home, then we will know each other better than others know us [110] since we have signs that we alone understand, signs that are hidden from others."

That's what Penelope said. Much-enduring godlike Odysseus smiled, and at once he spoke to Telemachus with winged words, "Telemachus, leave your mother in the hall so that she may scrutinize me and come to know with certainty who I am. Ah, but now because I am dirty and wear wretched clothing, she dishonors me and will not yet admit who I am.

"But you and I must plan how everything can turn out well—for if a man kills another man among the people in the land, even if the man slain leaves behind only a few relatives to avenge him, [120] he nevertheless goes into exile, abandoning his kinsman and homeland. But we have killed those who were the pillars of the city, the very best young men of Ithaca. This I bid you to consider."

123-152 *Telemachus demurs, noting that his father is the one with the reputation for wisdom and counsel. Odysseus suggests a ruse. The people will pretend a wedding feast is happening within the walls of the courtyard and the house until they have the chance to make it out of the city to their farm in the countryside. And so that's what happens. The many bathe, dress, and dance, and when people pass by outside the walls, they believe that Penelope has finally chosen to marry.*

153-216 But within the house, the housekeeper Eurynome bathed great-hearted Odysseus, anointed him with olive oil, and cast around his shoulders a beautiful cloak and tunic. And Athena poured abundant beauty upon his head, making him taller and stronger to behold, and she made flowing locks of curls fall from his head like the hyacinth flower. As when a man overlays silver with gold, [160] a skillful workman whom Hephaestus and Pallas Athena have trained in every art, and he produces work that is full of grace, even so did the goddess pour grace upon his head and shoulders. Odysseus stepped out of the bath appearing in form like the immortals.

Then he sat down again on the chair from which he had risen, and, facing his wife, he spoke to her these words, "God-possessed woman! Those who have their homes on Olympus have given you—beyond all women—a stubborn heart. No other woman would harden her spirit as you do, nor stand apart from her husband, one who after much unfortunate suffering and grievous toil [170] has come to his homeland after twenty years. Come, then, good nurse, and make ready a bed for me so that I may lay down—since the heart in her chest is made of iron."

Then thoughtful Penelope said to him, "God-possessed man! I am in no way proud, nor do I scorn you, nor am I inordinately amazed. Rather, I know well what kind of a man you were when you went in the long-oared ship from Ithaca. Yet come, Eurycleia, make up his massive bed outside the well-built bridal chamber that he built himself. Move its massive frame and throw bedding upon it—[180] fleeces, bed-cloaks, and coverings."

That's what Penelope said in order to test her husband. But Odysseus, frustrated and angry, said to his diligent wife, "Woman, these are bitter words that you have spoken! Who has put my bed in another place? It would be hard for one man alone to do this, however skilled he is—unless a god came and willed to move it with ease to another spot. But among the living there is no mortal man alive, however young or strong, who would be able to easily force it from its place. No, a great sign was built into the adorned bed. I know because I built it—no one else. [190] There grew a long-leafed olive tree within the courtyard. It was strong and vigorous, its girth much like a pillar. And around this tree I built my chamber until I had finished it. I built it with close-set stones, roofing it over well, and adding to it close-fitting doors. Then I cut away the leafy branches of the long-leafed olive tree. And trimming the trunk from the root, I smoothed it around with a bronze axe, well and skillfully, and made it straight to the line. In this way I fashioned the bedpost. Then I drilled holes in it with the auger. Beginning with these, I carved out my bed until I had finished it. [200] And I decorated it with inlaid gold, silver, and ivory. Over it I stretched oxhide straps, bright with purple. And this is the sign I declare to you. Even so, I do not know, woman, whether my bed still stands where it was or whether someone has set it somewhere else by cutting the olive tree's trunk."

That's what Odysseus said, and right then Penelope's knees were loosened beneath her, and her dear heart was unstrung as she recognized the certain signs that he pointed out. Then bursting into tears, she ran straight toward him, threw her arms around his neck and kissed his head, saying, "Do not be angry with me, Odysseus, since in all other things [210] you were always the most circumspect of men. The gods gave us suffering. The gods begrudged the enjoyment of our youth, not allowing us to stay together and come to the threshold of old age. Ah, but do not be angry with me for this! And do not feel indignation because I did not greet you with affection when I first saw you. I say this because the spirit within my dear chest always shuddered with fear that some mortal man would come here and beguile me, cheating me with words."

217-230 This is how men behave, Penelope asserts. Many scheme for gain. She mentions Argive Helen's shameful deed in sleeping with a foreign man—an act that led to their own misery. But now that Odysseus has made known the sign—that only he, Penelope, and the servant Actor knew about—she is persuaded. She believes it is her husband Odysseus.

231-240 That's what Penelope said. And doing so she aroused in him the longing to weep. And he cried, holding in his arms his heart-pleasing wife, she with diligent thoughts. And welcome as the sight of land is to swimming men, those whose well-built ship Poseidon has wrecked on the sea as it was driven on by the wind and breaking waves, and just a few escape by swimming from the gray sea to land, their skin covered with salt, and gladly they step ashore having escaped misfortune—even so, welcome to Penelope was her husband as she gazed upon him. [240] She could not drop her white arms from around his neck.

241-247 *They both weep. And they would have gone on weeping until dawn if Athena did not pause the passing of night by refusing Dawn the ability to harness Lampus and Phaethon, the horses who bring light to men. Odysseus turns to Penelope and speaks.*

248-255 "Wife, we have not yet reached the end of all our trials. There is yet a considerable amount of work and pain yet to come, [250] long and hard to bear, that I have to accomplish until it is finished to the very end. It is what the phantom-soul of Tiresias prophesied to me on the day I went down into the house of Hades to learn about my own homecoming and that of my comrades. But come, wife, let us go to bed so that, falling asleep together, we may delight in sweet sleep."

256-284 *Penelope agrees to go to bed, but first asks her husband about the trials to come. Odysseus tells all—how he must go inland until he reaches a people ignorant of the sea and of salt and of ships that fly upon the sea with oars. When someone calls his oar a winnowing-fan, then he is to plant it in the earth and make offerings to Poseidon. And returning home, he is to sacrifice hecatombs to the other immortal gods. And when he is old, a very gentle death will come to Odysseus away from the sea. His people will live in happy prosperity around him. This, he finishes, is what Tiresias told him.*

285-287 Then thoughtful Penelope said to him, "If the gods will bring about for you a better old age, then there is hope that you will escape this misfortune."

288-299 *Eurynome and Eurycleia prepare their bed, and Odysseus and Penelope go to sleep. As for the rest—Telemachus, Philoetius, Eumaeus, and all the women, they also stop their dancing and go to bed.*

300-309 When the two had taken their pleasure in delightful love, they relished in speaking to each other and telling stories.

She, divine among women, told about everything she had endured in the halls while looking upon the wasteful crowd of suitors, who—for her, they said—slaughtered many animals, cattle and fat sheep, and drew much wine out of many wine jars.

And god-born Odysseus recounted all the trouble he had brought to other men and all the woe he himself had suffered. Penelope was glad to listen. Sleep did not fall on her eyelids until he told the whole tale.

310-358 *From the beginning, Odysseus tells Penelope his story—about the Cicones, the Lotus-eaters, and his revenge upon the Cyclops. And about the stormy winds of Aeolus, and the land of the Laestrygonians, where all but one of his ships were destroyed. And about Circe's deception and his voyage to speak with Tiresias in Hades, where he met his mother and saw many of his comrades. And about the Siren's song, and the Wandering Rocks, and his harrowing scrape with Scylla and Charybdis. And how his men slaughtered the cattle of the Sun and perished for it thanks to Zeus' burning thunderbolt. And how he by himself came to Calypso's island, Ogygia, and stayed with her there for many years. She said she would make him immortal and ageless, but she never convinced him. And finally, about how he came to the Phaeacians, who honored him as a god and escorted him home. With the last, he falls into a sweet sleep that loosens the cares of his spirit.*

When Athena judges that Odysseus has had enough of love and sleep, she rouses Dawn, who brings light to men. Waking up, he bids Penelope to take care of the wealth in his halls. As for the flocks lost to the suitors, he will have the Achaeans resupply them. Then he reveals the plan.

359-372 "But I will go now to my well-wooded farm [360] to see my noble father, who, for my sake, has suffered much distress. As for you, wife, wise as you are, I give you this instruction. When the sun rises, a report will spread about the suitors I killed in the hall. Go then to the upper chamber with your handmaids and stay there, looking out at no one and asking no questions."

He spoke and fastened his beautiful armor around his shoulders. Then he awakened Telemachus, the cowherd, and the swineherd and ordered them to take in hand their weapons. They did not disobey, arming themselves with bronze. [370] They opened the doors and went out. Odysseus led the way.

By now, there was light over the earth—but Athena concealed them with night and swiftly led them away from the city.

BOOK 24

THE LAST BATTLE
PEACE AT LAST

IN BRIEF: *The souls of the suitors descend to Hades and encounter Achilles and Agamemnon, among others. Agamemnon speaks with Amphimedon and praises Penelope. Odysseus meets his father Laertes and, after testing him, reveals himself. The suitors' relatives meet in the assembly place to discuss what to do. Half, led by Eupeithes, want to find Odysseus to seek revenge. The other half, persuaded by Medon and Halitherses, do not fight. Those led by Eupeithes march off to one last battle. In the end, Zeus and Athena engineer a peace settlement.*

MEANWHILE, CYLLENIAN HERMES summoned the souls of the suitors *with his beautiful wand of gold.* And they went with him, babbling nonsense, crying, *as bats do when they exit a cave.* The protector Hermes led them along the dark and moldy pathway. They went past Oceanus' streams and the White Rock, and past the Gates of Helios, the portal of the Sun, and the land of dreams. And quickly they reached the field of asphodel, where souls dwell, the phantom-images of men who no longer toil. There they found the soul of Achilles, the son of Peleus, and the souls of Patroclus, blameless Antilochus, and Ajax, the best of the Danaans in beauty and stature after the blameless son of Peleus. These souls were joined in company with Achilles. And [20] the soul of Agamemnon, the son of Atreus, drew near to them, sorrowing.

21-190 Achilles turns to Agamemnon and laments the shameful way he perished by the hands of Aegisthus, his wife's lover. If only he had died gloriously on the battlefield before Troy, then the Achaeans would have fittingly honored him. In reply, Agamemnon recalls the day Achilles died—how the Achaeans bravely fought for his corpse, and how his mother, the immortal nymph Thetis, and all the Achaeans wept for him to the accompaniment of the Muses' plaintive dirge, and finally gave his body to the flames of a great funeral pyre. They eventually gathered his white bones and set them in a golden urn alongside Patroclus' bones—though apart from Antilochus, Agamemnon explains, the man Achilles honored most after Patroclus. Then they piled high a tomb over the urn that can be seen from the sea, one that men to come will see. Later, Thetis set out prizes for athletic games in honor of Achilles, who was dear to all the gods. There-fore, Agamemnon concludes, "Not even in death did you lose your name." *No, he goes on,* "Your glory will always be great among men."

As they are speaking, Hermes arrives trailing the suitors' phantom-spirits. Noticing them, and particularly one, Amphimedon, the son of Melaneus, Agamemnon asks him what has happened. What a large num-ber of men, he remarks. And the best. Did Poseidon sink your ship? Or did "hostile men" *kill you while you were cattle raiding or sacking their town in the hope of carrying off their women? He reminds Amphimedon of the time when he came with Menelaus to Ithaca to urge Odysseus to follow them to Troy. It was hard to win him over, he recalls.*

Amphimedon declares that he remembers their visit. Then he recounts the suitors' whole story from the moment they attempted to woo Penelope, long after Odysseus sailed for Troy. She neither said yes nor no, he ex-plains; rather, she "contrived death and black doom for us." *She tricked them with the plan to weave Laertes' burial shroud during the day and unravel it at night. It worked for three years, until in the fourth, one of her handmaids betrayed her and we made her finish the shroud, one that shines like the sun or moon. And now some wicked god brought Odysseus home. When he came to the house with the swineherd, he appeared like a beggar, and so we reviled him. At last, he took up the bow contrary to our or-ders—all of us but for Telemachus. And shooting Antinous first, he fired arrow after arrow, and they slaughtered us. Our bodies are still there in his house, uncared for in pools of blood, since no one has given the message to our friends and families that we are dead.*

191-202 Then the soul of the son of Atreus addressed Amphimedon, saying, "Happy son of Laertes, much-able Odysseus! You acquired for yourself an excellent wife, one of great worth. How good was the heart in blameless Penelope, the daughter of Icarius. How faithful in mind to Odysseus, her wedded husband. The glory of her excellence will never fade, but the immortals will make among men on earth a graceful song for thoughtful Penelope. She didn't plot evil works like the daughter of Tyndareus, [200] who killed her wedded husband. Her song will be hated among men—and harsh will be the judgment that follows womankind, bringing a bad reputation even to those women who are upright."

203-314 So finishes the conversation in the house of Hades. Meanwhile, Odysseus and the others come to Laertes' farm in the countryside, where an old Sicilian woman lives with the old man, looking after him. Ordering Telemachus, Eumaeus, and Philoetius to prepare a meal, Odysseus goes off in search of his father—to see if he will recognize him, he explains, or fail to know his son, who has been absent so long. He eventually discovers him alone, without his servant Dolius, hard at work in his vineyard, dressed in leather leggings, gloves, and a goatskin cap. Laertes appears old and worn. And stopping beneath a tall pear tree, Odysseus weeps. Now the question comes into his mind whether he should immediately greet his father with affection or test him. He decides to probe him.

Odysseus walks up to the old man who is digging around a vine in the soil, and he speaks to him. Old man, he begins—and he goes on to compliment him on his gardening skill but blame him for his ragged and worn appearance. How could your master cast you aside with all your skill? he queries. And in appearance you seem like a king rather than a slave. He proceeds to ask him who his master is and whether this is, indeed, Ithaca, as another man has already told him. Then, for one last time, Odysseus launches into a story. He's hoping to visit the son of Laertes, he declares, if he has not yet gone down to Hades. He explains that Odysseus once visited him in his own land, and he gave him many fitting guest-gifts made of gold and silver, as well as textiles and four women.

Laertes responds with tears. You're in Ithaca, he confirms, but that man is no longer here. Instead, arrogant men rule in his place. If he had been here, he would have given you due gifts. But tell me, he requests, when did you host him—"the wretched guest, who is my son," who has likely been eaten

*by animals on land or fish in the sea? We never had the chance to mourn for
him and give him a dead man's due. Anyway, who are you, who are your
people, and where are you from? And where is your ship?*

*Odysseus goes on with the story. He is from Alybas. He's the son of
Apheidas, the son of Polypemon. My name is Eperitus, he reveals. Some
god drove me from Sicania against my will—my ship is anchored just past
the city. As for Odysseus, he visited five years ago. When he departed, the
bird signs were favorable—all on the right. Ah, the ill-fated man!*

315-329 That's what Odysseus said, and a dark cloud of grief cov-
ered Laertes. And with both hands, he scooped up the smoky dust
and poured it over his gray head, groaning again and again.

At this, Odysseus' spirit was stirred, and a sharp pain shot up
through his nostrils as he looked upon his dear father. [320] He
sprang toward him, and embracing and kissing him, he said, "I am
that man, father—I myself, the one you search for! I have returned
to my homeland in the twentieth year. So, restrain this weeping and
tearful wailing, and I will tell you everything, though I must hurry.
I have killed the suitors in the halls of our house, punishing their
offensive insult and wicked deeds."

In reply, Laertes said to him, "If you are indeed my son Odys-
seus standing before me at home once again, then give me a clear
sign so that I may be persuaded."

330-344 *Odysseus first presents the boar-inflicted scar as evidence. Then he
offers to identify the trees his father gave him long ago—thirteen pear, ten
apple, and forty fig trees, as well as fifty rows of cluster-filled grapevines.*

345-360 That's what Odysseus said, and right then his father's
knees were loosened beneath him, and his dear heart was unstrung
as he recognized the certain signs that Odysseus pointed out. And
Laertes threw his arms around his dear son, and much-enduring
godlike Odysseus held him up as he was fainting.

When his father revived, his spirit returning again to his heart,
[350] Laertes once again replied to him, saying, "Father Zeus—surely
there are gods on high Olympus if in fact the suitors have paid for

their reckless arrogance. And yet now a dreadful fear has washed over my heart that all the men of Ithaca may come here against us at once—and that they'll send messengers to every Cephallenian city."

In reply, Odysseus of many counsels said to him, "Take courage and do not let these matters distress your heart. Instead, let's go to the house that stands by the orchard. I sent Telemachus ahead there, and the cowherd and swineherd, [360] so that they might quickly prepare a meal."

361-411 The two, father and son, walk to Laertes' farmhouse where Telemachus, the swineherd, and the cowherd are carving meat and pouring wine. When they arrive, the Sicilian woman bathes Laertes, and Athena makes him taller and stronger in appearance, like one of the immortal gods. When Odysseus declares as much, Laertes wishes he was the same as when he led the Cephallenians to sack Nericus on the mainland, or that he could have stood by him armed as he beat the suitors.

Eventually, they all sit down to eat while the Sicilian woman goes to call her husband Dolius and their six sons. They come and Dolius recognizes Odysseus right away. He rejoices and welcomes him, as do his sons. They sit down to eat.

412-486 The men ate their meal in this manner in the halls. Meanwhile, the messenger Rumor rushed swiftly throughout the whole city, reporting the miserable death and doom of the suitors. Hearing the news together, the people gathered from everywhere in front of Odysseus' house, moaning and groaning. And carrying the corpses away from the house, they honored the dead with funeral rites. As for the dead from other cities, they sent each corpse home upon the swift ships of fishermen. [420] Then they all went together to the assembly place, sad at heart.

Now, when they all had assembled and come together, Eupeithes stood and spoke among them. He did so because an inextinguishable sorrow had taken hold of his heart for his son, Antinous, the first man godlike Odysseus had slain. Shedding tears, he addressed the assembly, saying, "Friends, this man has plotted a monstrous deed against the Achaeans. Some of our men he led off in his ships—many men and noble. When he lost the hollow ships, he lost all the men. And now he has come and killed the very best of the Cephallenians. [430] Up then! Come before the man swiftly goes to Pylos or to divine Elis, where the Epeians rule. Let's go or our eyes will always be downcast in the future. We'll be shamed in future times if we do not take revenge on those who murdered our sons and brothers. In my mind, living would then no longer be sweet. Instead, I would rather die at once and be among the dead. But come! Let's go or they will escape from us across the sea!"

That's what Eupeithes said, tears pouring down his face, and pity took hold of all the Achaeans. Medon now drew near them, along with the divine bard. [440] They came from Odysseus' halls when sleep released them. They stood in the middle of the assembly, and astonishment seized each man while Medon, a man of understanding, spoke among them. "Listen to me now, men of Ithaca. It was not against the will of the immortal gods that Odysseus plotted these deeds. No, I myself spotted an immortal god by his side—one who appeared like Mentor in every way. And this immortal god stood before Odysseus, encouraging him at times and raging through the hall at others, scaring the suitors as they fell in heaps."

[450] That's what Medon said. And hearing him, pale fear took hold of them all. Then the old hero Halitherses, the son of Mastor, spoke among them. He alone saw before and after, and with kind intentions he spoke to the assembly, saying among them, "Listen to me, men of Ithaca, so that I may speak to you. These things have been done thanks to your own cowardly weakness, friends. You were not persuaded by me to stop your own sons' thoughtless deeds—nor did you listen to Mentor, the shepherd of men. What they did in reckless wickedness was monstrous—wasting the wealth and dishonoring the wife [460] of the best of men. They said he would never return. But let it be. And listen to my counsel. Let's not go—otherwise you may discover some misfortune drawn down upon your head."

That's what Halitherses said, but more than half of them sprang up with loud cries, since his speech did not agree with their own thoughts, while the others stayed in their seats. Those who rose were persuaded by Eupeithes. And at once they rushed for their arms. Then, when they had clothed their bodies in gleaming bronze, they gathered together in front of the spacious city. And Eupeithes foolishly led them. [470] His hope was to avenge his son's murder—yet he himself was doomed to never return home. Instead, he would meet his own destined end.

Yet Athena said to Zeus, the son of Cronus, "Father of us all, the son of Cronus, highest ruler, announce to me what I ask. What do you now hide deep within your mind? Will you stir them on to destructive war again, to the dread sound of battle, or will you establish them in friendship?"

In reply, cloud-gathering Zeus said to her, "Why do you question me closely and inquire into this? Did you yourself not propose the plan [480] to have Odysseus come and punish these men? So, do as you wish. Still, I will tell you what is fitting. Now that godlike Odysseus has taken vengeance on the suitors, let them swear a trustworthy oath, and let him always be king. As for our part, let us cause them to forget the murder of their sons and brothers. And let them love one another in friendship as they did before. And let wealth and peace appear in abundance."

487-493 Roused to action, Athena dashes down from Olympus. As she does so, Odysseus and the others are finishing their meal. Satisfied, Odysseus asks someone to go keep watch for the men. Dolius goes and sees that Eupeithes and his men are drawing near.

494-548 At once, Dolius called out with winged words, "They're here, close at hand! Quickly, let us arm!"

That's what Dolius said, and they rose up and put on armor. Odysseus with his men were four, and there were the six sons of Dolius. And among them, Laertes and Dolius also armed themselves even though they were gray, since all warriors were a necessity. [500] Then when they had clothed their bodies in gleaming bronze, they opened the doors and went out with Odysseus in the lead.

And Athena, the daughter of Zeus, drew near them. She was like Mentor in form and voice. Much-enduring godlike Odysseus saw her and was glad. And at once he said to Telemachus, his dear son, "Having come to battle where the best of men are separated in distinction from the rest, now you will learn never to shame your family line, for we have always excelled in might and manhood throughout all the land."

[510] In turn mindful Telemachus answered him, "If you wish, dear father, you will see me—given my present spirit—bring no shame on the family line, as you say."

That's what Telemachus said, and glad, Laertes spoke, saying, "What kind of day is this for me, dear gods? I absolutely rejoice! My son and my son's son are battling over excellence!"

Then bright-eyed Athena came near Laertes and said, "Son of Arceisius, by far the dearest of all my comrades, make a prayer to the bright-eyed maiden and to father Zeus. Then draw your long spear back at once and let it fly."

[520] That's what Pallas Athena said, and she breathed into him great might. And Laertes prayed to the daughter of great Zeus, drew his long spear back at once, and let it fly. The spear struck Eupeithes—hitting his helmet where the bronze defends the cheek. But the helmet didn't save him from the spear. No, the bronze point passed through the helmet, and Eupeithes fell with a thud! And when he fell, his armor rattled and clanged all around him.

Then Odysseus and his glorious son attacked the men out front, thrusting spears sharpened at both ends and slicing at them with their swords. And now they would have killed them all, cutting off their return home, if Athena, the daughter of aegis-bearing Zeus, [530] had not shouted aloud and held back all the men, saying, "Hold back from painful war, men of Ithaca! Hold back so that you may quickly separate from one another without shedding blood!"

That's what Athena said, and pale fear took hold of them. Their weapons fell from their trembling hands and dropped to the ground as the goddess shouted. And they turned toward the city, longing to save their lives.

Then, with a terrible cry, much-enduring godlike Odysseus gathered himself together and swooped down upon them like a high-flying eagle. But at that moment, the son of Cronus cast a flaming thunderbolt—[540] and down it fell before the bright-eyed daughter of the mighty father.

And bright-eyed Athena said to Odysseus, "God-born son of Laertes, much-able Odysseus, restrain yourself and stop the strife of war, common to all men, so that the far-seeing son of Cronus may not be moved to anger!"

That's what Athena said, and rejoicing in his spirit, Odysseus obeyed. And for the time to come, Pallas Athena established peace between them—Athena, the daughter of aegis-bearing Zeus, who was like Mentor in form and voice.

POINTS OF WISDOM
& WAYS OF PRACTICE
FROM HOMER

- Plan of Life Following Homer

- Points of Wisdom from Homer

- Ways of Practice Following Homer

PLAN OF LIFE
FOLLOWING HOMER

AS WITH ANY other plan, a plan of life is made to accomplish many goals or possibly just one significant goal. In the case of the "Plan of Life Following Homer," the goal is bare survival on the one side and happiness and thriving on the other—for we do not merely wish to live but to live well (as a later Greek philosopher would say). The following plan consists of the most significant Homeric goals and practices from both the Iliad *and* Odyssey.

1. **Act to survive.** Keep in mind that bare life is worth more than any amount of silver or gold. When life is gone, it is gone forever. Even a simple life is a good life. Cherish life. Be. Live.

2. **Be the best; act to thrive.** Strive for excellence, to be outstanding. Do your best to speak and act well in every situation. Flourish! Seek happiness, which is the satisfaction of what you truly desire. Take delight in abundance and the many good things of life. Generously request the happiness of others.

3. **Act for glory; be noble and honorable.** Flee from disgrace. Do what is necessary to build a noble reputation. Most of all, do that which is noble and honorable so that yours will be a glorious memorial. Readily acknowledge the honor and glory of others.

4. **Be home oriented.** Clearly define what home is for you—your family, your community, an ideal, a way of life. Beware of that which causes you to forget home. Yearn for home. Return home.

5. **Cooperate with others to survive and thrive.** Be loyal to your family. Be a faithful friend. Fulfill your duty as an ally. Fight alongside. Stand guard. Work together. Kindly host others. Be an amenable guest. Rule when necessary; submit to the rule of others (again, when necessary). Give advice; receive counsel. Whatever it is, play your role well and faithfully.

6. **Compete with others to survive and thrive.** Be courageous. Fight forward. Take a stand. Be angry when necessary—but quick to make amends and reconcile. Be careful when boasting. Engage in battle—but only if you must. Be fair.

7. **Cultivate your own strengths and skills.** Keep in mind human variation, that different people have different strengths and skills. Know yours. Graciously recognize those of others. Grasping the wisdom of difference, perform your own function well.

8. **Practice wisdom; deliberate well.** Pursue knowledge. Hunt for good counsel. Know in order to deliberate; deliberate in order to resolve; resolve in order to act. Think and speak in order to act.

9. **Be reconciled to the human condition.** Remember that humans are not gods, that we suffer pain and hardship and grow old and die. Choose to embrace these facts. Such a reconciliation paradoxically fosters a sense of freedom—the liberty to be human, the freedom to live the *when, how,* and *where* of one's fated role.

10. **Endure well.** Cultivate a spirit that can endure suffering, sorrow, and misfortune. Employ Odysseus' four-point endurance method: self-talk, recollection, deliberation, and command. Remember you must endure—you have no other choice.

11. **Desire well.** Learn how to deal with temptation in order to restrain your desires. Practice moderation—measure. Sail by the Island of the Sun; don't stop. Bear in mind that recklessness, which is often caused by out-of-control desires, leads to destruction. Restraint, by contrast, is liberating. Moderation will get you home.

12. **Acknowledge the divine.** Recognize the power that is behind all things. Strong and wise, it is how all things have come into existence. Dynamic, it is at peace. Concerned, it remains aloof. The divine cares for justice. Look to the divine for guidance, for the divine knows all things. Pray with hands outstretched to heaven.

POINTS OF WISDOM
FROM HOMER

The following points of wisdom come from Homer's Iliad *and* Odyssey. *Each begins in italics with a single word or more indicating the point's topic. For more points of wisdom from Homer organized by topic, read The Classics Cave's* The Wisdom & Way of Homer.

Happiness. Odysseus said, "Lord Zeus, may Telemachus be happy among men, and may everything happen as he desires in his heart."

The happiness of marriage. Odysseus said to Nausicaa, "May the gods grant you as much as your heart eagerly desires—a man for a husband, and a house. And may a noble unity of mind and feeling accompany these. For nothing is greater and nothing better than when a man and woman dwell in their household with the same feelings, thoughts, and mind—a huge pain to their enemies and joy to their friends. Their glory is very well known."

Human delight. "Different men delight in different things."

True delight. Odysseus said, "There is nothing sweeter to a man than his own homeland and his parents. . . . I declare that there is nothing better or more delightful than when a whole people join in merry festivity, with the guests sitting side by side listening to the singer, while before them the table is loaded with bread and meats, and the cupbearer draws wine from the mixing bowl and pours it into all the goblets. In my mind, this seems to be the most beautiful thing."

Fulfilment. Menelaus said, "I declare that all things find satisfaction—sleep, love, sweet song, and the stately dance. With these things a man hopes to find fulfilment."

The excellence imperative. Nestor said, "Old Peleus insistently ordered his son Achilles to always be the best and to stand out among other men."

The glory imperative. Hector said, "I have learned always to be brave and to fight in the front ranks among the Trojans, winning great glory for my father and myself. . . . Let me not then die ingloriously and without a struggle, but let me first do some great thing that men to come will hear about!"

True glory. Laodamas said, "There is no greater glory than that which a man has from the accomplishments of his own hands and feet."

The human condition. Glaucus said, "Men come and go as the leaves do year after year upon the trees. The wind sheds the autumn leaves upon the ground, but when the spring returns, the forest buds again with fresh ones. The generations of mankind are like this. The new generation springs up as the old is passing away."

The human condition. Apollo said, "Miserable mortals flourish now like green leaves in springtime, eating whatever the earth provides, but soon waste away and decay, falling lifeless to the ground."

Human variety. Polydamas said to Hector, "Some god has granted you skill in war, but . . . you can't win in everything. The gods have given to one man skill in war and to another skill in the dance. To others they've given the ability to play the lyre or sing. To still others far-seeing Zeus gives a noble mind."

Death. Athena said to Telemachus, "Death that is common to all men is certain. Not even the gods have the power to defend a loved man against it when the destructive fate of death finally drops a man to the dust."

The gods. Menelaus said, "The gods know all things. . . . Father Zeus— you are, they say, above all the other gods and men in wisdom, and by whom all these things have come into existence."

Human need for the gods. Peisistratus said, "All men need the gods."

God-dependent life. Hector said, "Everything rests with the gods."

God-dependent delight. Eumaeus said, "Eat and enjoy the food we have. The god gives on the one hand and withholds on the other depending on his spirit's wish, for the god is able to do all things."

God-dependent happiness and wealth. Odysseus said, "As for the happiness of wealth, it's up to the gods to give it or not."

Inescapable fate. Hector said, "No man has gone down to Hades beyond what Fate had decreed. But I declare that from the moment of his birth, no man has ever been able to run away from his own fate, neither the coward nor the brave man."

Zeus' two jars of fortune. Achilles said to Priam, the king of Troy, "On the floor of Zeus' house there are two jars from which he gives gifts. The one is filled with evil and the other with good. To whomever Zeus, who delights in thunder, mixes and gives out both, that man will meet now with good and now with evil fortune. But for the man who only receives evil gifts—ah, that man will suffer shameful treatment. Evil poverty and hunger will drive him back and forth over the earth, and neither the gods nor men will honor him."

Life's great value. Achilles said, "My life is worth more to me than all the wealth of Ilium, the riches it had before the Achaeans attacked it, when there was yet peace. It is worth more than all the treasure that lies on the stone floor of Apollo's temple beneath the cliffs of Pytho. Cattle and fat sheep may be carried off as booty, and tripods and yellow-headed horses may be acquired, but when a man's life has once left him, it cannot be brought back again or won by force."

The high price of excessive riches. Menelaus said, "I have wandered and suffered much over eight years to bring these riches home in my ships. . . . If only I had stayed home! I wish that I had only a third of my possessions and that all those who perished on the plain of Troy, far from horse-nourishing Argos, were still safe and alive."

Simple life is better than death. Achilles said, "Do not speak to me lightly about death, glorious Odysseus. If only I could, I would choose to live upon the earth, working as a day laborer for some other man, some landless man who doesn't have much of what it takes to live. I'd rather be that man, Odysseus, than rule over all the rotting dead."

Hunger. Odysseus said, "There is nothing more shameful and dog-like than one's hateful belly. It calls upon a man to remember it by absolute necessity, even if he is very oppressed and is bearing much grief and misfortune in his heart and mind, as I am now carrying all the sorrow in mine. My belly always insists that I eat and drink, and bids me lay aside all memory of my sorrows and dwell on re-plenishing itself. . . . There is no hiding a hungry belly. It is an ac-cursed, destructive thing, which introduces many evils to all men. It is because of hunger that well-benched ships are made ready to sail the barren sea and carry misery and sorrow to hostile men."

Human responsibility. Zeus said to the gods, "How shameful it is that the mortals even now blame the gods! From us, they say, come all sorts of bad things. But it is through their own recklessness that they have sorrows beyond those which are fated."

The need to restrain desire. Tiresias said to Odysseus, "You may still reach home, though suffering misfortune, if you will choose to restrain your own desires and curb those of your comrades when you reach the island of Thrinacia. . . . There you will find the grazing cattle and fat sheep of Helios the Sun . . . . If you leave these alone, . . . then you may still reach Ithaca, though suffering hardship and misfortune. But if you hurt them, then I predict ruin—destruction—for your ship and death for your comrades."

The endurance rule. Odysseus said, "But pity me . . . I have come upon you first after much suffering and toil." In reply, Nausicaa said, "Stranger, . . . since Olympian Zeus himself dispenses fortune and happiness to men, to both the good and the bad as he wills, whether he be brave or a coward, noble or base—so I believe that surely he has given misfortune to you. Regardless, you must endure it either way."

The need to endure. Athena said to Odysseus, "You must endure the trouble and pain—you have no choice. . . . In silence suffer all the pain and distress, and patiently bear the violent abuse of men."

Being weak, humans must endure. Odysseus said to Amphinomus, "Of all things that breathe and move along the earth, there's nothing weaker than a human being—I tell you, the earth nurtures no frailer thing. For as long as the gods give him excellence, and as long as his knees stand strong, he thinks he'll never suffer misfortune in the days to come. But when the blessed gods send him misery, he must bear it with an enduring spirit even though it is against his will."

Craft over strength. The gods . . . beheld the artful skill of inventive Hephaestus. And glancing at the other one would say, "Bad deeds do not thrive. The slow overtakes the swift—just as now Hephaestus, slow as he is, has seized Ares, even though he is the swiftest of the gods who hold Olympus. Lame, he has seized him by cunning craft. Ares must pay the fine for adultery."

Wisdom and cunning. Nestor said to Antilochus, "The horses making up the other teams are swifter than yours are, but the other men do not know how to plan a race better than you do. Therefore, dear son, fill your mind with wisdom and cunning of every sort so that you don't lose out on winning a prize. The woodcutter is far better because of wisdom and cunning than he is because of strength. And by wisdom and cunning, too, does a steersman rightly guide a swift ship that is buffeted by the winds on the wine-faced sea. And by wisdom and cunning does one charioteer prevail over another."

Act! Patroclus said to Meriones, "Why do you . . . speak in this way? The Trojans will not fall back from the corpse just because you speak words of reproach to them. . . . Rather, in our hands is the battle's outcome. . . . So, we must not multiply words, but we must fight."

Act! Nestor said to the Achaeans, "Talking will get us nowhere. Stand, therefore, son of Atreus, and lead the Argives into battle."

Strife. Strife, who causes much sorrow, rejoiced as she beheld the two armies. . . . Strife is man-slaying Ares' sister and comrade. She starts small and grows bigger and taller until her head is sky-high, and her feet drag along the earth. Strife lobbed distressful contention between them, and when it came among them, it increased their lamentation.

May strife perish! Achilles said to Thetis, "May strife utterly perish from among both the gods and men, and anger that incites a wise man to be savagely upset—an anger that drips like very sweet honey and expands like smoke in the breast of a man, growing ever larger. Even so has the lord of men Agamemnon now provoked me to anger."

Conquering anger. Phoenix said to Achilles, "You must conquer your great and angry temper, Achilles. It is not fitting to have a ruthless heart. No, even the gods are able to bend, the gods who are better."

Courage. "The bold and courageous man does better in all things."

Be brave! The son of Atreus, Agamemnon, ranged among the throng of men and called out, "Be men, friends! Have a brave heart! And feel shame before one another when you are fighting. More men live when there's such shame. But when men shamelessly flee, there's neither glory nor strength to avert danger."

Cooperate for strength. "Remember, battle excellence comes even for very weak and cowardly men when they band together."

Two is better than one. Diomedes said, "If some other man were to go along with me, there would be greater hope and confidence. When two go together, one apprehends before the other whatever advantage there may be. On the other hand, if one is alone, even when he discerns something, his mind is slow, and his cunning is inadequate."

WAYS OF PRACTICE
FOLLOWING HOMER

The following ways of practice, inspired by Homer's Odyssey, *are offered with the goal of practice in mind, the application of ancient wisdom to our contemporary ways and lives. We hope they will serve, in some small measure, as a source of inspiration and motivation. Use them to contemplate your life—where you are now, where you are going, and how you can better get there. For these exercises and practices and other similar ones, look for the Cave's* Homer Workbook & Journal. *One last note. You will likely find that the space given for responses is not enough. If so, jot your thoughts and practices down in a separate place.*

PRACTICE 1: RELYING ON WISDOM AND CUNNING
(INSTEAD OF PHYSICAL SUPERIORITY)

Odysseus is a man of "many counsels." Like the goddess Athena, he is "wise and cunning." When he relies on these noble qualities, he does well. His wisdom and cunning rescue him from things that are physically superior—the Cyclops, the many suitors. When he doesn't—when he falls asleep, for instance—, things don't go well.

We see the same with the god Hephaestus, who is physically disabled relative to the war god Ares, who is "handsome and has quick feet." Even so, Hephaestus wisely and skillfully captures Ares when he sleeps with his wife, Aphrodite, and makes him pay. As one of the gods observes: "Bad deeds do not thrive. The slow overtakes the swift—just as now Hephaestus, slow as he is, has seized Ares, even though he is the swiftest of the gods who hold Olympus. Lame, he has seized him by craft. Ares must pay the fine for adultery."

Nestor, in advising his son, Antilochus, makes the same point in the *Iliad*. "The horses making up the other *chariot* teams are swifter than yours are, but the other men do not know how to plan a race better than you do. Therefore, dear son, fill your mind with wisdom and cunning of every sort so that you don't lose out on winning a prize. The woodcutter is far better because of wisdom and cunning than he is because of strength. And by wisdom and cunning, too, does a steersman rightly guide a swift ship that is buffeted by the winds on the wine-faced sea. And by wisdom and cunning does one charioteer prevail over another."

Have a Redo • Recall a time in your life when you could have better employed wisdom (counsel, cunning, skill, craft) to end up with a better result. How could you have done so? Be specific.

_____

_____

_____

_____

Using Wisdom Now • Pinpoint an area in your life _right now_ in which you can better employ wisdom (counsel, cunning, skill, craft). How can you do so? Be specific.

_____

_____

_____

_____

MY WISDOM RULE

In the future, I will employ wisdom (etc.) in the following three ways:

Way 1: _____

_____

Way 2: _____

_____

Way 3: _____

_____

PRACTICE 2: RESISTING DESIRE AND DEALING WITH TEMPTATION

If we quietly listen to our deepest desire (or desires), we realize that it—like Odysseus yearning for his homeland—longs for true satisfaction or fulfillment. The problem is we have other desires for massively enticing things—such as the dreamy forgetfulness of the lotus flower, or the lazy abundance provided by Circe, or the sweet song of the Sirens, or the hunger-quieting flesh of the cattle of the Sun. At the moment, these desires feel overwhelmingly compelling as their satisfaction can be instant. Right now! Yet given the difference between their satisfaction and the satisfaction that home will bring, we must know—we must *choose* to know—that ultimately their satisfaction will not be truly satisfying. In fact, such a satisfaction will be harmful, destructive. The solution: we must somehow resist these latter desires and so deal with temptation to better satisfy our deepest desire(s).

As the seer Tiresias says to Odysseus: "Glorious Odysseus, you seek out an easy return home—honey-sweet. . . . But let me tell you, a god will make it hard for you. . . . Even so you may still reach home, though suffering misfortune, if you will choose to restrain your own desires and curb those of your comrades when you reach the island of Thrinacia. . . . There you will find the grazing cattle and fat sheep of Helios the Sun, who sees and hears everything. If you leave these alone, unharmed, keeping in mind your return home, then you may still reach Ithaca, though suffering hardship and misfortune. But if you hurt them, then I predict ruin—destruction—for your ship and death for your comrades."

Locate home • Quietly listen to your deepest desire(s). What is "home" for you? What do you truly desire? What offers you real satisfaction?—a steady and ongoing fulfillment?

_____

_____

_____

Disclose obstacles • What desires (or satisfactions of desires) serve as obstacles or distractions or pitfalls to you reaching home or true satisfaction? What temptations waylay you? How so? Be specific.

Desire or temptation 1: _____

_____

Desire or temptation 2: _____

_____

Desire or temptation 3: _____

_____

CIRCLE ONE • Keeping in mind the above words of Tiresias,

I <u>am</u> / <u>am not</u>

prepared to "suffer misfortune" to "reach home" — that is,
I <u>am</u> or <u>am not</u> prepared to experience (some) dissatisfaction to
know true satisfaction or fulfillment.

Resisting desire and dealing with temptation • Describe one specific, concrete *way* you can resist and deal with the above three desires or temptations. *Practice* each way over the next few days or week.

Way and practice 1: _____

_____

_____

Way and practice 2: _____

_____

_____

Way and practice 3: _____

_____

_____

PRACTICE 3: THE ENDURANCE RULE — TRAINING TO ENDURE

Whatever good happens in life, we must at times bear with suffering and hardship. So, we must follow "the endurance rule." We *must endure it.*

We learn the endurance rule from Nausicaa and Athena. After Odysseus reveals all the "sorrow that is hard to bear," "misfortune," and "suffering and toil" he has experienced and will experience, Nausicaa pronounces, "Stranger, since you do not seem to be a base or senseless man, and since Olympian Zeus himself dispenses fortune and happiness to men, to both the good and the bad as he wills, . . . so I believe that surely he has given misfortune to you. Regardless, *you must* nevertheless *endure it.*" Similarly, Athena declares, "Nevertheless, *you must endure the trouble and pain,* Odysseus—you have no choice. . . . In silence suffer all the pain and distress, and patiently bear the violent abuse of men."

This endurance, of course, is easier said or commanded than done. How, then, might we endure? What method can we follow? We discern a way to endure in the following passage (with added numbers):

> Odysseus lay sleepless there, contemplating misfortune for the suitors in his spirit. And the women came out from the hall—those who mixed in love with the suitors. They were laughing and making merry with one another. Odysseus' spirit stirred within his dear chest, and he considered in his heart and spirit whether he should rush upon them and kill each one or let them mix in love with the arrogant suitors one last time. His heart howled and barked within him at their evil deeds. . . .
>
> Even so, **(1)** he struck his chest and admonished his heart, saying, "Endure, my heart! **(2)** You once endured an even worse thing than this when the irresistible Cyclops devoured your mighty comrades. But you endured until **(3)** your cunning wisdom led you out from the cave where you imagined you would die." That's what Odysseus said, addressing the dear heart in his chest. And **(4)** in complete obedience his heart continued to endure even though he himself tossed from side to side.

ODYSSEUS' FOUR-STEP METHOD OF ENDURANCE
each point or step is numbered in the above passage

1. **Engage in "self-talk."** Begin by encouraging yourself to endure.
2. **Recall a specific time** in the past during which you had to bear with something horrible. Remind yourself that if you could *then* put up with *that* something, then *now* you can put up with *this* something.
3. **Use the wisdom you have.** Deliberate and form a plan for how you will escape or deal with whatever misfortune you're experiencing.
4. **Finish with simple obedience.** Resolutely command yourself to endure no matter how you feel. As Nausicaa says, "You must endure."

Apply it • How might you have better endured something in the past by using Odysseus' four-step method of endurance? Analyze the challenging event in terms of each step. What could you have said to yourself? What specific time would have you recalled? What wisdom would you have used? How would you have finished?

_____

_____

_____

_____

Practice • Are you suffering right now? Must you endure? Walk yourself through the four steps of Odysseus' method of endurance.

Step 1: _____

_____

Step 2: _____

_____

Step 3: _____

_____

Step 4: _____

_____

OTHER MATTERS OF INTEREST
RELATED TO HOMER'S *ODYSSEY*

THE CAST OF GODS AND MEN
A QUICK REFERENCE

GENERAL CATEGORIES OF BEINGS

GODS are human-like beings that are immortal and ageless because of their consumption of wine-like nectar and bread-like ambrosia. In general, the gods are more powerful than humans. They are glorious beings who live an easy and blessed life without care.

HUMAN BEINGS are mortals (their defining attribute). They age and die (in part at least) because they drink wine and eat bread. Although some humans live a relatively easy life, human life is generally marked by toil and struggle, misfortune and wretchedness.

IMMORTAL GODS AND GODDESSES

Gods or goddesses with significant roles in the Odyssey

AEOLUS (Aiolos): son of Hippotas. Aeolus, the master of winds, lives on a floating island, Aeolia, with his wife and twelve children (six boys and six girls, who are paired off in marriage). Odysseus visits and feasts with him and his family for a month. As a parting gift, Aeolus gives his guest a bagful of winds to speed him on his way home. When they are near to Ithaca, Odysseus' men open the bag—jealously suspecting it is full of silver and gold. The winds escape and drive them far away from their homeland again, back toward Aeolus' island. Meeting them, Aeolus refuses to receive and host them again.

ATHENA (Athēnē): daughter of Zeus (and Metis), Athena was born from her father's head. In the form of Mentes at times and Mentor at others, though operating all along as the goddess she is, Athena encourages and helps Telemachus in his journey to discover news of his father's fate. She also serves as Odysseus' chief advocate among the assembly of the gods, arguing on his behalf that he should be able to return home. Athena helps Odysseus along the way, taking on various forms. She works alongside him and his men when he is battling and slaughtering the suitors. Finally, at the prodding of Zeus, she joins Odysseus and the vengeance-seeking relatives of the suitors in peace, friendship, and abundance.

CALYPSO (Kalupsō or Kalypsō): daughter of Atlas. After Odysseus' men perish on the sea, the goddess Calypso hosts Odysseus on her faraway island, Ogygia, for seven years, promising to make him immortal and ageless, as well as her husband. Nevertheless, at the insistence of the other gods expressed in a message given by Hermes, she sends him homeward on a raft in the eighth year.

CHARYBDIS: daughter of Gaia and Poseidon; a monster. Three times every day Charybdis sucks down the water that surrounds her, and three times again she sends it up. After leaving the enchantress Circe, Odysseus and his men avoid Charybdis by sailing beneath Scylla instead. Later, Odysseus avoids her sucking pull by hanging on to the branch of a fig tree on the cliff above her monstrous whirlpool. When Charybdis spits up his raft again, he paddles away with his hands.

CIRCE (Kirkē): daughter of Helios and Perse; sister of Aeetes. When Odysseus and his men come to Aeaea, the goddess Circe's island, the enchantress Circe gives half a drink mixed with a drug that causes them to forget their homeland and turns them into swine. With the help of Hermes and the protection of the herb called moly, Odysseus forces Circe to free his men. Friends now, they remain with the goddess feasting for a year. At year's end, and before they depart, she explains how Odysseus must talk to Tiresias in Hades. Later, after they return from Hades, she warns him about the dangers of the voyage ahead—the Sirens, Scylla and Charybdis, and that they must avoid the island of the sun god Helios.

EIDOTHEA: daughter of Proteus. Eidothea pities and saves Mene-laus and his men. She commands Menelaus to take hold of her di-vine father, the old man of the sea, by stealth when he is resting among his seals. She promises that he will tell the stranded man everything he needs to know to make it home.

HELIOS (Hyperion), the Sun: son of the Titan Hyperion and the Ti-taness Theia; with Perse the father of Circe; with Neaera the father of the shepherd-nymphs Phaethusa and Lampetia. The sun god, Helios threatens to withdraw his light from the living and shine on the dead alone in Hades after Odysseus' men slaughter and eat the best of his cattle. Zeus convinces him to keep shining on the living by promising to strike down Odysseus' men.

HERMES: son of Zeus and Maia. The messenger of his father, Her-mes frequently carries Zeus' important commands to others. On a mission from his father before the *Odyssey* begins, he advises Ae-gisthus not to seduce Clytemnestra, Agamemnon's wife. Later, he orders Calypso to release Odysseus. One of the handful of gods who show up to view Aphrodite tied up with Ares, Hermes assures Apollo he would willingly be trapped like Ares if he could sleep with Aphrodite. Serving as psychopomp, Hermes escorts the suit-ors to the Underworld.

INO: daughter of Cadmus, the king of Thebes. Called Leukothea, the White Goddess (elsewhere), the once human and now immortal sea nymph Ino advises Odysseus to leave his raft and swim for Scheria, the island of the Phaeacians. She gives him an immortal veil that serves as a life preserver.

POSEIDON: son of Cronus and Rhea; brother of Zeus; with Thoōsa the father of the Cyclops Polyphemus; the forefather of the Phaeacian king and queen Alcinous and Arete. Called the Earth-shaker, Posei-don is angry with and harasses Odysseus during his journey home for blinding his son Polyphemus. When the Phaeacians sail Odys-seus to Ithaca, Poseidon punishes them by turning the offending ship into stone and covering over their island with a mountain.

PROTEUS (the old man of the sea): father of the sea nymph Eidothea. A shapeshifting sea god, who lives on the island of Pharos, off Egypt, Proteus reveals to Menelaus what he and his men must do to return home.

SCYLLA: daughter of Crataeis. A monster with twelve feet, six necks and heads, each with three rows of teeth, and living in a cave on the side of a cliff, Scylla fishes for dolphins and seadogs and whatever other great fish or sea monsters she may happen to catch. When Odysseus sails nearby, she snatches up six of his men and devours them.

SIRENS: the two Sirens (two in the *Odyssey*) cast a spell on men when they pass by their island in their ships. They do so by their clear singing, their sweet-sounding song. The result, contrary to hope, is death, when the Sirens draw the enchanted men to themselves. When Odysseus and his men row by, Odysseus safely listens to their song—this, thanks to Circe, who forewarned him, directing him to tie himself to the mast of his ship and have all his men press beeswax into their ears.

ZEUS: son of Cronus and Rhea; brother of Poseidon; father of Athena; the father of gods and men. Zeus blames men such as Aegisthus for their own destruction. With Athena, he plans Odysseus' homecoming and later recommends peace and friendship for Odysseus and the suitors. Zeus destroys Odysseus' men with a blast of lightning after they eat the cattle of the sun god Helios.

Gods or goddesses who appear in the Odyssey
without a significant role

APHRODITE: daughter of Zeus and Dione; the wife of Hephaestus (in the *Odyssey*). The bard Demodocus sings the story of the adulterous love affair between Ares and Aphrodite, and how Hephaestus cleverly caught them in the middle of the act. Odysseus' wife, Penelope, is frequently compared to Aphrodite in terms of her great beauty.

APOLLO: son of Zeus and Leto; twin brother of Artemis. Odysseus prays to Apollo for the glory-boast when he is battling the suitors. Otherwise, Apollo shows up in many small ways in the *Odyssey*, from sending a positive omen to Telemachus, to laughing at Ares and Aphrodite with the other gods, to figuring into Eumaeus' story about his homeland, Syria, in that he and his sister Artemis gently slay the inhabitants in old age.

ARES: son of Zeus and Hera. Ares is the handsome and speedy god of war. The bard Demodocus sings the story about the adulterous love affair between Ares and Aphrodite, and how Hephaestus cleverly outdoes them by catching them in the middle of the act.

ARTEMIS: daughter of Zeus and Leto; twin sister of Apollo. The swineherd Eumaeus explains that Artemis hit his nurse with one of her many arrows of disease when they were sailing away from Syria, his homeland, with Phoenician merchants. Both Penelope and Nausicaa are compared to Artemis in terms of beauty.

BOREAS, THE NORTH WIND: the divine wind that oftentimes blows a ship where it needs to go. Odysseus shelters from Boreas when he first reaches Scheria, the island of the Phaeacians.

CRONUS (Kronos): father of Zeus. Homer calls the god "scheming" Cronus, the one whose counsels are crooked.

DAWN (Ēōs): wife of Tithonos. Dawn brings light to mortal human beings and the immortal gods in the early morning, at the moment when night turns into day. She is "early-born rosy-fingered Dawn," representing the colorful rays of the sun first shining over the earth. Lampus and Phaethon are the horses that pull her chariot.

EUROS, THE EAST WIND: Homer explains that Euros, the East Wind, melts the snow after Zephyrus, the West Wind, has dumped it.

The FATES (the Spinners) (Klōthes): Homer presents the Spinners as the ones who spin out a man's fate "with their flaxen thread when he came to be on the day his mother gave birth to him."

HADES: son of Cronus and Rhea; husband of Persephone. Hades is the god of the Underworld, the "house of Hades." "Hades" is synonymous with the destination and dwelling place of the dead. Odysseus visits Hades to speak with the seer Tiresias.

HEPHAESTUS: son of Zeus and Hera; husband of Aphrodite (the Grace Charis is his wife in the *Iliad*). Hephaestus is the skillful and inventive fire-smith god who makes, in the *Iliad*, Achilles' shield and armor. In the *Odyssey*, he is responsible for the immortal and ageless golden and silver dogs that stand guard outside Alcinous' palace. Limited by various bodily deformities, including disabled legs and feet, Hephaestus is a wise god who offers counsel and outsmarts other gods. When he catches and punishes Ares, who is having an affair with Aphrodite, the bard Demodocus states, "Bad deeds do not thrive. The slow overtakes the swift—just as now Hephaestus, slow as he is, has seized Ares, even though he is the swiftest of the gods who hold Olympus. Lame, he has seized him by craft. Ares must pay the fine for adultery."

MUSE: daughter of Zeus or Apollo (as Odysseus speculates). Homer calls on the Muse to reveal to him the story of Odysseus' painful wanderings and return home. It is the Muse who gifts bards with their song. The phantom-soul of Agamemnon reveals that all nine Muses wept over Achilles after he died.

NAIAD NYMPHS (the Naiads): daughters of Zeus. Odysseus hides his treasure in a cave on Ithaca that belongs to the Naiad Nymphs, ones to whom he offered hecatombs before he left for Troy.

NOTOS, THE SOUTH WIND: storms occasionally arise on sea thanks to Notos, the South Wind.

PHAETHUSA AND LAMPETIA: daughters of Helios Hyperion (the sun god) and Neaera. Nymphs with beautiful long locks of hair, they are the divine shepherdesses who watch over the cattle and sheep of the Sun.

ZEPHYRUS, THE WEST WIND: Aeolus sends Zephyrus to blow Odysseus and his men home. Athena sends him to carry Telemachus across the sea. Homer reveals that Zephyrus brings snow; thus, the West Wind can be very cold. Though Zephyrus can be a fair wind, he oftentimes brings stormy winds.

HUMAN BEINGS

ACHILLES: son of the mortal man Peleus and the goddess Thetis; father of Neoptolemus. When Odysseus encounters Achilles in the Underworld, Achilles tells him he would rather be a landless man than one who rules over the dead.

AEGISTHUS (Aigisthos): son of Thyestes. After killing the bard who had been tasked with guarding her, Aegisthus seduces Clytemnestra and eventually murders Agamemnon, her husband, upon his return home from Troy. Agamemnon's son Orestes later takes revenge by killing him.

AGAMEMNON: son of Atreus; husband of Clytemnestra; father of Orestes; brother of Menelaus; leader of the allied Achaean army in Troy. Agamemnon is murdered by Aegisthus upon his return home from Troy. He praises Penelope's faithfulness and curses Clytemnestra's treachery.

AGELAUS: son of Damastor; a suitor. Agelaus bids Telemachus to ask Penelope to choose and marry the best of the suitors. Agelaus takes the lead with several of the other suitors after Antinous and

Eurymachus die during the slaughter of the suitors. Odysseus kills him by running him through with his spear.

ALCINOUS (Alkinoos): son of Nausithous; grandson of the god Poseidon; husband of Arete; father of Nausicaa and Laodamas, among other children. Alcinous is the ruler of the Phaeacians. He and his wife host Odysseus when he comes to their island, Scheria. He boasts that the Phaeacians are excellent at foot racing, dancing, singing, and sailing, among other activities. When Alcinous notices Odysseus weeping at the telling of several tales, he asks his guest to explain who he is and what troubles he has endured. After a night of feasting and storytelling, he sends Odysseus off in a Phaeacian ship to Ithaca with many gifts. When Poseidon punishes the Phaeacians for escorting Odysseus home against his will, Alcinous explains that the turning of the ship into stone is the fulfilment of an ancient prophecy.

AMPHIMEDON: son of Melaneus; a suitor. Struck down by Telemachus during the slaughter of the suitors, he encounters Agamemnon when he goes down to Hades and converses with him. Amphimedon explains why so many men have come down to the house of the dead—how Penelope deceived the suitors and how Odysseus returned home and slaughtered them.

AMPHINOMUS: son of Nisus; a suitor. Amphinomus advises the suitors not to kill Telemachus, "the offspring of a king." When Odysseus defeats the beggar Irus, Amphinomus offers him bread and wine and blesses him with future happiness. Odysseus attempts to warn him of the coming destruction, but Amphinomus fails to leave for his own home. Later, he calls on all the suitors to stop abusing the wandering stranger (Odysseus). Of all the suitors, Penelope likes him the best. During the slaughter of the suitors, Telemachus spears Amphinomus from behind as he is rushing at Odysseus with sword drawn.

ANTICLEIA: daughter of Autolycus; wife of Laertes; mother of

Odysseus. Odysseus encounters his mother Anticleia in the Underworld. She explains that she perished thanks to her longing for Odysseus' return and for his counsels.

ANTINOUS (Antinoos): son of Eupeithes. One of the "best of the suitors," Antinous defends the behavior of the suitors, blaming it on Penelope's own tricks. Several times he advises the suitors to slay Telemachus. Penelope abhors Antinous, criticizing him for his lack of care for suppliants. She later prays for his death. Antinous upbraids the swineherd Eumaeus for bringing a stranger (Odysseus) to the house. He later throws a footstool at the stranger in anger after the stranger censures him for his stinginess. Amphinomus is the first to die during the slaughter of the suitors. Odysseus shoots him with an arrow through his throat.

ARETE: daughter of Rhexenor; granddaughter of Poseidon; wife of Alcinous; mother of Nausicaa and Laodamas, among other children. Throwing his arms around her knees, Odysseus first supplicates noble-minded Arete for help when he comes to Scheria. Along with Alcinous, Arete questions Odysseus. She praises him for his mind and looks and suggests the Phaeacians give him more gifts.

CLYTEMNESTRA (Klutaimnēstrē): daughter of Tyndareus; wife of Agamemnon and later Aegisthus; mother of Orestes. Clytemnestra is seduced by Aegisthus and subsequently plots to kill Agamemnon.

CTESIPPUS: son of Polytherses; a suitor. At the prodding of Athena, Ctesippus throws an ox-hoof at Odysseus. During the slaughter of the suitors, the cowherd Philoetius spears him in the chest, declaring the spear is meant to make up for the ox-hoof.

DEMODOCUS: the blind Phaeacian bard who plays the lyre and, thanks to the Muse, beautifully sings when Odysseus visits Alcinous and Arete and the rest of the Phaeacians. He is "honored by the people." Among other tales, he sings about Odysseus' quarrel with

Achilles, about Hephaestus trapping Ares in his affair with Aphrodite, and about the Trojan horse and the battle for Troy. Odysseus praises him for his skill, even though Demodocus' singing and storytelling makes the hero weep.

DIOCLES: son of Ortilochus. Telemachus and Peisistratus stay at Diocles' house in Pherae on the way to and from Menelaus' house in Sparta.

DOLIUS: husband of a Sicilian woman. Dolius and his six sons ally with Odysseus, Telemachus, and Laertes during the final confrontation with the relatives of the suitors.

ELPENOR: One of Odysseus' men, Elpenor is a young man who falls from Circe's roof and breaks his neck when he is drunk. After encountering him dead in the Underworld, Odysseus and his men return to Circe's island in order to properly send him off.

EUMAEUS (Eumaios): son of Ctesius; grandson of Ormenus. Thanks to the treacherous cooperation of his nurse, Eumaeus was taken by Phoenician men from his homeland island of Syria and sold to Laertes. He is Odysseus' swineherd, who faithfully watches over his master's property while he is gone. Eumaeus generously hosts the wandering stranger (Odysseus) when he comes to his dwelling, though he is skeptical of any news he has regarding Odysseus. He later carries Odysseus' bow to him during the great contest for Penelope, and allies with Odysseus, Telemachus, and Philoetius during the slaughter of the suitors and the final confrontation with the relatives of the suitors.

EUPEITHES: father of Antinous. Eupeithes leads the relatives of the suitors who want revenge into battle against Odysseus and his allies. Laertes kills him with his spear.

EURYCLEIA: Both Odysseus' and Telemachus' nurse (she was purchased and prized by Laertes), Eurycleia helps Telemachus in his preparations and is sworn to silence when he leaves for Pylos and Sparta. When Odysseus returns home (disguised as a wandering beggar), she recognizes him by means of a scar above his knee. She later rejoices after the slaughter of the suitors and identifies those servants who have been unfaithful to Odysseus. Eurycleia often works to calm Penelope. She tells Penelope that her husband has finally returned home.

EURYLOCHUS: relative of Odysseus by marriage. Eurylochus leads the group of men who go to investigate what turns out to be Circe's house. When Circe turns them into swine, Eurylochus, who remained apart from his men, reports what has happened to them. Later, Eurylochus advises Odysseus' men to slaughter and consume the cattle of the sun god Helios.

EURYMACHUS: son of Polybus; a suitor. Along with Antinous, he is the leader of the suitors. Melantho is his lover. When the wandering stranger (Odysseus) insults him in response to his own abuse, he throws a footstool at him. After Odysseus slays Antinous, Eurymachus attempts to negotiate peace with him, including full compensation. Odysseus refuses the offer and drops him with an arrow.

EURYNOME: along with Autonoe and Hippodameia, Eurynome is a trusted handmaid of Penelope.

HELEN: daughter of Zeus (or the mortal man Tyndareus) and Leda, wife of Menelaus, though in the *Iliad* the wife of Paris. Her abduction by the Trojan Paris leads to the Achaean invasion of Troy and therefore the Trojan War. In the *Odyssey*, Helen, now back home in Sparta with Menelaus, hosts Telemachus and Peisistratus. She tells the story of Odysseus' entry into Troy disguised as a beggar. When everyone is full of sorrow, she slips a drug into the wine bowl, one that quiets heartache and anger.

IRUS (Iros): also called Arnaeus (his birth name), the beggar Irus attempts to remove the wandering stranger (Odysseus) from his own usual spot for begging. When Odysseus refuses to move, Irus challenges him to a fight. They end up boxing at the instigation of the suitors. Odysseus beats him with one punch and drags him off.

LAERTES: son of Arceisius; husband of Anticleia; father of Odysseus. Once wealthy, by the time Odysseus returns home, Laertes is living outdoors among the slaves, quietly farming. An old Sicilian woman, the wife of Dolius, takes care of him. He pines for Odysseus' return and worries greatly when Telemachus leaves to visit Pylos and Sparta. In the final confrontation with the relatives of the suitors, Laertes spears the father of Antinous, Eupeithes.

LAODAMAS: son of Alcinous and Arete. One of the best of the Phaeacians of his generation, his brothers are Halius, Clytoneus, Euryalus (who taunts Odysseus), Elatreus, and his sister is Nausicaa. Laodamas wins in boxing when Odysseus visits. He encourages Odysseus to compete in the games. Laodamas and Halius expertly perform the ball dance.

MELANTHIUS: son of Dolius. The goatherd Melanthius abuses the wandering stranger (Odysseus) and the swineherd Eumaeus several times. He sits next to the suitor Eurymachus during the feasting and carries out various chores for the suitors, such as serving the wine and building a fire. During the slaughter of the suitors, Melanthius retrieves arms for the suitors from the storeroom. Eumaeus and Philoetius later capture him there, and after the slaughter, they and Telemachus torture and brutally kill him.

MELANTHO: daughter of Dolius. Even though Penelope raised and cherished her, Melantho does not feel sorry for Penelope's situation. She is the suitor Eurymachus' lover. Melantho upbraids the wandering stranger (Odysseus) a number of times. After the slaughter of the suitors, Melantho is hanged alongside many other unfaithful serving women.

MENELAUS: son of Atreus; brother of Agamemnon; husband of

Helen. Menelaus hosts Telemachus and Peisistratus when they come to Sparta. He tells his guests about Agamemnon's murder; and how he, Menelaus, was stuck in Egypt and eventually got away; and how Odysseus is trapped on an island with the nymph Calypso.

MENTES: son of Anchialus; leader of the Taphians. Athena visits Telemachus disguised as Mentes. Mentes explains that he is friends with Odysseus, even as his father was friends with Laertes. Angry at the suitors' behavior, he tells Telemachus that Odysseus is on his way home.

MENTOR: the friend of Odysseus and the man who was given charge of Odysseus' house during his absence, Mentor rebukes the suitors during the assembly called by Telemachus. Disguised as Mentor, Athena helps and advises Telemachus during his journey abroad. She also—as Mentor—allies with Odysseus, Telemachus, and the other men during the slaughter of the suitors and stands with them during the final confrontation with the relatives of the suitors.

NAUSICAA: daughter of Alcinous and Arete. While washing laundry and playing ball, the beautiful princess Nausicaa first welcomes Odysseus to Scheria, the island of the Phaeacians, and wisely directs him to her parents' house. Her nurse is Eurymedusa.

NESTOR: son of Neleus; husband of Eurydice; father of Peisistratus and Antilochus, among others. Nestor hosts Telemachus, telling him about the great suffering the Achaeans endured at Troy, and about the successful and unsuccessful homecomings of the many heroes. He relates how Agamemnon was murdered by Aegisthus, and how Orestes, in turn, took revenge and killed his father's murderers. He sends his son Peisistratus to escort Telemachus to Sparta.

ODYSSEUS: son of Laertes and Anticleia; grandson of Autolycus and Amphithea; brother of his sister Ctimene; husband of

Penelope; father of Telemachus. The *Odyssey* relates the story of Odysseus' return home to Ithaca after the ten year-long war with the Trojans at Troy. Major encounters along the way include those with the Cicones (or Ciconians), the Lotus-eaters, the Cyclops Polyphemus (to whom he self-identifies as "Nobody"), the stormy winds of Aeolus, the Laestrygonians, the enchantress Circe, the voyage to Hades, the Sirens, the monster Scylla, the cattle of the Sun, the goddess Calypso, and the Phaeacians. Upon returning home, Odysseus disguises himself in order to reconnoiter and slaughter the suitors. Odysseus is finally reunited with Penelope before the final confrontation with the relatives of the suitors.

PEISISTRATUS: son of Nestor. Peisistratus accompanies Telemachus when he visits Menelaus in Sparta.

PENELOPE: daughter of Icarius; wife of Odysseus; mother of Telemachus. The object of the suitors' interests, Penelope puts them off for years by weaving (and unweaving) a burial shroud for Laertes. Though she remains faithful to Odysseus for twenty years, she finally announces a contest for her hand. Odysseus (disguised as a wandering stranger) takes advantage of the contest to take up his old bow and slaughter the suitors. Penelope is nevertheless wary of the stranger until he reveals to her the sign of their bed. It is then that she accepts him as Odysseus, her husband returned home.

PHILOETIUS: the cowherd Philoetius blesses the wandering stranger (Odysseus) when he first meets up with him because he reminds him of his master Odysseus, who must likewise be roaming or dead in Hades, he says. When Odysseus predicts his own return and the suitors' slaying, Philoetius prays for the prediction's fulfillment and assures him he will help him in the fight. He allies with Odysseus, Telemachus, and Eumaeus during the slaughter of the suitors and the final confrontation with the relatives of the suitors.

TELEMACHUS: son of Odysseus and Penelope; grandson of Laertes and Anticleia. Unhappy with the suitors, Telemachus calls for an assembly and accuses them of improper behavior, of wasting his household wealth. With the help of Athena disguised as Mentor, Telemachus journeys to visit Nestor in Pylos and Menelaus in Sparta in order to gather news about his father. Upon returning home to Ithaca, he discovers his father's return and joins him in the slaughter of the suitors and the final confrontation with the relatives of the suitors.

THEOCLYMENUS: son of the seer Polypheides. On the run as one who has killed a man of his own tribe, Theoclymenus approaches Telemachus as a suppliant. He interprets a bird sign in favor of his host's house, and later states that Odysseus is already home, planning evil for all the suitors. Still later, he has a vision of the suitors' destruction, complete with blood dripping down the walls of the great hall and many souls descending down to the Underworld.

TIRESIAS: the blind seer from Thebes renowned for his wisdom. When Odysseus visits Tiresias in Hades, the seer tells him what he must suffer before returning home, how he will slaughter the suitors, and about the final journey he must make.

OTHER BEINGS & PEOPLES

ANTIPHATES: king of the man-eating Laestrygonians, Antiphates leads the hunt for Odysseus' men, spearing them like fish.

ARGOS: dog of Odysseus. Though miserable and resting upon a dunghill, Argos happily recognizes and greets Odysseus upon his return home — then he dies.

LAMPUS AND PHAETHON: the two horses of Dawn that bring light to earth.

POLYPHEMUS (Poluphēmos) THE CYCLOPS (Kuklōps, the singular of Kuklōpes or Cyclopes): son of the god Poseidon and the nymph Thoōsa. The Cyclops Polyphemus dwells among many other

Cyclopes. When he hosts Odysseus in his cave, he kills and eats a number of his men, promising to eat Odysseus last (as his guest-gift to him). In response, Odysseus blinds the Cyclops and escapes by clinging to the underbelly of one of Polyphemus' rams. Polyphemus prays to his father Poseidon for revenge.

HOMER'S *ODYSSEY* IN BRIEF
BOOK SUMMARIES

BOOK 1 ▪ THE GODS IN ASSEMBLY—ATHENA AND TELEMACHUS The action opens with the "man" Odysseus struggling to return home from Troy. He's trapped and depressed on Calypso's island. Many of the Achaeans have returned; many have not—the ones who are now dead. Although men typically blame the gods for such ill fortune, Zeus, in assembly with the other gods, declares their destruction is the result of their own foolish recklessness. Such is the case with Aegisthus, who wooed Agamemnon's wife contrary to the advice of Zeus. Thanks to Athena's prodding, the conversation turns to how Odysseus will return home from Calypso's island, Ogygia. Once a decision is reached, Athena flies down to Ithaca disguised as Mentes to motivate Telemachus, the son of Odysseus, to act. There she encounters the suitors, who want Penelope and her wealth now that her husband, Odysseus, is presumably dead. Athena-Mentes speaks with Telemachus. Once she departs, Telemachus boldly calls for an assembly.

BOOK 2 ▪ THE ASSEMBLY AT ITHACA—TELEMACHUS STANDS UP Old and wise Aegyptius wonders why the assembly has been called and who called for it. Telemachus rises to explain why he has called them together. He accuses the suitors of improper behavior, of wasting his wealth. The suitor Antinous in turn blames Penelope for tricking the suitors and putting them off with the burial shroud she was making for Laertes. She must marry one of them, he demands. Telemachus prays for revenge. In response, Zeus sends two eagles to foretell the suitors' destruction. The birdwatcher Halitherses stands to confirm the bird sign and states that Odysseus is nearby and ready to slaughter the suitors. The suitor Eurymachus expresses skepticism. Telemachus asks for a ship to go and search for information regarding his father. Mentor stands to rebuke the suitors and the others who have let the suitors behave as they do. Odysseus will return, he asserts. The suitor Leiocritus declares they'll fight Odysseus if he returns. Then he breaks up the assembly. Telemachus prays to Athena, who appears as Mentor. She gathers a ship and men for the young man while he gathers provisions. Finally, they set sail for the mainland to gather news about his father.

BOOK 3 • TELEMACHUS WITH NESTOR IN PYLOS—THE YOUNG MAN LEARNS TO SPEAK First stop, Pylos. With the encouragement of Athena-Mentor, Telemachus meets up with Nestor, who hosts him, telling him about the great suffering the Achaeans endured at Troy, and about the successful and unsuccessful homecomings of the many heroes. He relates how Agamemnon was murdered by Aegisthus, and how Orestes took revenge and killed his father's murderers. He tells of Menelaus' journey to Egypt and of all the gold he gathered there. After an overnight stay, Telemachus departs by chariot with Nestor's son Peisistratus to visit Menelaus in Sparta.

BOOK 4 • TELEMACHUS WITH MENELAUS IN SPARTA—THE SUITORS PLOT TO AMBUSH THE YOUNG MAN Menelaus and Helen host Telemachus in Sparta. During a feast, they recall all the tragedy of the past. Menelaus doubts whether the wealth he has gathered is worth all the suffering he and the others endured at Troy and afterward. He mournfully speaks of his brother Agamemnon's murder, and about how he grieves for his good friend Odysseus. Hearing this, Telemachus weeps and is revealed as Odysseus' son. They all weep. After telling Menelaus about the suitors' behavior, Telemachus asks him if he has any news of his father. Promising the full truth, Menelaus tells of his time stuck in Egypt and his eventual getaway thanks to the help of Proteus, the old man of the sea. As for Odysseus, he explains that Proteus told him he was trapped with the nymph Calypso on her island. Meanwhile, the suitors conspire to kill Telemachus by means of an ambush at sea. Penelope hears of the plot and swoons.

BOOK 5 • ODYSSEUS SAILS TO SCHERIA (THE PHAEACIANS)—THE PLOTTING OF THE GODS The gods assemble and decide what to do with Odysseus. Hermes carries out their plan by telling Calypso that she must let him leave her island home. After initially protesting, she does. Odysseus sails off on a raft. All is well for seventeen days until Poseidon spots him and angrily raises a dark storm. The sea nymph Ino advises and saves Odysseus. Although the going is rough, he makes it to Scheria, the island of the Phaeacians, and falls asleep beneath a pair of shrubs.

BOOK 6 ▪ ODYSSEUS MEETS NAUSICAA—THE ENCOUNTER BY THE RIVER STREAM At Athena's prodding in a dream, the princess Nausicaa goes to wash her and her family's clothing in a stream near to where Odysseus is sleeping. When he awakens, he approaches Nausicaa and blesses her. She gives him directions to her house where the Phaeacian king and queen, her father and mother, live. She also tells him what to do once there. They set off for the palace.

BOOK 7 ▪ THE HOUSE OF ALCINOUS—ODYSSEUS MEETS ALCINOUS AND ARETE Thanks to Athena's help, Odysseus comes before Alcinous and Arete. They treat him honorably as a guest-friend. After the hero briefly explains who he is and how much he has suffered, Alcinous offers his daughter Nausicaa to him in marriage. Not wishing to restrain him, however, he also offers him conveyance home in a fast Phaeacian ship.

BOOK 8 ▪ FEASTING WITH THE PHAEACIANS— SONGS, GAMES, AND SORROW Alcinous calls an assembly and reveals the plan to sail Odysseus home. He invites the other sceptered kings to a feast. They eat and listen to the blind bard Demodocus. He sings about Odysseus' quarrel with Achilles, and Odysseus quietly weeps. Soon after, the Phaeacians compete in games—Odysseus reluctantly and angrily, after Euryalus insults him. He throws a discus farther than any other man. The Phaeacians dance, accompanied by the bard, who sings about the love affair between Ares and Aphrodite, Hephaestus' wife. They later feast and listen to the bard again. Euryalus makes amends with Odysseus. They all return to the palace to feast again and listen to Demodocus recount the tale of the Trojan horse and the battle in Troy, including Odysseus' fight with Deiphobus. Hearing this, tears fall down Odysseus' cheeks. Alcinous notices and asks him who he really is.

BOOK 9 ▪ DISASTER ON THE WAY HOME—THE CICONES, THE LOTUS EATERS, AND THE CYCLOPS Odysseus reveals himself and explains all the suffering he's endured since leaving Troy—the battle against the Cicones; the dreamy lethargy of the Lotus Eaters; the horror of the man-eating Cyclops, Polyphemus. Odysseus wisely escapes the Cyclops by blinding him and using the name, Nobody. In doing so, however, he incurs the wrath of the Cyclops' father, Poseidon.

BOOK 10 ▪ A YEAR WITH CIRCE—AEOLUS, THE LAESTRYGONIANS, AND CIRCE Odysseus and his men nearly reach Ithaca and home after a prolonged stay with Aeolus and his family, but Odysseus' men open the bag of winds that drive them off again. They next meet up with the monstrous man-eating Laestrygonians, who kill and eat many of them, destroying all the ships but one. They sail to Circe's island. The goddess turns half of his men into pigs with a magical potion. Nevertheless, Odysseus, with the help of Hermes, forces her to return their manly form, and they all become friends. They feast for a year until his men remind Odysseus of his fatherland and he resolves to leave for home. Still, Circe tells him he must make one last voyage—to the end of the world and Hades in order to speak with the seer Tiresias.

BOOK 11 ▪ THE UNDERWORLD—SPEAKING WITH THE DEAD Odysseus and his men sail to the edge of the world to communicate with the dead in Hades. After pouring out a libation and sacrificing two sheep, Odysseus speaks with the seer Tiresias, who tells him what he must suffer before returning home, how he will slaughter the suitors, and about the final journey he must make. After speaking with him, he converses with many women, including his mother, and sees many more—among them, Epicaste, the mother-wife of Oedipus, and Leda, the wife of Tyndareus. After the Phaeacians ask to hear more, Odysseus reports his conversation with Achilles, his attempted reconciliation with Telamonian Ajax, and how he saw many others—Minos, Orion, Tityus, Tantalus, Sisyphus, and Heracles.

BOOK 12 ▪ A VOYAGE WITH MANY DANGERS—THE SIRENS, SCYLLA AND CHARYBDIS, AND THE ISLAND OF THE SUN Odysseus and his men return from Hades to Circe's island to bury Elpenor. Circe warns Odysseus about the dangers of the voyage ahead and, as Tiresias did, she warns him to stay away from the island of the sun god Helios and his cattle. Departing the following morning, they first encounter the Sirens before passing between Scylla and Charybdis. They eventually approach the island of the Sun and stop for the night. It is a big mistake. There will be no homecoming for Odysseus' men after they slaughter and eat some of Helios' cattle. Finally, Odysseus survives an encounter with Charybdis and drifts to Calypso's island.

BOOK 13 ▪ **ITHACA AT LAST—ODYSSEUS AND ATHENA** Odysseus feasts one last time with the Phaeacians before they speed him home with many gifts while he sleeps. Poseidon punishes the Phaeacians. When Odysseus awakes in Ithaca, he doesn't recognize where he is until Athena, at first disguised as a young shepherd, shows him that he's home. Now he's full of joy! Still, until Athena reveals herself as she truly is and that he is truly home, Odysseus prevaricates with a story. Once Athena changes form, she reveals all the suffering he must endure and the work he has to do. They hide the many gifts in a cave, then Athena and Odysseus plan how the suitors will be punished. But first, the hero must endure much sorrow and pain. The goddess changes his appearance.

BOOK 14 ▪ **THE SWINEHERD EUMAEUS—LOYALTY AND HOSPITALITY** The wandering, old stranger Odysseus visits the loyal swineherd Eumaeus, who behaves as an ideal host. When asked who he is and where he has come from, Odysseus lies, saying he is from Crete and fought next to Idomeneus at Troy. He cunningly relates how he has come to Ithaca after several misadventures—one in Egypt, another in Phoenicia. Eumaeus doubts the news the stranger offers about Odysseus' homecoming—that he will soon be home. He believes his master is dead. Not only that but many others have offered similar tales, he explains. They feast on boar's meat and sleep after Odysseus tells one last story to win a warm covering for the night. Eumaeus sleeps apart from the others with the boars.

BOOK 15 ▪ **STORIES AND RETURNS—TELEMACHUS SPEEDS HOME, EUMAEUS GIVES HIS STORY** Leaving Menelaus and Helen in Sparta and avoiding contact with Nestor in Pylos given his need to speed home, Telemachus returns to Ithaca from his long journey abroad gathering information and earning a reputation. The seer Theoclymenus joins him. Meanwhile, Odysseus tests Eumaeus' loyalty. The swineherd passes the test and tells of his past life—how, with the help of his nurse, he was taken by Phoenician men from the island Syria and his kingly father and sold to Laertes. When Telemachus reaches Ithaca, he goes to see Eumaeus.

BOOK 16 ▪ FATHER AND SON—ODYSSEUS REVEALS HIMSELF TO TELEM-
ACHUS Telemachus comes to Eumaeus' shelter. He asks the swineherd
about the stranger. Telemachus is upset he cannot host him in his own
house thanks to the suitors. The stranger Odysseus expresses anger at
the suitors. Telemachus sends Eumaeus to report his homecoming to
Penelope. Athena appears to Odysseus and strengthens him. In turn,
he reveals himself to his son, and they plan how they will deal with the
many suitors. Meanwhile, the suitors plot against Telemachus in the
place of assembly. When they come back to the house, Penelope re-
bukes them for their insolent behavior. Eumaeus returns to his shelter.

BOOK 17 ▪ THE STRANGER AND THE SUITORS—ODYSSEUS RETURNS TO
HIS HOUSE Telemachus returns to the city where he meets up with his
mother, Penelope, and the seer Theoclymenus, who foretells Odys-
seus' return and plan for revenge. Odysseus and Eumaeus journey to
town and the house. On the way, the goatherd Melanthius verbally
abuses them. After seeing the dog Argos, Odysseus enters the house
and begs for food. When Telemachus gives him some, he prays for his
happiness, that he may get what he desires. Begging some more, Odys-
seus is battered by the suitor Antinous. Penelope curses the suitors and
sends Eumaeus to fetch the stranger. Odysseus suggests they talk later
in the evening.

BOOK 18 ▪ NAVIGATING A DANGEROUS HOUSE—ODYSSEUS BOXES IRUS
AND DEALS WITH THE SUITORS The beggar Irus arrives and is rude to
Odysseus. With the encouragement of the suitors, Odysseus boxes
with him, knocking him out, thereby winning a prize and their bless-
ings—at least for the moment. Odysseus warns Amphinomus that the
fortunes of men rapidly change. He was once wealthy, he claims, but
after behaving recklessly, he lost everything. The suitors should be
careful. Penelope shows herself to the suitors. They are awed by her.
After she chastises them for pursuing her contrary to custom, they
bring her gifts. Later, the housemaid Melantho shamefully upbraids
Odysseus. In turn, he threatens her with what Telemachus will do to
her. The suitor Eurymachus makes fun of Odysseus. After his defen-
sive response, the suitor throws a stool at him, but Odysseus ducks.
There is such a racket that Telemachus orders them all to leave.

Amphinomus backs him up, advising them not to abuse the stranger anymore. After one more drink, they depart.

BOOK 19 ▪ THE STRANGER SPEAKS WITH PENELOPE—ODYSSEUS PLANS FOR THE SUITORS' DEATH At the direction of Odysseus, Telemachus stores the weapons away from the suitors. Penelope enters the hall from her chamber. The handmaid Melantho abuses Odysseus. After reprimanding her handmaid, Penelope interviews the stranger, who praises her for her well-known glory. She explains her misfortune—how now, after having deceived them for so long, she must marry one of the suitors. When asked about himself, Odysseus claims he is Aethon from Crete. He says he once hosted Odysseus and gives proof. Not only that, he declares, but Odysseus is on his way home. Penelope is skeptical. The old nurse Eurycleia washes Odysseus and recognizes him by the scar above his knee. He swears her to silence. Penelope tells the stranger about the dream she had of the eagle that killed her geese. Odysseus confirms its truth—the suitors will die. No, says Penelope, he won't come home. Instead, she will hold a great contest to determine the suitor she will marry. They go to sleep.

BOOK 20 ▪ ODYSSEUS ENDURES—THE SUITORS' DESTRUCTION WILL COME Odysseus endures the insolent women in his halls. Athena encourages him when he worries about how he will fight so many men. With her, she promises, he can accomplish the deed. Still, Odysseus asks for a sign. In response, Zeus sends an omen—thunder and the words of a woman—portending destruction for the suitors. The herdsman Philoetius meets the stranger Odysseus, wishing him well and explaining his own plight with the suitors. When the stranger predicts Odysseus' return and the slaying of the suitors, Philoetius prays for fulfillment. And, he assures him, he'll help in the fight! Within the hall, the suitors are amazed at Telemachus and his bold words. Athena drives them on in their foolishness. The seer Theoclymenus sees blood on the walls and dead men descending to Hades. Soon the suitors will pay.

BOOK 21 ▪ THE CONTEST OF THE GREAT BOW—ODYSSEUS PARTICIPATES Penelope retrieves and presents the great bow of Odysseus to the suitors for a contest. Whoever strings the bow and shoots an arrow through twelve axes will win her hand in marriage. The suitors try without success. Meanwhile, Odysseus reveals himself to Eumaeus and Philoetius, who assure him of their loyalty and willingness to fight. Contrary to the suitors' wishes, he takes up and attempts to string the bow.

BOOK 22 ▪ SLAUGHTER IN THE HALL—THE SUITORS PAY Odysseus and his men—Telemachus, Eumaeus, and Philoetius—kill the suitors, showing mercy only to a few. After the slaughter, and after Eurycleia identifies the women who betrayed Odysseus, the twelve guilty serving women clean the hall. They punish these same women with a shameful death, as well as the goatherd Melanthius. Once the work of revenge and cleansing is complete, the other women, including Penelope, come into the hall and see Odysseus for the first time.

BOOK 23 ▪ ODYSSEUS AND PENELOPE—SIGNS AND RECOGNITION Eurycleia reports Odysseus' homecoming to Penelope, who is still doubtful. Penelope goes to see for herself, and though she is standoffish at first, she finally comes to believe the stranger is her husband when Odysseus reveals the sign of the olive tree bedpost. And so, they are finally happily reunited. Lying in bed in love, they tell each other what has happened over the past twenty years. In the morning, Odysseus arms with Telemachus, Eumaeus, and Philoetius. They leave the city for the fields.

BOOK 24 ▪ THE LAST BATTLE—PEACE AT LAST The souls of the suitors descend to Hades and encounter Achilles and Agamemnon, among others. Agamemnon speaks with Amphimedon and praises Penelope. Odysseus meets his father Laertes and, after testing him, reveals himself. The suitors' relatives meet in the assembly place to discuss what to do. Half, led by Eupeithes, want to find Odysseus to seek revenge. The other half, persuaded by Medon and Halitherses, do not fight. Those led by Eupeithes march off to one last battle. In the end, Zeus and Athena engineer a peace settlement.

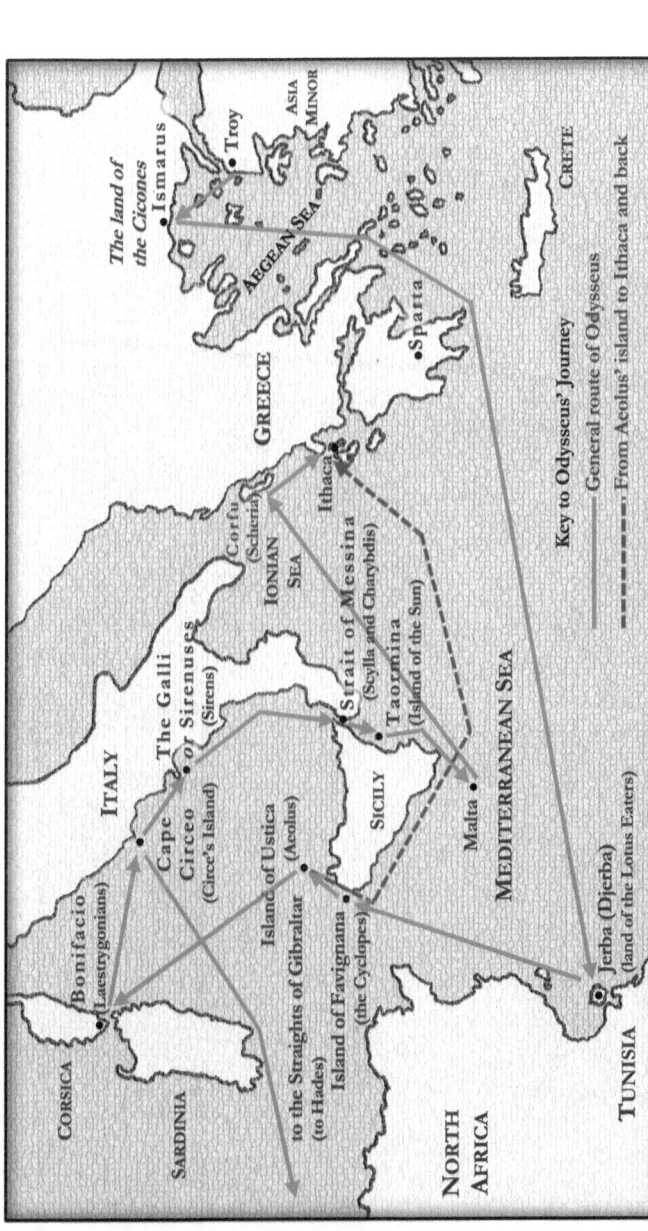

The Journey of Odysseus (A Possible Reconstruction*) (Map 1)

The above reconstruction, however fanciful and despite the criticism of some scholars, offers some idea of where Odysseus and his men may have ventured.

*Based on the mid-twentieth century voyages and reconstruction of yachtsman Ernle Bradford.

Note: some modern place names are given for purposes of orientation.

The Journey of Telemachus (Map 2)

Beginning in Ithaca, Telemachus sails to Pylos to speak with Nestor. From Pylos, he travels by chariot to Sparta, with Peisistratus, the son of Nestor, to confer with Menelaus. On the way, they stay in Pherae with Diocles, the son of Ortilochus. The return journey is virtually identical. The identity and location of Odysseus' town on Ithaca are unknown.

Note: some modern place names are given for purposes of orientation.

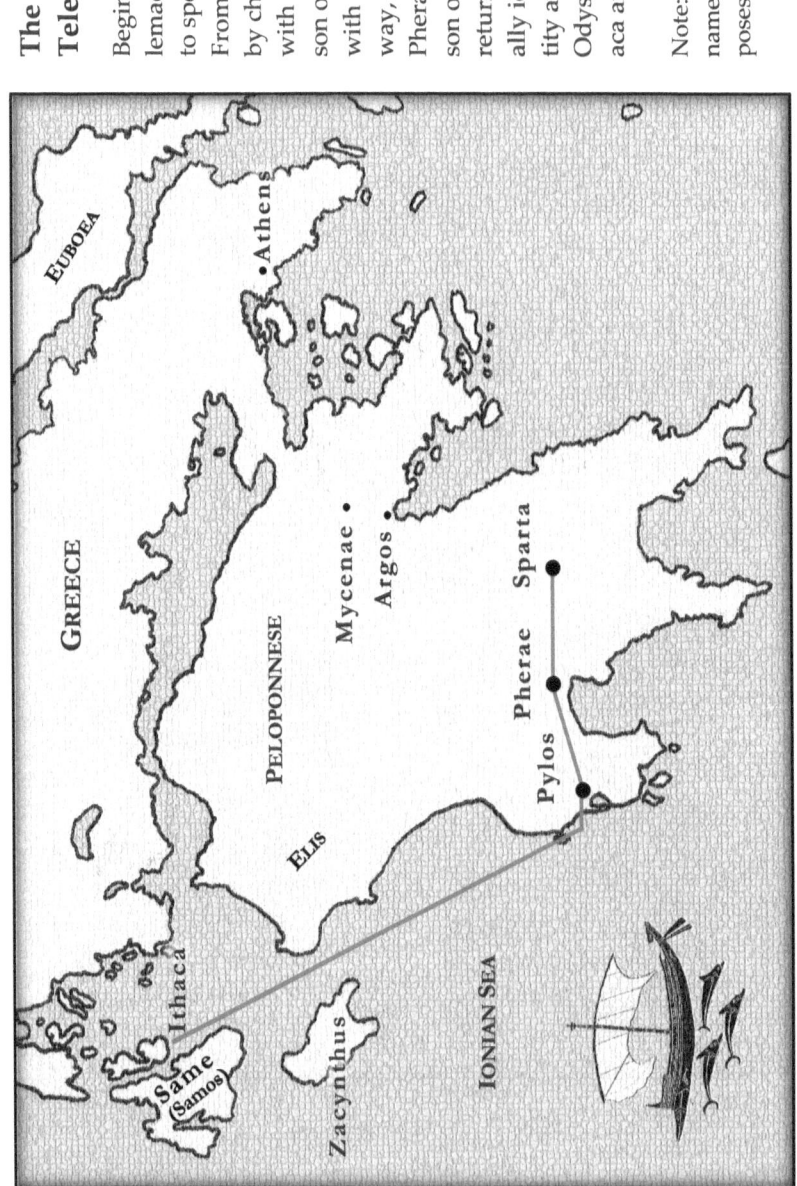

GLOSSARY

OF ENGLISH WORDS AND GREEK EQUIVALENTS
THAT APPEAR IN HOMER'S *ODYSSEY*

Ageless: *agēraos* (ἀγήραος).

Assembly; an assembly of the people; the place of assembly: *agora* (ἀγορά).

Bad, evil; worthless, ignoble, base; trouble, misfortune: *kakos* (κακός).

Ball: *sphaira* (σφαῖρα).

Bard; singer: *aoidos* (ἀοιδός).

Battle, combat, fight: *machē* (μάχη). To battle, fight: *machomai* (μάχομαι).

Best, most excellent: *aristos* (ἄριστος).

Beautiful, fair: *kalos* (καλός).

Beggar: *ptōchos* (πτωχός).

To **blame,** accuse: *aitiaomai* (αἰτιάομαι).

Blameless, excellent: *amumōn* (ἀμύμων).

Blessed, happy: *makar* (μάκαρ).

Care, trouble, sorrow: *kēdos* (κῆδος).

Comrade, friend, companion in arms: *hetairos* (ἑταῖρος).

Counsel: *boulē* (βουλή).

To hold **counsel,** deliberate: *bouleuō* (βουλεύω).

Courage, confidence, boldness, audacity: *tharsos* (θάρσος).

Cowardly; vile, worthless; miserable, luckless, wretched: *deilos* (δειλός).

Cowardice; badness, baseness, wickedness: *kakotēs* (κακότης).

Cowherd; herdsman: *boukolos* (βουκόλος).

Cunning; wisdom; counsel; craft, skill: *mētis* (μῆτις). **Of many counsels;** crafty, shrewd: *polumētis* (πολύμητις).

Dear (dear one), friend, beloved: *philos* (φίλος).

Death (the allotted time of death); one's fate, lot: *potmos* (πότμος).

To **delight,** enjoy, take pleasure in: *terpō* (τέρπω).

Desire: *eros* (ἔρος).

To **desire eagerly:** *menoinaō* (μενοινάω).

Destruction, ruin: *olethros* (ὄλεθρος).

Dog: *kuōn* (κυῶν).

Doom, lot, fate: *moros* (μόρος). To be **doomed to a sad end:** *ainomoros* (αἰνόμορος).

Drug, medicine: *pharmakon* (φάρμακον).

To **endure:** *tlaō* (τλάω) or *tolmaō* (τολμάω).

Enemy, hostile (man): *dusmenēs* or *dysmenēs* (δυσμενής).

Evil, bad; worthless, ignoble, base; trouble, misfortune: *kakos* (κακός).

Excellence (esp. manly excellence), goodness, virtue; valor, prowess, merit: *aretē* (ἀρετή).

Faithful, loyal, trusty: *eriēros* (ἐρίηρος).

Falsehood: *pseudos* (ψεῦδος).

Fate (personified); fate, portion: *Moira* or *moira* (μοῖρα).

Feast: *daitē* (δαίτη).

Food; grain; bread; meat: *sitos* (σῖτος) or *eidar* (εἶδαρ).

Friend, guest-friend, stranger: *xenos* (ξένος).

Glory, fame, report: *kleos* (κλέος).

Glory: *kudos* (κῦδος).

Glory-boast, the boast: *euchos* (εὖχος).

God: *theos* (θεός).

Good, noble, brave: *agathos* (ἀγαθός) or *esthlos* (ἐσθλός).

Guest-gift; a host's gift to a departing guest: *xeinēion* (ξεινήιον).

Hall; house: *megaron* (μέγαρον).

Happiness, fortune, riches: *olbos* (ὄλβος).

Happy, blessed: *olbios* (ὄλβιος).

Homeland, fatherland (land of one's fathers): *patris gaia* (πατρίς γαῖα), which shows up as *patridos aiēs* (πατρίδος αἴης).

Honor: *timē* (τιμή); to **honor,** prize, deem worthy: *timaō* (τιμάω).

Hospitality shown to a guest-friend: *xenia* (ξενία).

House, household: *oikos* (οἶκος).

Human being; man: *anthrōpos* (ἄνθρωπος).

Illustrious, glorious: *klutos* (κλυτός).

Immortal, undying; everlasting: *athanatos* (ἀθάνατος). The immortals (the gods): *athanatoi* (ἀθάνατοι).

Inferior, worse: *cheirōn* (χείρων).

Insolence, arrogance, wantonness: *hubris* (ὕβρις).

King, chief; prince: *basileus* (βασιλεύς).

Life, soul, breath, spirit, phantom-life: *psuchē* or *psychē* (ψυχή).

Lord, master: *anax* (ἄναξ).

Loyal, faithful, trusty: *eriēros* (ἐρίηρος).

Man: *anēr* (ἀνήρ).

Meat: *kreas* (κρέας).

Mortal; liable to death: *thnētos* (θνητός). A **mortal human being**: *brotos* (βροτός).

Much-able; ever-ready, resourceful, full of resources; inventive: *polumēchanos* (πολυμήχανος).

Necessity, constraint: *anankē* (ἀνάγκη).

Nobody or No one or No man; the name Odysseus gives to himself when Polyphemus asks for his name: *Outis* (Οὖτις).

Observant of custom, civilized; righteous: *dikaios* (δίκαιος).

Pain of body or mind; sorrow; distress; trouble: *algos* (ἄλγος).

Portion, fate: *moira* (μοῖρα).

Prize: *athlon* (ἄθλον).

Property or possessions: *ktēma* (κτῆμα).

Recklessness; presumptuous sin; arrogance: *atasthalia* (ἀτασθαλία).

To **rejoice**: *gētheō* (γηθέω).

Return home, return homeward; travel, journey: *nostos* (νόστος).

To take **revenge** or **vengeance**; to pay a price: *tinō* (τίνω).

Salt: *hals* (ἅλς).

Sea: *thalassa* (θάλασσα).

Shame: *aidōs* (αἰδώς).

Shield: *aspis* (ἀσπίς).

Ship: *naus* (ναῦς).

Sleep: *hupnos* (ὕπνος).

Soul; life, breath, spirit, phantom-life: *psuchē* or *psychē* (ψυχή)

Spear: *doru* (δόρυ).

Spirit, passion, desire for something: *thumos* (θυμός).

Stranger; guest-friend, friend: *xenos* (ξένος).

Strength, power, might: *bia* (βία).

Strength, vigor, courage: *kartos* (κάρτος).

Strife, a quarrel, contention: *eris* (ἔρις).

Suffering; misery: *pēma* (πῆμα). To **suffer**, toil: *mogeō* (μογέω).

Sweet: *glukeros* (γλυκερός).

Swineherd: *subōtēs* (συβώτης).

To **take**, seize, and slay: *haireō* (αἱρέω).

True: *etumos* (ἔτυμος); truth: *alētheia* (ἀληθεία).

Unhappy, miserable, wretched: *dustēnos* or *dystēnos* (δύστηνος).

Victory: *nikē* (νίκη); to **be victorious**: *nikaō* (νικάω).

Wanderer: *alōmenos* (ἀλώμενος). To **wander**, roam: (ἀλάομαι).

Wave: *kuma* (κῦμα).

Wealth, riches: *ploutos* (πλοῦτος).

Wine: *oinos* (οἶνος).

Wisdom; counsel; craft, skill; cunning: *mētis* (μῆτις).

Wrath: *mēnis* (μῆνις).

Wretched, unhappy: *deilos* (δειλός).

SOURCES AND FURTHER READING

This Classics Cave rendition of Homer's *Odyssey* was made using the critical edition of T.W. Allen (*Homeri Opera*, vols. III-IV, Oxford: Oxford University Press, 1917 and 1919), as well as the Greek texts and other immensely helpful tools found online at the Perseus Digital Library (www.perseus.tufts.edu), The Chicago Homer (http://homer.library.northwestern.edu/html/application.html), and elsewhere.

Otherwise, the Cave checked its own version of the *Odyssey* against many other translations, new and old, including Alexander Pope's early eighteenth century version in heroic couplets (1725), the late Victorian translations of George Herbert Palmer (1884) and Samuel Butler (1900), A.T. Murray's early Loeb version (1919), and the more recent translations of Robert Fitzgerald (1961), Richmond Lattimore (1965), A.T. Murray and George Dimock (1998, the most recent Loeb version), Robert Fagles (1990), and Stanley Lombardo (2000). Where the translations of the *Odyssey* in the public domain were suitable, The Classics Cave occasionally made use of them with little to no alteration.

OTHER ANCIENT LITERATURE RELATED TO HOMER OR THE EPIC CYCLE

Greek Epic Fragments: From the Seventh to the Fifth Centuries BC. Edited and translated by Martin L. West. Cambridge: Harvard University Press, 2003.

Homeric Hymns, Homeric Apocrypha, Lives of Homer. Edited and translated by Martin L. West. Cambridge: Harvard University Press, 2003.

Porphyry. *Porphyry on the Cave of the Nymphs.* Translated by Robert Lamberton. Barrytown: Station Hill Press, 1983.

∎ ∎ ∎

SUGGESTIONS FOR FURTHER READING

Adkins, A.W.H. *Moral Values and Political Behavior in Ancient Greece: From Homer to the End of the Fifth Century.* New York: W.W. Norton & Company, 1972.

Anderson, Øivind. "Happiness in Homer." Symbolae Osloensis 85, no. 1: 2-16. *Academic Search Complete*, EBSCOhost (accessed May 25, 2015).

Boardman, John, Jasper Griffin, and Oswyn Murray. *The Oxford History of Greece and the Hellenistic World.* Oxford: Oxford University Press, 2001.

Bowra, C.M. *Homer.* London: Gerald Duckworth & Company, Ltd., 1972.

Bradford, Ernle. *Ulysses Found.* Phoenix Mill: Sutton Publishing Limited, 2004. (Originally published by Hodder and Stoughton, 1963.)

Burkert, Walter. *Greek Religion.* Translated by John Raffan. Cambridge: Harvard University Press, 1985.

Finkelberg, Margalit. *Greeks and Pre-Greeks: Aegean Prehistory and Greek Heroic Tradition.* Cambridge: Cambridge University Press, 2007.

Finley, M.I. *The World of Odysseus.* New York: New York Review of Books with Viking Penguin, 1982.

Fischer, Norman. *Sailing Home: Using the Wisdom of Homer's Odyssey to Navigate Life's Perils and Pitfalls.* New York: Free Press, 2008.

Fowler, Robert ed. *The Cambridge Guide to Homer.* Cambridge: Cambridge University Press, 2004.

Grant, Michael. *The Rise of the Greeks.* New York: Charles Scribner's Sons, 1988.

Greene, William Chase. *Moira: Fate, Good, and Evil in Greek Thought.* New York: Harper Torchbooks, 1963. (Originally published by Harvard University Press, 1944.)

Hall, Jonathan M. *A History of the Archaic Greek World ca. 1200-479 BCE.* Malden: Blackwell Publishing, 2007.

Jenkyns, Richard. *Classical Literature: An Epic Journey from Homer to Virgil and Beyond.* New York: Basic Books, 2016.

Kirk, G.S. *The Songs of Homer.* Cambridge: Cambridge University Press, 1962.

Lesky, Albin. *A History of Greek Literature.* Translated by Cornelis de Heer and James Willes. Indianapolis: Hackett Publishing Company, 1996.

MacDonald, Dennis Ronald. *Christianizing Homer: The Odyssey, Plato, and The Acts of Andrew.* Oxford: Oxford University Press, 1994.

Martin, Thomas R. *Ancient Greece: From Prehistoric to Hellenistic Times.* New Haven: Yale University Press, 1996.

McAuslan, Ian, and Peter Walcot, eds. *Homer (Greece & Rome Studies IV).* Oxford: Oxford University Press, 1998.

Morford, P.O. Mark, and Robert J. Lenardon. *Classical Mythology.* 4th ed. New York: Longman Publishing Group, 1991.

Nagy, Gregory. *The Best of the Achaeans: Concepts of the Hero in Archaic Greek Poetry.* Rev. ed. Baltimore: The Johns Hopkins University Press, 1999.

———. *The Ancient Greek Hero in 24 Hours.* Cambridge: Harvard University Press, 2013.

Nicolson, Adam. *Why Homer Matters.* New York: Picador, 2014.

Parry, M. *The Making of Homeric Verse: The Collected Papers.* Oxford: Oxford University Press, 1971.

Rohde, Erwin. *Psyche: The Cult of Souls and Belief in Immortality among the Greeks.* 2 vols. Translated by W.B. Hillis. New York: Harper Torchbooks, 1966.

Schofield, Louise. *The Mycenaeans.* London: The British Museum Press, 2007.

Snodgrass, Anthony. *Homer and the Artists: Text and Picture in Early Greek Art.* Cambridge: Cambridge University Press, 1998.

West, Martin L. *Indo-European Poetry and Myth.* Oxford: Oxford University Press, 2007.

———. *The East Face of Helicon: West Asiatic Elements in Greek Poetry and Myth.* Oxford: Oxford University Press, 1997.

Whitman, Cedric H. *Homer and the Heroic Tradition*. New York: W.W. Norton & Company, 1965.

Young, Tim J. *A Hero's Wish: What Homer Believed about Happiness and the Good Life*. Sugar Land: EuZōn Media, 2015.

Will you help the Cave? Here's how . . .

- **Buy** a book. **Join** a club. **Sponsor** the Cave. **Give** a donation.
  - **Talk** to friends and family about Cave books and the free online Cave content at the Cave (www.theclassicscave.com).
- Leave a **positive review** online—if possible, **five stars** with a **brief remark** about what you liked. This truly helps!
- **Write us** at contact@theclassicscave.com to let us know how you've benefited from our work. This inspires us to do more!

THE CLASSICS CAVE is a small, shoestring operation, on fire to spread the wisdom and ways of ancient Greek literature. We **rely on you**, the friend of the Cave, to let people know how you liked and benefited from what we're doing. We also **depend on you** to **improve our books**. Did you see something that requires editing? Something we got wrong? Something we need to add? Despite our great effort and care to get everything right, it happens. So please **let us know** by emailing us at contact@theclassicscave.com. Otherwise, **visit** the Cave to benefit from our ever-growing collection of free online content at www.theclassicscave.com. And don't forget to **support our mission** to spread the wisdom and ways of ancient Greek literature by **buying** and **reading** Cave Books, **enjoying** Cave Gear, **joining** The BAGL Club or AAGS, or by **sponsoring** or **giving** to the Cave. **Thanks!**

Read and enjoy more from **Homer**!

If you benefited from reading *The Best of Homer's Odyssey*, you may wish to pick up another Cave book related to Homer. There are many now available or in the works.

Visit the Cave at . . .

www.theclassicscave.com

www.theclassicscave.com

Looking for the **best books** ever?
And new ways to read and benefit from them?

Hunting for **wisdom** and **ways** that
are time-tested and people-approved?

READ A CAVE BOOK

VISIT THE CAVE ONLINE
www.theclassicscave.com

When you read a Cave book, an ancient classic,
you'll have a better idea about where you're
going in life and how to get there.

You'll feel smarter. Be wiser.
And if you practice what you've encountered,
you'll live a better life. Be a little happier.

Enjoy the Cave's **free online content**. Or **choose a book** from one
of **our series**. The Cave Best of Series. The Cave Wisdom & Way
Series. The Cave Workbook & Journal Series. And more!
You'll be glad you did!

www.theclassicscave.com